Fodor's

Spanish for Travelers

Random House Gift 4/29/99 7.00

Fodor's
Spanish for Travelers
PHRASEBOOK DICTIONARY

From the editors of

LIVING LANGUAGE®
A Random House Company

Fodor's Travel Publications, Inc.
New York • Toronto • London • Sydney • Auckland
Visit us on the Web at http://www.fodors.com/

PREVIOUSLY PUBLISHED AS *LIVING LANGUAGE TRAVELTALK™ SPANISH*

While every care has been taken to ensure the accuracy of the information in this guide, time brings change, and consequently, the publisher cannot accept responsibility for errors that may occur. Always call ahead to verify information that is important to you.

ISBN 0-679-03415-3

Acknowledgments
Cover photo: Nik Wheeler/CORBIS Photo Researcher: Jolie Novak
Cover design: Guido Caroti

Special Sales
Fodor's Travel Publications are available at special discounts for bulk purchases (100 copies or more) for sales promotions or premiums. Special editions, including personalized covers, excerpts of existing guides, and corporate imprints, can be created in large quantities for special needs. For more information, write to Special Marketing, Fodor's Travel Publications, 201 East 50th St., New York, NY 10022. Inquiries from Canada should be sent to Random House of Canada Ltd., Marketing Department, 1265 Aerowood Drive, Mississauga, Ontario L4W 1B9. Inquiries from the United Kingdom should be sent to Fodor's Travel Publications, 20 Vauxhall Bridge Rd., London, England SW1V 2SA.

Printed in the United States of America
10 9 8 7 6

CONTENTS

PREFACE

You don't need to know Spanish to get along in the Spanish-speaking world. The 2,200 Spanish phrases in this guide will see you through almost every situation you encounter as a tourist. Each expression is followed by a phonetic transcription, and all you have to do to make yourself understood is to read the phonetics as you would any English sentence. You don't even need Fodor's *Spanish for Travelers* cassette, on which native speakers pronounce the guide's key Spanish dialogues, although the cassette will help you polish your pronunciation.

Before you start practicing, familiarize yourself with the main features of the guide:

Pronunciation Guide The transcription system for this volume is presented in this section through the use of simple English examples and explanations. Reading through it first will enable you to use the phrases in subsequent chapters with full confidence that your pronunciation will be understood.

Chapter 1: Useful Expressions Many common phrases are likely to be used quite frequently in a variety of contexts. For your convenience, these phrases have been grouped together in one brief chapter.

Chapters 2–13 From arrival at the airport to saying farewell to new friends, Fodor's *Spanish for Travelers* provides a comprehensive resource for every important context of your visit.

Sample Dialogues Beginning most chapters, these give you a sense of how the language sounds in conversation.

Travel Tips and Cultural Highlights Interspersed throughout the chapters is solid information on cultural attractions from Fodor's resident-writers to help you get the most out of your visit. Mexico and Spain are highlighted throughout the book; however, most material is applicable to other Spanish-speaking areas as well.

General Information   To ease your transition into a new setting, the guide includes legal holidays, metric conversion tables, important signs, common abbreviations, and clothing and shoe-size conversion charts.

Two-Way 1,600-Word Dictionary   For easy reference, all key words in the book appear here, grouped in English-Spanish and Spanish-English sections. Both sections include the phonetic transcription of each Spanish word and phrase to help you pronounce them.

Grammar in Brief   This concise section summarizes Spanish grammar for those who want to understand the structure of the language and begin to learn it on their own.

¡Buen viaje (Bwehn VYAH-heh)! Have a good trip!

ACKNOWLEDGMENTS

We wish to acknowledge the resources, organizations, and individuals who were helpful to us in the preparation of this work. First of all, we thank The Experiment Press and Crown Publishers, both of whom permitted us to draw materials from several sources: the *Living in Mexico* and *Living in Spain* series, edited by Alvino E. Fantini, The Experiment Press, Brattleboro, Vermont, 1987; *Conversational Spanish*, by Ralph Weiman and O. A. Succar, Crown Publishers, Inc., 1985; and *Crown Insiders' Guide to Mexico*, Crown Publishers, Inc., 1987. All of these works provided a great deal of useful information.

We are also grateful to the directors of both the Mexican and the Spanish national offices of The Experiment in International Living—a nonprofit international educational exchange organization—for their help in reviewing this work for accuracy of language and content. In particular, we cite Bárbara B. de Gómez, Arturo Gómez, and Natividad Solana. In addition, we are grateful to Alex Silverman, Director of the Master of Arts in Teaching Program of the School for International Training, Brattleboro, Vermont, who helped to devise the format; to Shirley Capron, Research Librarian of the Donald B. Watt Library of the School for International Training; to our student assistants, Víctor Múzquiz and Patrick Smith; to Kathryn Mintz, Publisher, Crown Publishers, who helped to develop the work; and especially to Carla A. Fantini, who lent a helping hand at various stages during the preparation of this work. *Dedicamos este libro muy especialmente a "Carlina."*

ABOUT THE SPANISH LANGUAGE

Spanish belongs to the family of Romance languages—along with French, Italian, Portuguese, and several others. These languages are all basically variations of the spoken Latin of the Roman Empire. Other languages have also exerted their own influence on Spanish. Through the seven-century domination of Spain by the Arabs, Arabic became the principal outside influence on Spanish. With the discovery of the New World, Spanish was brought to the American continent. Here, over the centuries, it has borrowed many words from the indigenous languages. In modern times, French and Italian have made significant contributions. And in recent years, Spanish has also borrowed heavily from English, while also contributing many of its own words to the English language. It is no wonder that many Spanish words appear familiar to you.

Nearly 300 million people speak Spanish—the world's fourth major language. Spanish is spoken over a vast area, including Spain, Mexico, Central America, the Caribbean, South America (except, largely, Brazil), and many parts of the United States.

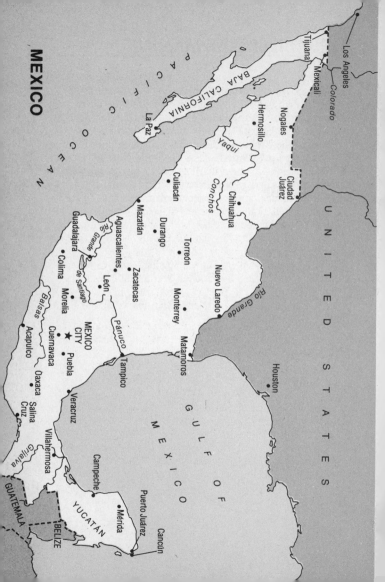

PRONUNCIATION GUIDE

Each English word and phrase in this book is presented with a Spanish equivalent. An easy-to-follow sound key (transcription) guides you to the correct pronunciation of the Spanish word. Simply read the sound key as you would in English. Although English and Spanish sounds are often not identical, the result should be fairly comprehensible to most Spanish speakers. To sharpen up your pronunciation, use the accompanying audiocassette, which contains dialogues by native speakers. Listen and repeat what you hear on the recording and try to imitate their pronunciation as best you can.

PRONUNCIATION CHART

The chart below will be your guide to transcriptions used in this book. Review the chart to see how Spanish sounds are properly pronounced. As you use this book, you will become more familiar with the spelling of Spanish words and the sound key. Eventually you may be able to read the words without referring to the guide at all.

Four points should be stressed about pronouncing Spanish: First, since the Spanish spelling system is much more phonetic than English spelling, it is easier to tell, by reading it, how a word should be pronounced. Second, pay special attention to vowels since they affect the overall pronunciation of a word and are crucial to making yourself understood. Third, note that vowels in Spanish are generally more flat than in English. The long *o* sound in particular does not carry the *w* sound that usually accompanies it in English. Fourth, in the chart below—and throughout the book—note that the syllable stressed in a word appears in capital letters in the phonetic transcription, as in *taco* (TAH-koh), the first example below.

Vowels

Spanish Spelling	Approximate Sound in English	Phonetic Symbol	Example–Transcription
a	(f<u>a</u>ther)	ah	**taco** (<u>TAH</u>-koh)
e	(m<u>e</u>t)	eh	**cerca** (<u>SEHR</u>-kah) or **donde** (DOHN-d<u>eh</u>)
i	(b<u>ee</u>t)	ee	**día** (<u>DEE</u>-ah)
o	(b<u>o</u>th)	oh	**foto** (<u>FOH</u>-toh)
u	(b<u>oo</u>th)	oo	**mucho** (<u>MOO</u>-choh)
y	(f<u>ee</u>t)	ee	**y** (only a vowel when standing alone)

Frequent Vowel Combinations (Diphthongs)

Spanish Spelling	Approximate Sound in English	Phonetic Symbol	Example–Transcription
au	n<u>ow</u>	ow	**auto** (<u>OW</u>-toh)
ai/ay	ripe	ahy	**bailar** (b<u>ahy</u>-LAHR) **hay** (<u>ahy</u>)
ei	(m<u>ay</u>)	ay	**peine** (<u>PAY</u>-neh)
ia	(<u>ya</u>rn)	yah	**gracias** (GRAH-s<u>yah</u>s)
ie	(<u>ye</u>t)	yeh	**siempre** (S<u>YEH</u>M-preh)
io	(<u>yo</u>del)	yoh	**adiós** (ah-D<u>YOHS</u>)
iu	(<u>you</u>)	yoo	**ciudad** (s<u>yoo</u>-DAHD)
oy	(s<u>oy</u> sauce)	oy	**estoy** (ehs-T<u>OY</u>)
ua	(<u>wa</u>nd)	wah	**cuando** (K<u>WAH</u>N-doh)
ue	(<u>we</u>t)	weh	**bueno** (B<u>WEH</u>-noh)
ui/uy	(s<u>wee</u>t)	wee	**ruido** (R<u>WEE</u>-doh) or **muy** (m<u>wee</u>)

Consonants

Spanish Spelling		Approximate Sound in English	
b/d/k/l/m/n/p/s/t		similar to English	

Spanish Spelling	Approximate Sound in English	Phonetic Symbol	Example–Transcription
c* (before e/i)	s (<u>c</u>ertain)	s	cine (<u>SEE</u>-neh)
c (before a/o/u)	k (<u>c</u>atch)	k	como (<u>K</u>OH-moh)
cc	cks (a<u>cc</u>ent)	k-s	lección (lehk-<u>S</u>YOHN)
ch	ch (<u>ch</u>amp)	ch	mucho (MOO-<u>ch</u>oh)
g (before a/o/u)	hard g (<u>g</u>o)	g	gato (<u>G</u>AH-toh)
g (before e/i)	hard h (<u>h</u>at)	h	gente (<u>H</u>EN-teh)
h	always silent	—	hasta (AHS-tah)
i	hard h (<u>h</u>at)	h	jefe (<u>H</u>EH-feh)
ll	y (<u>y</u>ard)	y	silla (SEE-<u>y</u>ah)
ñ	ny (ca<u>ny</u>on)	ny	señor (seh-<u>NY</u>OHR)
qu	k (<u>k</u>ite)	k	que (<u>k</u>eh)
r	[single trill] (th<u>r</u>ow)	r	pero (PEH-<u>r</u>oh)
r	[double trill]	rr	rosa (<u>RR</u>OH-sah)
rr	[double trill]	rr	arroz (ah-<u>RR</u>OHS)
v	v (<u>v</u>ote, but softer, almost like <u>b</u>)	v	vaca (<u>V</u>AH-kah)
x	cks (ro<u>cks</u>)	ks	taxi (TAH<u>K</u>-see)
z*	s	s	zona (<u>S</u>OH-nah)

*In parts of Spain, z—and also c before e or i—is pronounced like English th. Examples: zona (THON-nah), cera (THEH-rah), cinco (THEEN-koh). In this book, however, Latin American pronunciation is used throughout, as described in the chart above.

1/USEFUL EXPRESSIONS
COURTESY

Please.	**Por favor.**	pohr fah-VOHR
Thank you.	**Gracias.**	GRAH-syahs
You're welcome.	**De nada.**	deh NAH-dah
Sorry (excuse me).	**Disculpe.**	dees-KOOL-peh
Excuse me.	**Con permiso.** (*or*) **Perdón.**	kohn pehr-MEE-soh pehr-DOHN
It doesn't matter.	**No importa.**	noh eem-POHR-tah

GREETINGS

Good morning.	**Buenos días.**	BWEHN-nohs DEE-ahs
Good afternoon.	**Buenas tardes.**	BWEHN-nahs TAHR-dehs
Good evening.	**Buenas noches.***	BWEHN-nahs NOH-chehs
Good night.	**Buenas noches.***	BWEHN-nas NOH-chehs
Hello.	**Hola.**	OH-lah
Good-bye.	**Adiós.**	ah-DYOHS
See you soon.	**Hasta pronto.**	AHS-tah PROHN-tah
See you later.	**Hasta luego.** (*or*) **Hasta la vista.** (*or*) **Hasta más tarde.**	AHS-tah LWEH-goh AHS-tah lah VEES-tah AHS-tah mahs TAHR-deh
See you tomorrow.	**Hasta mañana.**	AHS-tah mah-NYAH-nah

*In Spanish, *buenas noches* is used both when arriving and when leaving, after around 6:00 P.M.

APPROACHING SOMEONE FOR HELP

Excuse me,	**Perdón,**	pehr-DOHN
• sir.	• **señor.**	• seh-NYOHR
• ma'am.	• **señora.**	• seh-NYOH-rah
• miss/ms.	• **señorita.**	• seh-nyoh-REE-tah
Do you speak English?	**¿Habla usted inglés?**	AH-blah oos-TEHD een-GLEHS?
Do you understand English?	**¿Comprende inglés?**	kohm-PREN-deh een-GLEHS?
Yes./No.	**Sí./No.**	see/noh
I'm sorry.	**Lo siento.**	loh SYEHN-toh
I'm a tourist.	**Soy turista.**	soy too-REES-tah
I don't speak Spanish.	**No hablo español.**	noh AH-bloh ehs-pah-NYOHL
I speak very little Spanish.	**Hablo muy poco español.**	AH-bloh mwee POH-koh ehs-pah-NYOHL
I don't understand.	**No comprendo.**	noh kohm-PREHN-doh
I understand a little.	**Comprendo un poco.**	kohm-PREHN-doh oon POH-koh
Please speak more slowly.	**Hable más despacio, por favor.**	AH-bleh mahs des-PAH-syoh, pohr fah-VOHR
Please repeat.	**Repita, por favor.**	rreh-PEE-tah, pohr fah-VOHR
May I ask a question?	**Una pregunta, por favor.**	OO-nah preh-GOON-tah, pohr fah-VOHR
Could you please help me?	**¿Podría ayudarme?**	poh-DREE-ah ah-yoo-DAHR-meh?
Where is the bathroom?	**¿Dónde está el baño?**	DOHN-deh ehs-TAH ehl BAH-nyoh?
Thank you very much.	**Muchas gracias.**	MOO-chas GRAH-syahs*

Note: In Spanish, although there are some exceptions (*turista,* for example), most nouns and adjectives end in -o for males and -a for females, with the corresponding plurals -os and -as. Use -os when including both males and females. So, if you're an American male, you'd say, *Soy norteamericano.* If you're an American female, you'd say, *Soy norteamericana.* A group of females might say, *Somos norteamericanas,* and a mixed group would say, *Somos norteamericanos.*

QUESTION WORDS

Who?	**¿Quién?**	kyehn?
Who? (plural)	**¿Quiénes?**	KYEH-nehs?
What?	**¿Qué?**	keh?
Why?	**¿Por qué?**	pohr KEH?
When?	**¿Cuándo?**	KWAHN-doh?
Where?	**¿Dónde?**	DOHN-deh?
Where from?	**¿De dónde?**	deh DOHN-deh?
Where to?	**¿Adónde?**	ah-DOHN-deh?
How?	**¿Cómo?**	KOH-moh?
How much?	**¿Cuánto?**	KWAHN-toh?

NUMBERS

Take the time to learn how to count in Spanish. You'll find that knowing the numbers will make everything easier during your trip.

zero	**cero**	SEH-roh
one	**uno**	OO-noh
two	**dos**	dohs
three	**tres**	trehs
four	**cuatro**	KWAH-troh
five	**cinco**	SEEN-koh
six	**seis**	says
seven	**siete**	SYEH-teh
eight	**ocho**	OH-choh
nine	**nueve**	NWEH-veh
ten	**diez**	dyes

eleven	**once**	OHN-seh
twelve	**doce**	DOH-seh
thirteen	**trece**	TREH-seh
fourteen	**catorce**	kah-TOHR-seh
fifteen	**quince**	KEEN-seh
sixteen	**dieciséis**	dyeh-see-says
seventeen	**diecisiete**	dyeh-see-SYEH-teh
eighteen	**dieciocho**	dyeh-see-OH-choh
nineteen	**diecinueve**	dyeh-see-NWEH-veh
twenty	**veinte**	VAYN-teh
twenty-one	**veintiuno**	vayn-tee-OO-noh
twenty-two	**veintidós**	vayn-tee-DOHS
twenty-three . . .	**veintitrés . . .**	vayn-tee-TREHS
thirty	**treinta**	TRAYN-tah
forty	**cuarenta**	kwah-REHN-tah
fifty	**cincuenta**	seen-KWEN-tah
sixty	**sesenta**	seh-SEHN-tah
seventy	**setenta**	seh-TEHN-tah
eighty	**ochenta**	oh-CHEHN-tah
ninety	**noventa**	noh-VEHN-tah
one hundred	**cien**	SYEHN
one hundred one	**ciento uno**	SYEHN-toh OO-noh
one hundred two . . .	**ciento dos . . .**	SYEHN-toh dohs
one hundred twenty . . .	**ciento veinte . . .**	SYEHN-toh VAYN-teh
one hundred thirty . . .	**ciento treinta . . .**	SYEHN-toh TRAYN-tah
two hundred	**doscientos(-as)**	dohs-SYEHN-tohs (-tahs)
three hundred	**trescientos(-as)**	trehs-SYEHN-tohs (-tahs)
four hundred	**cuatrocientos(-as)**	kwah-troh-SYEHN-tohs (-tahs)
five hundred	**quinientos(-as)**	kee-NYEHN-tohs (-tahs)
six hundred	**seiscientos(-as)**	says-SYEHN-tohs (-tahs)

9

seven hundred	**setecientos(-as)**	seh-teh-SYEHN-tohs (-tahs)
eight hundred	**ochocientos(-as)**	oh-choh-SYEHN-tohs (-tahs)
nine hundred	**novecientos(-as)**	noh-veh-SYEHN-tohs (-tas)
one thousand	**mil**	meel
two thousand	**dos mil**	dohs meel
three thousand . . .	**tres mil . . .**	trehs meel
one million	**un millón**	oon mee-YOHN
two million . . .	**dos millones . . .**	dohs mee-YOH-nehs

Ordinal Numbers

first	**primero**	pree-MEH-roh
	primer(-a)	pree-MEHR (MEHR-ah)
second	**segundo(-a)**	seh-GOON-doh(-dah)
third	**tercero**	tehr-SEH-roh
	tercer(-a)	tehr-SEHR (-SEH-rah)
fourth	**cuarto(-a)**	KWAHR-toh(-tah)
fifth	**quinto(-a)**	KEEN-toh(-tah)
sixth	**sexto(-a)**	SEHKS-toh(-tah)
seventh	**séptimo(-a)**	SEHP-tee-moh(-mah)
eighth	**octavo(-a)**	ohk-TAH-voh(-vah)
ninth	**noveno(-a)**	noh-VEH-noh(-nah)
tenth	**décimo(-a)**	DEH-see-moh(-mah)

QUANTITIES

once	**una vez**	OO-nah vehs
twice	**dos veces**	dohs VEH-sehs
last	**último**	OOL-tee-moh
half	**medio**	MEH-dyoh
a half	**una mitad**	OO-nah mee-TAHD
one-third	**un tercio**	oon TEHR-syoh
one-quarter	**un cuarto**	oon KWAHR-toh
percent	**por ciento**	pohr-SYEN-toh

Note: In Spanish, decimal points are indicated by commas. For example, *6,5* would be written *6,5* and pronounced "says KOH-mah SEEN-koh."

10

ABOUT THE CURRENCY

In Mexico, the currency is the *nuevo peso* (noo-EH-vo PEH-soh), or new peso, indicated as NP$ and containing 100 *centavos* (sen-TAH-vos). The official currency in Spain is the *peseta* (peh-SEH-tah), abbreviated *pta*, with 100 *céntimos* (SEHN-tee-mohs or THEHN-tee-mohs) in each *peseta*.

Banks in Mexico are generally open weekdays 9 A.M. to 1:30 P.M.—but later and on weekends in some large cities. In Spain, banks are open in summer on weekdays 8:30 A.M. to 1 P.M. and the rest of the year, weekdays 8:30 A.M. to 2 P.M. and Saturdays 8:30 A.M. to 1 P.M.

Although you can exchange money at special exchange offices and at some hotels, rates are usually best at banks and at ATMs in the Cirrus and Plus networks. Remember that at banks, you usually need your passport to change money. At ATMs in both Spain and Mexico, you can use only four-digit PIN numbers (so you may need to change your PIN before departure); note that transaction fees may be higher than at home. Make sure your credit cards have been programmed for use at ATMs if you want to use them to get cash advances.

CHANGING MONEY

Where can I change	¿Dónde puedo cambiar	DOHN-deh PWEH-doh kahm-BYAHR
• some money?	• algún dinero?	• ahl-GOON dee-NEH-roh?
• dollars?	• dólares?	• DOH-lah-rehs?
• this check?	• este cheque?	• EHS-teh CHEH-keh?
• traveler's checks?	• cheques de viajero?	• CHEH-kehs deh vyah-HEH-roh?
Is the bank open now?	¿El banco está abierto ahora?	ehl BAHN-koh ehs-TAH ah-BYEHR-toh ah-OH-rah?

11

No, it's closed.	**No, está cerrado.**	noh ehs-TAH seh-RRAH-doh
But the currency exchange is open.	**Pero la oficina de cambio está abierta.**	PEH-roh lah oh-fee-SEE-nah deh KAHM-byoh ehs-TAH ah-BYEHR-tah
Do you accept • personal checks? • a bank draft (cashier's check)? • a money order?	**¿Acepta** • **cheques personales?** • **un giro bancario?** • **una órden de pago?**	ah-SEHP-tah • cheh-kehs pehr-soh-nah-lehs? • oon HEE-roh bahn-KAH-ryoh? • OO-nah OHR-dehn deh PAH-goh?
How much is the . . . worth? • dollar • peso • peseta	**¿A cómo está** • **el dólar?** • **el peso?** • **la peseta?**	ah KOH-moh ehs-TAH • ehl DOH-lahr? • ehl PEH-soh? • lah peh-SEH-tah?
Do you need • identification? • my passport? • other documents?	**¿Necesita** • **identificación?** • **mi pasaporte?** • **otros documentos?**	neh-seh-SEE-tah • ee-dehn-tee-fee-kah-SYOHN? • mee pah-sah-POHR-teh? • Oh-trohs doh-koo-MEHN-tohs?
Where do I sign?	**¿Dónde firmo?**	DOHN-deh FEER-moh?
May I have • small bills? • large bills? • some large and small bills? • some coins? • the rest in change?	**¿Puede darme** • **billetes chicos?** • **billetes grandes?** • **billetes grandes y chicos?** • **algunas monedas?** • **el resto en cambio?**	PWEH-deh DAHR-meh • bee-YEH-tehs CHEE-kohs? • bee-YEH-tehs GRAHN-dehs? • bee-YEH-tehs GRAHN-dehs ee CHEE-kohs? • ahl-GOO-nahs moh-NEH-dahs? • ehl rrehs-toh ehn KAHM-byoh?

TIPPING

Service charges are fairly common in better restaurants in both Spain and Mexico. This may amount to about 10 to 15 percent. A tip may be added to the service charge in accordance with the level of service provided. When no service charge is added to the bill, you should leave about 15 percent tip in better restaurants and 10 percent in less expensive restaurants and in smaller towns.

Tips are also given for a variety of other services. The following chart will serve as a general guide.

Service	Spain	Mexico
Waiter	small change	15% plus small change
Bellboy/porter	125 pesetas per suitcase	7.50 pesos per suitcase
Chambermaid	125 pesetas per day	7.50 pesos per day
Usher	125 pesetas	7.50 pesos
Taxi driver	small change	optional, small change
Barber/hairdresser	375 pesetas	15 pesos
Shoeshine	small change	small change
Bathroom attendant	60 pesetas	small change

PAYING THE BILL

How much does it cost?	**¿Cuánto cuesta?**	KWAHN-toh KWEHS-tah?
The bill, please.	**La cuenta, por favor.**	lah KWEN-tah pohr fah-VOHR
How much do I owe you?	**¿Cuánto le debo?**	KWAN-toh leh DEH-boh?

13

| Is service included? | ¿El servicio está incluido? | ehl sehr-VEE-syoh ehs-TAH een-kloo-EE-doh? |
| This is for you. | Esto es para usted. | EHS-toh ehs pah-rah oos-TEHD |

TELLING TIME

What time is it?	¿Qué hora es?	keh OH-rah ehs?
At what time?	¿A qué hora?	ah keh OH-rah?
It's	Es	ehs
• one o'clock.	• la una.	• lah OO-nah
• 1:15.	• la una y cuarto.	• lah OO-nah ee KWAHR-toh
• 1:30.	• la una y media.	• lah OO-nah ee MEH-dyah
It's	Son las	sohn lahs
• 1:45.*	• dos menos cuarto.	• dohs MEH-nos KWAHR-toh
• two o'clock.	• dos.	• dohs
• two o'clock in the morning.	• dos de la mañana.	• dohs deh lah mah-NYAH-nah
• two o'clock in the afternoon.	• dos de la tarde.	• dohs deh lah TAHR-deh
• 2:10.	• dos y diez.	• dohs ee dyehs
• 2:50.*	• tres menos diez.	• trehs MEH-nohs dyehs
• three o'clock.	• tres.	• trehs
• four o'clock.	• cuatro.	• KWAH-troh
• five o'clock.	• cinco.	• SEEN-koh
• six o'clock.	• seis.	• says
• seven o'clock.	• siete.	• SYEH-teh
• eight o'clock.	• ocho.	• OO-choh
• nine o'clock.	• nueve.	• NWEH-veh
• ten o'clock.	• diez.	• dyehs
• eleven o'clock.	• once.	• OHN-seh
• twelve o'clock.	• doce.	• DOH-seh
It's midnight	Es media noche	ehs MEH-dyah NOH-cheh

14

It's noon	**Es el mediodía**	ehs ehl meh-dyoh-DEE-ah
Five minutes ago	**Hace cinco minutos**	AH-seh SEEN-koh mee-NOO-tohs
In a half hour	**En media hora**	ehn MEH-dyah OH-rah
After 8 P.M.	**Después de las ocho de la noche**	dehs-PWEHS deh lahs OH-choh deh lah NOH-cheh
Before 9 A.M.	**Antes de las nueve de la mañana**	AHN-tehs deh lahs NWEH-veh deh lah mah-NYAH-nah
When does it begin?	**¿Cuándo empieza?**	KWAHN-doh ehm-PYEH-sah?
He came.	**El llegó.**	ehl yeh-GOH
• on time.	• **a tiempo.**	• ah TYEHM-poh
• early.	• **temprano.**	• tehm-PRAH-noh
• late.	• **tarde.**	• TAHR-deh

*After the half hour on the clock, minutes are subtracted from the next hour. The literal translation of the Spanish for 1:45 is "two minus a quarter" (of an hour).

In Spanish-speaking countries, the 24-hour system, familiar in the United States as "military time," is often used in official listings, such as transportation schedules and theater times (3:00 P.M. is 12 plus 3, or 15:00, and so on, until 24:00, which is midnight). Midnight is also expressed as 00:00, and minutes past midnight are expressed as 00:01, and so forth, until 01:00.

You can use the following chart for quick reference.

THE 24-HOUR SYSTEM

1 A.M.	01:00	**la una**	lah OO-nah
2 A.M.	02:00	**las dos**	lahs dohs
3 A.M.	03:00	**las tres**	lahs trehs
4 A.M.	04:00	**las cuatro**	lahs KWAH-troh
5 A.M.	05:00	**las cinco**	lahs SEEN-koh

15

6 A.M.	06:00	**las seis**	lahs says
7 A.M.	07:00	**las siete**	lahs SYEH-teh
8 A.M.	08:00	**las ocho**	lahs OH-choh
9 A.M.	09:00	**las nueve**	lahs NWEH-veh
10 A.M.	10:00	**las diez**	lahs dyehs
11 A.M.	11:00	**las once**	lahs OHN-seh
12 noon	12:00	**las doce**	lahs DOH-seh
1 P.M.	13:00	**las trece**	lahs TREH-seh
2 P.M.	14:00	**las catorce**	lahs kah-TOHR-seh
3 P.M.	15:00	**las quince**	lahs KEEN-seh
4 P.M.	16:00	**las dieciséis**	lahs dyeh-see-SAYS
5 P.M.	17:00	**las diecisiete**	lahs dyeh-see-SYE-teh
6 P.M.	18:00	**las dieciocho**	lahs dyeh-see-OH-choh
7 P.M.	19:00	**las diecinueve**	lahs dyeh-see-NWEH-veh
8 P.M.	20:00	**las veinte**	lahs VAYN-teh
9 P.M.	21:00	**las veintiuno**	lahs vayn-tee-OO-noh
10 P.M.	22:00	**las veintidós**	lahs vayn-tee-DOHS
11 P.M.	23:00	**las veintitrés**	lahs vayn-tee-TREHS
12 mid-night	24:00	**las veinticuatro**	lahs vayn-tee-KWAH-troh

The show you're planning to see might start at 7:30 P.M. or 19:30 *(las diecinueve horas y treinta minutos)*.

2/AT THE AIRPORT

When you go through customs, most personal items—like clothing, tobacco products, alcohol, and perfume—are duty free. However, in Mexico, you may have to prove that electrical appliances—such as tape recorders and radios—are for personal use and not for resale in the country. Small appliances—hair dryers, electric razors, and the like—present no problem. Here's a typical dialogue you may encounter.

DIALOGUE: CUSTOMS AND IMMIGRATION (ADUANA E INMIGRACIÓN)

Empleado de inmigración:	**Buenos días. ¿Puedo ver su pasaporte?**	BWEH-nohs DEE-ahs. PWEH-doh vehr soo pah-sah-POHR-teh?
Turista:	**Sí, aquí lo tiene.**	see, ah-KEE luh TYEH-neh
Empleado:	**¿Es usted norteamericano(-a)?**	ehs oos-TEHD nohr-teh-ah-meh-ree KAH-noh(-nah)?
Turista:	**Sí, lo soy.**	see, loh soy
Empleado:	**¿Cuánto tiempo va a estar en el país?**	KWAHN-toh TYEHM-poh vah ah ehs-TAHR ehn ehl PAH-ees?
Turista:	**Voy a estar aquí por tres semanas.**	voy ah ehs-TAHR ah-KEE pohr trehs seh-MAH-nahs
. . . .		
Officer:	Hello. May I see your passport?	
Tourist:	Yes, here it is.	
Officer:	Are you American?	
Tourist:	Yes, I am.	

17

| Officer: | How long will you stay in the country? |
| Tourist: | I'll be here for three weeks. |

CLEARING CUSTOMS

What nationality are you?	¿Qué nacionalidad tiene?	Keh nah-syoh-nah-lee-DAHD TYEHN-eh?
I'm	Soy	soy
• American.	• norteamericano (-a).	• nohr-teh-ah-meh-ree-KAH-noh(-nah)
• Canadian.	• canadiense.	• kah-nah-DYEHN-seh
• English.	• inglés(-a).	• een-GLEHS(-GLEH-sah)
What's your name?	¿Cómo se llama?	KOH-moh seh YAH-mah?
My name is . . .	Me llamo . . .	Meh YAH-moh . . .
Where will you be staying?	¿Dónde va a quedarse?	DOHN-deh vah ah keh-DAHR-seh?
I am staying at the Rex hotel.	Estoy en el hotel Rex.	ehs-TOY ehn ehl oh-TEHL rrehks
Are you here on vacation?	¿Está de vacaciones?	ehs-TAH deh vah-kah-SYOH-nehs?
I'm just passing through.	Estoy de paso.	ehs-TOY deh PAH-soh
I'm here on a business trip.	Estoy aquí en viaje de negocios.	ehs-TOY ah-KEE ehn VYAH-heh deh neh-GOH-syohs
I'll be here for	Voy a estar aquí por	voy ah ehs-TAHR ah-KEE pohr
• a few days.	• unos días.	• OO-nohs DEE-ahs
• a week.	• una semana.	• OO-nah seh-MAH-nah
• several weeks.	• unas semanas.	• OO-nahs seh-MAH-nahs

18

English	Spanish	Pronunciation
• a month.	• un mes.	• oon mehs
Your passport, please.	Su pasaporte, por favor.	soo pah-sah-POHR-teh, pohr fah-VOHR
Do you have anything to declare?	¿Tiene algo para declarar?	TYEH-neh AHL-goh pah-rah deh-klah-RAHR?
No, I have nothing to declare.	No, no tengo nada para declarar.	noh, noh THEN-goh NAH-dah pah-rah deh-klah-RAHR
Can you open the bag?	¿Puede abrir la maleta?	PWEH-deh ah-BREER lah mah-LEH-tah?
Of course.	Por supuesto.	pohr soo-PWEHS-toh
What are these?	¿Qué son éstos?	keh sohn EHS-tohs?
They're • personal effects.	Son • efectos personales.	sohn • eh-FEHK-tohs pehr-soh-NAH-lehs
• gifts.	• regalos.	• rreh-GAH-lohs
Do I have to pay duty?	¿Tengo que pagar impuestos?	TEHN-goh keh pah-GAIIR eem-PWEHS-tohs?
Yes./No.	Sí./No.	see/noh
Have a nice stay.	¡Buena estadía!	BWEH-nah ehs-tah-DEE-ah!

LUGGAGE AND PORTERS

Porters are usually available at major airports and train stations. Some places may provide baggage carts to help you move your luggage to ground transportation. Give your luggage only to uniformed redcaps, noting his or her name or number. Be wary of bystanders who are not official employees.

English	Spanish	Pronunciation
I need • a porter.	Necesito • un maletero.	neh-seh-SEE-toh • oon mah-leh-TEH-roh

19

• a baggage cart.	• **un carrito para maletas.**	• oon kah-RREE-toh PAH-rah mah-LEH-tahs
Here is my luggage.	**Aquí están mis maletas.**	ah-KEE ehs-TAHN mees mah-LEH-tahs
Take my bags	**Lleve mis maletas**	YEH-veh mees mah-LEH-tahs
• to the taxi.	• **al taxi.**	• ahl TAHK-see
• to the bus.	• **al autobús.**	• ahl ow-toh-BOOS
• to the sidewalk.	• **a la acera.**	• ah lah ah-SEH-rah
Please be careful!	**¡Cuidado, por favor!**	kwee-DAH-doh, pohr fah-VOHR!
How much is it?	**¿Cuánto es?**	KWAHN-toh ehs?

AT THE AIRLINE COUNTER

Do you know where . . . is?	**¿Sabe dónde está la aerolínea**	SAH-beh DOHN-deh ehs-TAH lah ah-eh-roh-LEE-neh-ah
• Iberia	• **Iberia?**	• ee-BEHR-ee-ah?
• Mexicana	• **Mexicana?**	• meh-hee-KAH-nah?
Where is	**¿Dónde está**	DOHN-deh ehs-TAH
• the information booth?	• **el mostrador de información?**	• ehl mohs-trah-DOHR deh een-fohr-mah-SYON?
• the ticket counter?	• **el despacho de billetes?**	• ehl dehs-PAH-choh deh bee-YE-tehs?
• luggage check-in?	• **la entrega de equipaje?**	• lah en-TREH-gah deh eh-kee-PAH-heh?
the airport tax?	• **el lugar para pagar el impuesto de salida?**	• the place to pay • ehl loo-GAHR pah-rah pah-GAHR ehl eem-PWEHS-toh deh sah-LEE-dah?

COMMON AIRPORT TERMS AND SIGNS

vuelo directo	VWEH-loh dee-REHK-toh	direct flight (non-stop)

20

vuelo con escalas	VWEH-loh kohn ehs-KAH-lahs	direct flight (with stops)
número de vuelo	NOO-meh-roh deh VWEH-loh	flight number
viaje de ida	VYAH-heh deh EE-dah	one-way flight
viaje de ida y vuelta	VYAH-heh deh EE-dah ee VWEHL-tah	round trip
primera clase	pree-MEH-rah KLAH-seh	first class
clase turística	KLAH-seh too-REES-tee-kah	tourist class
asiento a la ventanilla	ah-SYEHN-toh ah lah vehn-tah-NEE-yah	window seat
asiento al pasillo	ah-SYEHN-toh ahl pah-SEE-yoh	aisle seat
número de asiento	NOO-meh-roh deh ah-SYEHN-toh	seat number
sección de fumar	sehk-SYOHN deh foo-MAHR	smoking section
equipaje de mano	eh-kee-PAH-heh deh MAH-noh	carry-on luggage
etiquetas	eh-tee-KEH-tahs	luggage tags
LINEAS NACIONALES	LEE-neh-ahs nah-syoh-NAH-lehs	NATIONAL AIRLINES
LINEAS INTERNA-CIONALES	LEE-neh-ahs een-tehr-nah-syoh-NAH-lehs	INTERNATIONAL AIRLINES
VUELOS NACIONALES	VWEH-lohs nah-syoh-NAH-lehs	NATIONAL FLIGHTS
VUELOS INTERNA-CIONALES	VWEH-lohs een-ter-nah-syoh-NAH-lehs	INTERNATIONAL FLIGHTS
SALIDAS	sah-LEE-dahs	DEPARTURES

LLEGADAS	yeh-GAH-dahs	ARRIVALS
NO FUMAR	noh foo-MAHR	NO SMOKING
PUERTA DE SALIDA	PWEHR-tah deh sah-LEE-dah	DEPARTURE GATE

AIRPORT SERVICES AND TRANSPORTATION

In cities like Mexico City or Madrid, look for booths that sell tickets for buses or taxis. This is usually better than paying the taxi driver directly. Fares generally vary by zones. Some taxis take two to three passengers and let them off in order of their destination on the route. If you prefer a private taxi, say so when buying your ticket and be prepared to pay a higher fare.

Where is	¿Dónde está	DOHN-deh ehs-TAH
• the lost-baggage office?	• **la sección de equipaje perdido?**	• lah sehk-SYOHN deh eh-kee-PAH-heh pehr-DEE-doh?
• the duty-free shop?	• **la tienda libre de impuestos?**	• lah TYEHN-dah lee-BREH deh eem-PWEHS-tohs?
• the money exchange?	• **la casa de cambio?**	• lah KAH-sah deh KAHM-byoh?
• a car rental agency?	• **una agencia de alquiler de autos?**	• OO-nah ah-HEHN-syah deh ahl-kee-LEHR deh ow-tohs?
• the bus stop?	• **la parada de autobuses?**	• lah pah-RAH-dah deh ow-toh-BOO-sehs?
• the taxi stand?	• **la parada de taxis?**	• lah pah-RAH-dah deh TAHK-sees?

3/FINDING YOUR WAY

TAKING A TAXI

Taxis in Spain are usually easy to identify; most display a logo
on the door or have a light on top. Sometimes, however, their
only distinction may be the color of the license plate. Taxis are
normally easy to find at airports near the baggage-claim areas.
From your hotel, taxis taken at a taxi stop (*una parada de
taxis*/OO-nah pah-RAH-dah deh TAHK-sees/) or just outside
the hotel may sometimes be a little more expensive than those
you can hail along the street. Some taxis charge by zones and
should display a map showing the fares by zone. Others charge
whatever appears on the meter. If there is no meter, you should
settle on the fare before getting in. Also watch for any special
regulations applying to charges for bags or supplemental fees
after certain hours. In Mexico, a small tip may be given, usually by rounding off the fare. A 10 percent tip is customary in
Spain.

DIALOGUE: TAKING A TAXI (COGER UN TAXI)

Turista:	**Buenos días. ¿Está libre?**	BWEH-nohs DEE-ahs. ehs-tah LEE-breh?
Chofer:	**Sí, ¿adónde va?**	see, ah-DOHN-deh vah?
Turista:	**A la estación de au-tobuses.**	ah lah ehs-tah-SYOHN deh ow-toh-BOO-sehs
Chofer:	**Está bien.**	ehs-TAH byehn
Turista:	**¿Cuánto demora?**	KWAHN-TOH deh-MOH-rah?
Chofer:	**Unos veinte minutos.**	OO-nohs VAYN-teh mee-NOO-tohs
Turista:	**Está bien. Muchas gracias.**	ehs-TAH byehn. MOO-chas GRAH-syahs
. . . .		
Tourist:	Good day. Is this taxi free?	

23

Driver:	Yes, where are you going?
Tourist:	To the bus station.
Driver:	Fine.
Tourist:	How long does it take?
Driver:	About twenty minutes.
Tourist:	That's fine. Thank you.

Is this taxi • free? • occupied?	¿Está • libre? • ocupado?	ehs-TAH • LEE-breh? • oh-koo-PAH-doh?
Do you know this address?	¿Conoce usted esta dirección?	koh-NOH-seh oos-TEHD EHS-tah dee-rehk-SYOHN?
Please take me	Lléveme, por favor,	YEH-veh-meh, pohr fah-VOHR,
• to the Hotel Rex.	• al hotel Rex.	• ahl oh-TEHL rrehks
• to the station.	• a la estación.	• ah lah ehs-tah-SYOHN
• to the main square.	• a la plaza principal.	• ah lah PLAH-sah preen-see-PAHL
• to the center (of town).	• al centro.	• ahl SEHN-troh
• to White Street.	• a la calle Blanca	• ah lah KAH-yeh BLAHN-kah
• to Royal Avenue.	• a la avenida Royal	• ah lah ah-veh-NEE-dah roy-AHL
Slower, please.	Más despacio, por favor.	mahs des-PAH-syoh, pohr fah-VOHR
Stop over there.	Pare allá.	PAH-reh ah-YAH
meter	el taxímetro	el tahk-SEE-meh-troh
fare	la tarifa	lah tah-REE-fah
fixed rate	la tarifa fija	lah tah-REE-fah FEE-hah
tip	la propina	lah proh-PEE-nah

24

ON THE BUS

The bus networks in Spain and Mexico are extensive. In both countries, intercity buses go where trains do not, service is frequent, and tickets can usually be purchased on the spot. First-class buses have televisions and, in Mexico, even hostess service. There are often several bus stations (*las terminales de autobuses*/lahs tehr-mee-NAH-lehs deh ow-toh-BOO-schs/) in different parts of the city; which you use depends on your destination.

Buses in Madrid and Mexico City are efficient. Most Latin American cities have extensive urban bus systems; however, buses do tend to be overcrowded.

Although it is usually easiest and fastest to take a taxi to your destination, there are good reasons to take a bus. It's inexpensive and you can sight-see at the same time. In Mexico City, another transportation option is the *pesero,* usually a taxi or small van that follows a fixed route and charges a fixed fare. Although they pick up and drop off passengers along the way, they are faster than the larger city buses.

I'm looking for the bus stop.	**Estoy buscando la parada de autobuses.**	ehs-TOY boos-KAHN-doh lah pah-RAH-dah deh ow-toh-BOO-sehs
What bus line goes	**¿Qué linea va**	keh LEE-neh-ah vah
• north?	• **al norte?**	• ahl NOHR-teh?
• south?	• **al sur?**	• ahl soor?
• east?	• **al este?**	• ahl EHS-teh?
• west?	• **al oeste?**	• ahl oh-EHS-teh?
What bus do I take to go to	**¿Qué autobús tomo para ir a**	keh ow-toh-BOOS TOH-moh PAH-rah eer ah
• Madrid?	• **Madrid?**	• mah-DREED?
• Mexico City?	• **la ciudad de México?**	• lah syoo-DAHD deh MEH-hee-koh?

25

How many stops until the Museum of Modern Art?	¿Cuántas paradas hasta el Museo de Arte Moderno?	KWAHN-tahs pah-RAH-dahs AHS-tah ehl moo-SEH-oh deh AHR-teh moh-DEHR-noh?
How long does it take to get to Seville?	¿Cuánto demora para ir hasta Sevilla?	KWAHN-toh deh-MOH-rah PAH-rah eer AHS-tah seh-VEE-yah?
Can you tell me when to get off?	¿Podría decirme cuando debo bajarme?	poh-DREE-ah deh-SEER-meh KWAN-doh DEH-boh bah-HAHR-meh?
How much is the fare?	¿Cuánto es el pasaje?	KWAHN-toh ehs ehl pah-SAH-heh?
Should I pay when I get on?	¿Debo pagar al subir?	DEH-boh pah-GAHR ahl soo-BEER?
Where do I take the bus to return?	¿Dónde se toma el autobús para regresar?	DOHN-deh seh TOH-mah ehl ow-toh-BOOS PAH-rah rreh-greh-SAHR?
How often do the return buses run?	¿Cada cuánto hay autobuses de regreso?	KAH-dah KWAHN-toh ahy ow-toh-BOO-sehs deh rreh-GREH-soh?
Which is the closest stop to the park?	¿Cuál es la parada más cercana al parque?	KWAHL ehs lah pah-RAH-dah mahs sehr-KAH-nah ahl PAHR-keh?
I would like • a ticket. • a receipt. • a reserved seat. • first class. • second class.	Quisiera • un boleto. • un compro-bante. • un asiento numerado. • primera clase. • segunda clase.	kee-SYEH-rah • oon boh-LEH-toh • oon kohm-proh-BAHN-teh • oon ah-SYEHN-toh noo-meh-RAH-doh • pree-MEH-rah KLAH-seh • seh-GOON-dah KLAH-seh

26

• a direct bus.	• **un autobús directo.**	• oon ow-toh-BOOS dee-REHK-toh
• an express bus.	• **un autobús expreso.**	• oon ow-toh-BOOS ehks-PREH-soh
• ticketed luggage.	• **equipaje facturado.**	• eh-kee-PAH-heh fahk-too-RAH-doh

USING THE SUBWAY

Metros, or subway systems, in Madrid, Barcelona, Mexico City, Caracas, and Buenos Aires are all quite efficient, and Mexico City's is especially beautiful. All will save you time and get you to all of the most important places. Like subways anywhere, the metro tends to be crowded, especially at rush hour.

Where can I buy a token?	**¿Dónde puedo comprar una ficha?**	DOHN-deh PWEH-doh kohm-PRAHR OO-nah FEE-chah?
How much are they?	**¿Cuánto cuestan?**	KWAHN-toh KWEHS-tahn?
Is there a map for the metro?	**¿Hay un mapa del metro?**	ahy oon MAH-pah dehl MEH-troh?
Which train do I take to go to . . . ?	**¿Que tren tomo para ir a . . . ?**	keh trehn TOH-moh PAH-rah eer ah . . . ?
Can you tell me when we arrive at . . . ?	**¿Me avisa cuando lleguemos a . . . ?**	meh ah-VEE-sah KWAHN-doh yeh-GEH-mohs ah . . . ?

GOING BY TRAIN
In Spain

Traveling by train in Spain is not only convenient, but also a great way to see the countryside if you travel by day, and a comfortable way to go overnight on a long stretch. Discounts are available for trips in accordance with the kilometers you travel. It's a good idea to make reservations, which can be done at travel agencies or at the railway station.

Train services in Spain are classified in several ways:

Expreso
(ehks-PREH-soh)
A long-distance night train with few stops.

Rápido
(RAH-pee-doh)
A fast train, but not nearly as fast as the Expreso, which makes more stops.

Talgo
(TAHL-goh)
Deluxe accommodations, reclining seats, and air conditioning. Travels between major cities, such as Madrid, Barcelona, Valencia, Sevilla, Cádiz, Málaga, and Bilbao.

Electrotren
(eh-LEHK-troh-trehn)
A luxury train, not as fast as the Talgo, with more stops, and also more economical.

TER
(teh eh eh-reh)
A luxury diesel express, like the Talgo, but with more stops.

TAF
(te ah eh-feh)
A second-class diesel train.

Ferrobuses
(feh-rroh-BOO-sehs)
Local trains.

In Mexico

For train buffs and the well composed, who don't mind if everything is absolutely off-schedule on a long trip, riding the rails in Mexico has its merits—glimpses of small villages, economical fares, and scenery that's sometimes spectacular. However, as first-class bus service proliferates throughout the country, the government is privatizing the luxury rail service that has been most attractive to tourists, and schedules are being cut, often with little notice. A good source of general information is the **Mexican National Railways,** Insurgente Norte, Avda. Eje # 1 Norte (tel. 52/5547-6593). Information and reservations are also available in the United States from **Mexico by Train** (tel. 210/725-3659 or 800/321-1699).

When does the train leave for Madrid?	¿Cuándo sale el tren para Madrid?	KWAN-doh SAH-leh ehl trehn PAH-rah mah-DREED?
Is it a . . . train?	¿Es un tren	ehs oon trehn
• local	• local?	• loh-KAHL?
• express	• expreso?	• eks-PREH-soh?
• through	• directo?	• dee-REHK-toh?
When does the train . . .	¿Cuándo . . . el tren?	KWAHN-doh . . . ehl trehn?
• leave?	• sale	• SAH-leh
• arrive?	• llega	• YEH-gah
Is the train	¿Está el tren	ehs-TAH ehl trehn
• on time?	• en hora?	• ehn OH-rah?
• late?	• retrasado?	• rreh-trah-SAH-doh?
From what platform does it leave?	¿De qué andén sale?	deh keh ahn-DEHN SAH-leh?
Does this train stop at	¿Este tren para en	ES-teh trehn PAH-rah ehn
• Cordoba?	• Córdoba?	• KOHR-doh-bah?
• Toledo?	• Toledo?	• toh-LEH-doh?
• Jerez?	• Jerez?	• heh-REHS?
Is there time to	¿Hay tiempo para	ahy TYEHM-poh PAH-rah
• eat something?	• comer algo?	• koh-MEHR AHL-goh?
• drink something?	• tomar algo?	• toh-MAHR AHL-goh?
• buy something?	• comprar algo?	• kohm-PRAHR AHL-goh?
• take pictures?	• tomar fotografías?	• toh-MAHR foh-toh-grah-FEE-ahs?
Is there a dining car?	¿Hay un coche-comedor?	ahy oon KOH-cheh koh-meh-DOHR?
Is there a sleeping car?	¿Hay un coche-cama?	ahy oon KOH-cheh KAH-mah?

I'd like a . . . ticket.	**Quisiera un billete de**	kee-SYEH-rah oon bee-YEH-teh deh
• round-trip	• **ida y vuelta.**	• EE-dah ee VWEHL-tah
• one-way	• **ida.**	• EE-dah
Is this seat taken?	**¿Está ocupado este asiento?**	ehs-TAH oh-koo-PAH-doh EHS-teh ah-SYEHN-toh?
Excuse me, I believe this is my seat.	**Perdón, creo que éste es mi asiento.**	pehr-DOHN, KREH-oh keh EHS-teh ehs mee ah-SYEHN-toh
Sorry, this seat is occupied.	**Perdón, este asiento está ocupado.**	pehr-DOHN, EHS-teh ah-SYEHN-toh ehs-TAH oh-koo-PAH-doh
No, it's not occupied.	**No, no está ocupado.**	noh, noh ehs-TAH oh-koo-PAH-doh
I would like a no-smoking compartment.	**Quisiera un compartimiento de no fumar.**	kee-SYEH-rah oon cohm-pahr-tih-MYEHN-toh deh noh foo-MAHR

WALKING AROUND

Do you have a map of the city?	**¿Tiene usted un mapa de la ciudad?**	TYEH-neh oos-TEHD OON MAH-pah deh lah syoo-DAHD?
Could you show me on the map?	**¿Puede usted indicármelo en el mapa?**	PWEH-deh oo-STEHD een-dee-KAHR-meh-loh ehn ehl MAH-pah?
Can I get there on foot?	**¿Puedo llegar allí a pie?**	PWEH-doh yeh-GAHR ah-YEE ah pyeh?
How far is it?	**¿A qué distancia es?**	ah keh dees-TAHN-syah ehs?
I'm lost.	**Estoy perdido(-a).**	ehs-TOY pehr-DEE-doh(-dah)

Where is	¿Dónde está	DOHN-deh ehs-TAH
• the Hotel Rex?	• el hotel Rex?	• ehl oh-TEHL rreks?
• . . . Street?	• la calle . . . ?	• lah KAH-yeh . . . ?
• . . . Avenue?	• la avenida . . . ?	• lah ah-veh-NEE-dah . . . ?

How can I get to	¿Cómo puedo ir a	KOH-moh PWEH-doh eer ah
• the train station?	• la estación de ferrocarril?	• lah ehs-tah-SYON deh feh-rroh-cah-RREEL?
• the bus stop?	• la parada de autobuses?	• lah pah-RAH-dah deh ow-toh-BOO-ses?
• the ticket office?	• la taquilla?	• lah tah-KEE-yah?
• the subway entrance?	• la entrada del metro?	• lah ehn-TRAH-dah dehl MEH-troh?
• the airport?	• el aeropuerto?	• ehl ah-eh-roh-PWEHR-toh?

straight ahead	derecho	deh-REH-choh
to the right	a la derecha	uh lah deh-REH-chah
to the left	a la izquierda	ah lah ees-KYEHR-dah
a block away	a una cuadra	ah OO-nah KWAH-drah
on the corner	en la esquina	ehn lah ehs-KEE-nah
on the square	en la plaza	ehn lah PLAH-sah
facing, opposite	enfrente	ehn-FREHN-teh
across	al frente	ahl FREHN-teh
next to	al lado	ahl LAH-doh
near	cerca	SEHR-kah
far	lejos	LEH-hohs

31

COMMON PUBLIC SIGNS

ENTRADA	ehn-TRAH-dah	ENTRANCE
SALIDA	sah-LEE-dah	EXIT
PARADA	pah-RAH-dah	(BUS) STOP
ABIERTO	ah-BYEHR-toh	OPEN
CERRADO	seh-RRAH-doh	CLOSED
BAJADA	bah-HAH-dah	DOWN
SUBIDA	soo-BEE-dah	UP
EMPUJE	ehm-POO-heh	PUSH
JALE (*Mexico*) (*or*) TIRE	HAH-leh TEE-reh	PULL
ALTO	AHL-toh	STOP
PELIGRO	peh-LEE-groh	DANGER
NO PASE	noh PAH-seh	DO NOT ENTER
SERVICIOS (*Spain*)	sehr-VEE-syohs	TOILETS
PRIVADO	pree-VAH-doh	PRIVATE
DAMAS	DAH-mahs	LADIES
SEÑORAS	seh-NYOH-rahs	WOMEN
CABALLEROS	kah-bah-YEH-rohs	GENTLEMEN
SEÑORES	seh-NYOH-rehs	MEN
BAÑOS	BAH-nyohs	BATHROOMS
LAVABO	lah-VAH-boh	SINK
AGUA NO POTABLE	AH-gwah noh poh-TAH-bleh	NOT DRINKING WATER
PROHIBIDO FUMAR	proh-ee-BEE-doh foo-MAHR	NO SMOKING

PROHIBIDO SACAR FOTO- GRAFIAS	proh-ee-BEE-doh sah- KAHR foh-toh-graf- FEE-ahs	NO PHOTOGRAPHS
PROHIBIDO TIRAR OBJETOS POR LA VENTANA	proh-ee-BEE-doh tee- RAHR ohb-HEH-tohs pohr lah vehn-TAH-nah	DO NOT THROW OBJECTS OUT OF THE WINDOW
SALIDA DE EMERGENCIA	sah-LEE-dah deh eh- mehr-HEHN-syah	EMERGENCY EXIT

4/ACCOMMODATIONS

In most cases, it's best to make hotel reservations in advance, especially if an important holiday or celebration is taking place in an area. In Spain, hotels include both new high-rises and lovely *paradors,* inns installed in castles, monasteries, and convents. You will find complete hotel information in the *Guía de Hoteles* (Hotel Guide), available at any branch of the Spanish National Tourist Office.

In Mexico, accommodations range from simple budget properties to modern high-rise hotels. You will also find *posadas,* or inns, which are often restored estates, haciendas, or monasteries dating from the 16th and 17th centuries but with modern amenities. All the better hotels have air-conditioning; the simpler ones have showers but not bathtubs.

In both Spain and Mexico, the government rates properties with one to five stars. Ratings reflect the number of facilities and amenities rather than the quality of the property.

hotel	**hotel**	oh-TEHL
pension (usually with meals)	**pensión**	pehn-SYOHN
small hotel	**albergue**	ahl-BEHR-geh
top-quality government hotel (*Spain*)	**parador**	pah-rah-DOHR
inn (usually in the countryside)	**refugio**	rreh-FOO-hyoh
inn	**posada**	poh-SAH-dah
student residence	**residencia estudiantil**	rreh-see-DEHN-syah ehs-too-dyahn-TEEL

DIALOGUE: AT THE FRONT DESK (EN LA RECEPCIÓN)

Turista:	**Quisiera una habitación doble, por favor.**	kee-SYEH-rah OO-nah ah-bee-tah-SYOHN DOH-bleh, pohr fah-VOHR
Recepcionista:	**¿Por cuánto tiempo?**	pohr KWAHN-toh TYEHM-poh?
Turista:	**Por cuatro noches.**	pohr KWAH-troh NOH-chehs
	¿Cuánto cuesta por noche?	KWAHN-toh KWEHS-tah pohr NOH-cheh?
Recepcionista:	**Cuesta 35.000 pesos por noche.**	KWEHS-tah trayn-tee-SEEN-koh meel PEH-sohs pohr NOH-cheh
Turista:	**Está bien. ¿Puedo anotarme?**	ehs-TAH byehn. PWEH-doh ah-noh-TAR-meh?
Recepcionista:	**Sí. Llene este for-mulario, por favor**	see. YEH-neh EHS-teh fohr-moo-LAH-ryoh, pohr fah-VOHR
Turista:	**¡Cómo no! Gracias.**	KOH-moh noh! GRAH-syahs

. . . .

Tourist:	I'd like a double room, please.
Clerk:	For how long?
Tourist:	For four nights. How much is it per night?
Clerk:	It's 35,000 pesos per night.
Tourist:	Fine. May I register?
Clerk:	Yes. Please fill out this form.
Tourist:	Of course. Thank you.

HOTEL ARRANGEMENTS AND SERVICES

I would like a room for | **Quisiera una habitación por** | kee-SYEH-rah OO-nah ah-bee-tah-SYOHN pohr

- one night.
- two nights.
- a week.

- two weeks.

- **una noche.**
- **dos noches.**
- **una semana.**

- **dos semanas.**

- OO-nah NOH-cheh
- dohs NOH-chehs
- OO-nah seh-MAH-nah
- dohs seh-MAH-nahs

How much is it
- for a day?
- for a week?

¿Cuánto es
- **por día?**
- **por una semana?**

KWAHN-toh ehs
- pohr DEE-ah?
- pohr OO-nah seh-MAH-nah?

Does that include tax? | **¿Incluye impuestos?** | een-KLOO-yeh eem-PWEHS-tohs?

I have a reservation. | **Tengo una reservación** | TEHN-goh OO-nah rreh-sehr-vah-SYOHN

| **(or) . . . una reserva. (Spain)** | . . . OO-nah rre-SEHR-vah

Do you have a room with
- a private bath?

- air-conditioning?

- heat?
- television?
- hot water?

- a balcony?
- a view facing the street?
- a view facing the ocean?

¿Tiene una habitación con
- **baño privado?**

- **aire acondicionado?**

- **calefacción?**
- **televisor?**
- **agua caliente?**

- **balcón?**
- **vista a la calle?**

- **vista al mar?**

TYEH-neh OO-nah ah-bee-tah-SYOHN kohn
- BAH-nyoh pree-VAH-doh?
- Y-reh ah-kohn-dee-syoh-NAH-doh?
- kah-leh-fak-SYOHN?
- teh-leh-vee-SOHR?
- AH-gwah kah-LYEHN-teh?
- bahl-KOHN?
- VEES-tah ah lah KAH-yeh?
- VEES-tah ahl mahr?

Does the hotel have

- a restaurant?

¿Tiene el hotel . . . ?

- **un restaurante**

TYEH-neh . . . ehl oh-TEHL

- oon rrehs-tow-RAHN-teh

• a bar?	• **un bar**	• oon bahr
• a swimming pool?	• **una piscina**	• OO-nah pee-SEE-nah
• room service?	• **servicio de habitación**	• sehr-VEE-syoh deh ah-bee-tah-SYOHN?
• a garage?	• **un garage**	• oon gah-RAH-heh
• a safe-deposit box?	• **una caja de valores**	• OO-nah KAH-hah deh vah-LOH-rehs
• laundry service?	• **servicio de lavandería**	• sehr-VEE-syoh deh lah-vahn-deh-REE-ah
I would like	**Quisiera**	kee-SYE-rah
• meals included.	• **con las comidas incluidas.**	• kohn lahs koh-MEE-dahs een-KLUEE-dahs
• breakfast only.	• **solamente con desayuno.**	• soh-lah-MEN-teh kohn deh-sah-YOO-noh
• no meals included.	• **sin comidas.**	• seen koh-MEE-dahs
• an extra bed.	• **una cama más.**	• OO-nah KAH-mah mahs
• a baby crib.	• **una çuna para bebé.**	• OO-nah KOO-nah PAH-rah beh-BEH
• another towel.	• **otra toalla.**	• OH-trah TWAH-yah
• soap.	• **jabón.**	• hah-BOHN
• clothes hangers.	• **ganchos de ropa.**	• GAHN-chohs deh RROH-pah
• another blanket.	• **otra manta.**	• OH-trah MAHN-tah
• drinking water.	• **agua para beber.**	• AH-gwah PAH-rah beh-BEHR
• toilet paper.	• **papel higiénico.**	• pah-PEHL ee-HYE-nee-koh
This room is very	**Esta habitación es muy**	EHS-tah ah-bee-tah-SYOHN ehs muee
• small.	• **pequeña.**	• peh-KEH-nyah
• cold.	• **fría.**	• FREE-ah
• hot.	• **caliente.**	• kah-LYEHN-teh
• dark.	• **oscura.**	• ohs-KOO-rah
• noisy.	• **ruidosa.**	• rruee-DOH-sah

The . . . does not work.	**No funciona**	noh foon-SYOH-nah
• light	• **la luz.**	• lah loos
• heat	• **la calefacción.**	• lah kah-leh-fahk-SYOHN
• toilet	• **el baño.**	• ehl BAH-nyoh
• the air conditioner	• **el aire acondicionado.**	• ehl AY-reh ah-kohn-dee-syo-NAH-doh
• key	• **la llave.**	• lah YAH-veh
• lock	• **el seguro.**	• ehl seh-GOO-roh
• fan	• **el ventilador.**	• ehl VEHN-tee-lah-DOHR
• outlet	• **el enchufe.**	• ehl ehn-CHOO-feh
• television	• **el televisor.**	• ehl teh-leh-vee-SOHR
May I change to another room?	**¿Podría cambiar de habitación?**	poh-DREE-ah kahm-BYAR deh ah-bee-tah-SYOHN?
Is there	**¿Hay**	ahy
• room service?	• **servicio de habitación?**	• sehr-VEE-syoh deh ah-bee-tah-SYOHN?
• laundry service?	• **servicio de lavandería?**	• sehr-VEE-syoh deh lah-vahn-deh-REE-ah?
• a beauty parlor?	• **un salón de belleza?**	• oon sah-LOHN deh beh-YEH-sah?
• a barber shop?	• **una peluquería?**	• OO-nah peh-loo-keh-REE-ah?
• a babysitter?	• **una niñera?**	• OO-nah nee-NYEH-rah?
• a gift shop?	• **una tienda de regalos?**	• OO-nah TYEHN-dah deh rreh-GAH-lohs?
I would like to place an order for room number four.	**Quisiera hacer un pedido para la habitación número cuatro.**	kee-SYEH-rah ah-SEHR oon peh-DEE-doh PAH-rah lah ah-bee-tah-SYOHN NOO-meh-roh KWAH-troh

Can you recommend a babysitter for my child?	¿Puede recomendarme una niñera para cuidar a mi hijo(a)?	PWEH-deh rreh-koh-mehn-DAHR-me OO-nah nee-NYEH-rah PAH-rah KUEE-dahr ah mee EE-hoh(-hah)?
How much do you charge?	¿Cuánto cobra?	KWAHN-toh KOH-brah?
Can you stay until midnight?	¿Puede quedarse hasta medianoche?	PWEH-deh keh-DAHR-seh AHS-tah meh-dyah-NOH-cheh?

USING THE HOTEL TELEPHONE

operator	operadora	oh-peh-rah-DOH-rah
May I have an outside line, please?	¿Me da la línea, por favor?	meh dah lah LEE-neh-ah, pohr fah-VOHR?
I would like to make	Quisiera hacer	kee-SYEH-rah ah-SEHR
• a long-distance call.	• una llamada de larga distancia.	• OO-nah yah-MAH-dah deh LAHR-gah dees-TAHN-syah
• a collect call.	• una llamada por cobrar.	• OO-nah yah-MAH-dah pohr koh-BRAHR
• a call with time and charges.	• una llamada con tiempo y costo.	• OO-nah yah-MAH-dah kohn TYEHM-poh ee KOHS-toh
• a person-to-person call.	• una llamada de persona a persona.	• OO-nah yah-MAH-dah deh pehr-SOH-nah ah pehr-SOH-nah
• a credit-card call.	• una llamada con tarjeta de crédito.	• OO-nah yah-MAH-dah kohn tahr-HEH-tah deh KREH-dee-toh
Please connect me with	Me comunica con	meh koh-moo-NEE-kah kohn
• room 203.	• la habitación doscientos tres.	• lah ah-bee-tah-SYOHN doh-SYEHN-tohs trehs

• the reception desk.	• **la recepción.**	• lah rreh-sehp-SYOHN
• the dining room.	• **el comedor.**	• ehl koh-meh-DOHR
• telephone number . . .	• **el teléfono número . . .**	• ehl teh-LEH-foh-noh NOO-meh-roh . . .
• room service.	• **el servicio de habitación.**	• ehl ser-VEE-syoh deh ah-bee-tah-SYOHN
• the bell captain.	• **el jefe de botones.**	• ehl HEH-feh deh boh-TOH-nehs
We're leaving now.	**Estamos saliendo ahora.**	ehs-TAH-mohs sah-LYEHN-doh ah-OH-rah
We need a porter for the luggage.	**Necesitamos un botones para las maletas.**	neh-seh-see-TAH-mohs oon boh-TOH-nehs PAH-rah lahs mah-LEH-tahs
The bill, please.	**La cuenta, por favor**	lah KWEHN-tah, pohr fah-VOHR
Could you call us a taxi, please?	**¿Podría lla-marnos un taxi, por favor?**	poh-DREE-ah yah-MAHR-nohs oon TAHK-see, pohr fah-VOHR?

5/SOCIALIZING

Meeting people and making friends give you the opportunity to learn about another culture and to discover important cultural differences regarding how Spanish speakers interact. While Spaniards tend to be a bit more formal than Latin Americans, you will quickly see that they are open and friendly.

You will notice that in Spain and Mexico—and elsewhere in Latin America—people generally shake hands upon meeting or leave-taking. Close friends often embrace, and women usually kiss each other. You may notice that Latin Americans and Spaniards stand closer to people they're talking to than do North Americans and Northern Europeans. This subtle difference in sense of personal space can be disconcerting at first, until you get used to it. But observing such norms can show your hosts that you respect their way of doing things.

Note that in Spanish, it is customary to use the title *señor, señora,* and *señorita* to show respect, especially when speaking to people who are not close friends. These titles may be used with the last name, or alone.

DIALOGUE: INTRODUCTIONS (PRESENTACIONES)

Turista:	**Buenos días, señor. Permítame presentarme. Soy Julie Adams.**	BWEH-nohs DEE-ahs, seh-NYOHR. pehr-MEE-tah-meh preh-sehn-TAHR-meh. soy Julie Adams.
Sr. Vargas:	**Encantado, señorita. Yo soy Juan Vargas.**	ehn-kahn-TAH-do, seh-NYOH-REE-tah. yoh soy HWAN VAHR-gahs.
Turista:	**Encantada.**	ehn-kahn-TAH-dah
Sr. Vargas:	**Está de vacaciones aquí?**	ehs-TAH deh vah-kah-SYOH-nehs ah-KEE?
Turista:	**Sí, estaré aquí por tres semanas.**	see, ehs-tah-REH ah-KEE pohr trehs seh-MAH-nahs

41

| Sr. Vargas: | ¡Qué bueno! ¡Que tenga una buena estadía! | keh BWEH-noh! keh TEHN-gah OO-nah BWEH-nah ehs-tah-DEE-ah! |
| Turista: | ¡Gracias! Adiós, señor. | GRAH-syahs. ah-DYOHS, seh-NYOR. |

Tourist:	Hello! May I introduce myself? My name is Julie Adams.
Mr. Vargas:	Pleased to meet you, miss. I'm Juan Vargas.
Tourist:	Pleased to meet you.
Mr. Vargas:	Are you here on vacation?
Tourist:	Yes, I'll be here for three weeks.
Mr. Vargas:	How nice! Have a good stay.
Tourist:	Thank you. Good-bye, sir.

INTRODUCTIONS

I'd like to introduce you to	Quisiera presentarle	kee-SYEH-rah preh-sehn-TAHR-leh
• Mr. Vargas.	• al señor Vargas.	• ahl seh-NYOHR VAHR-gahs
• Mrs. Vargas.	• a la señora Vargas.	• ah lah seh-NYOH-rah VAHR-gahs
• Miss/Ms. . . .	• a la señorita . . .	• ah lah seh-nyoh-REE-tah . . .
Pleased to meet you.	Encantado(-a).	ehn-kahn-TAH-doh (-dah)
A pleasure.	Mucho gusto.	MOO-choh GOOS-toh
What is your name?	¿Cómo se llama?	KOH-moh seh YAH-mah?
My name is . . .	Me llamo . . .	meh YAH-moh . . .
• John.	• Juan.	• HWAHN
• Mary.	• María.	• mah-REE-ah

• Mr. Vargas	• **Sr. Vargas.**	• seh-NYOHR VAHR-gahs
I am . . .	**Soy . . .**	soy . . .
This is my	**Es mi**	ehs mee
• husband.	• **esposo.**	• ehs-POH-soh
• wife.	• **esposa.**	• ehs-POH-sah
• colleague.	• **colega.**	• koh-LEH-gah
• friend (*male*).	• **amigo.**	• ah-MEE-goh
• friend (*female*).	• **amiga.**	• ah-MEE-gah
How are you?	**¿Cómo está usted?**	KOH-moh ehs-TAH oos-TEHD?
Fine, thanks. And you?	**Bien, gracias. ¿Y usted?**	BYEHN, GRAH-syahs. ee oos-TEHD?

FIRST CONTACT

Where do you live?	**¿Dónde vive?**	DOHN-deh VEE-veh?
I live in	**Vivo en**	VEE-voh ehn
• the United States.	• **los Estados Unidos.**	• lohs ehs-TAH-dohs oo NEE Juhs
• England.	• **Inglaterra.**	• een-glah-TEH-rrah
• Canada.	• **Canadá.**	• ka-nah-DAH
• New York.	• **Nueva York.**	• NWEH-vah yohrk
• California.	• **California.**	• kah-lee-FOHR-nyah
That's in the	**Está en el**	ehs-TAH ehn ehl
• north.	• **norte.**	• NOHR-teh
• south.	• **sur.**	• soor
• east.	• **este.**	• EHS-teh
• west.	• **oeste.**	• oh-EHS-teh
That's near	**Está cerca de**	ehs-TAH SEHR-kah deh
• the coast.	• **la costa.**	• lah KOHS-tah
• Canada.	• **Canadá.**	• kah-nah-DAH
• the border.	• **la frontera.**	• lah frohn-TEH-rah
• the ocean.	• **el mar.**	• ehl mahr
• the mountains.	• **las montañas.**	• lahs mohn-TAH-nyahs

43

I'm from New York.	**Soy de Nueva York.**	soy deh NWEH-vah yohrk
How long will you be here?	**¿Cuánto tiempo estará aquí?**	KWAHN-toh TYEHM-poh ehs-tah-RAH ah-KEE?
I'll be here for	**Estaré aquí por**	ehs-tah-REH ah-KEE pohr
• a week.	• **una semana.**	• OO-nah seh-MAH-nah
• another week.	• **otra semana.**	• OH-trah seh-MAH-nah
• three weeks.	• **tres semanas.**	• trehs seh-MAH-nahs
• a short while.	• **poco tiempo.**	• POH-koh TYEHM-poh
• a long while.	• **mucho tiempo.**	• MOO-choh TYEHM-poh
What hotel are you staying at?	**¿En qué hotel está?**	ehn keh oh-TEHL ehs-TAH?
I am at the . . . hotel.	**Estoy en el hotel . . .**	ehs-TOY ehn ehl oh-TEHL . . .
How do you like • Spain? • Mexico?	**¿Le gusta*** • **España?** • **México?**	leh GOOS-tah • ehs-PAH-nyah? • MEH-hee-koh?
I like it very much.	**Me gusta mucho.***	meh GOOS-tah MOO-choh
I just arrived.	**Acabo de llegar.**	ah-KAH-boh deh yeh-GAHR
I'm not sure yet.	**No estoy seguro(-a) todavía.**	noh ehs-TOY seh-GOO-roh(-rah) toh-dah-VEE-ah
I like the people very much.	**La gente me gusta mucho.***	lah HEHN-teh meh GOOS-tah MOO-choh
I like the countryside.	**Me gusta el campo.***	meh GOOS-tah ehl KAHM-poh

44

Everything is so	**Todo es muy**	TOH-doh ehs muee
• interesting.	• **interesante.**	• een-teh-reh-SAHN-teh
• different.	• **diferente.**	• dee-feh-REHN-teh
• pretty.	• **bonito.**	• boh-NEE-toh

*In Spanish, the verb *gustar* agrees with the object. The literal translation of *"Me gusta España"* is "Spain pleases me." "I like the shops here" would be translated as *"Me gustan las tiendas aquí"*—literally, "The shops here please me."

JOBS AND PROFESSIONS

Where do you work?	**¿Dónde trabaja?**	DOHN-deh trah-BAH-hah?
What do you do?	**¿En qué trabaja?**	ehn keh trah-BAH-hah?
What is your profession?*	**¿Cuál es su profesión?**	KWAHL ehs soo proh-feh-SYOHN?
I'm a • businessman.	**Soy** • **hombre de negocios.**	soy • OHM-breh deh neh-GOH-syohs
I'm retired.	**Estoy jubilado(-a).**	ehs-TOY hoo-bee-LAH-doh(-dah)
I'm not working any longer.	**Ya no trabajo.**	yah noh trah-BAH-hoh

*For a list of professions and occupations, see page 177.

MAKING FRIENDS

It's so good to see you.	**Un gusto verle.**	oon GOOS-toh VEHR-leh
It's nice to be here.	**Es un placer estar aquí.**	ehs oon plah-SEHR ehs-TAHR ah-KEE
Would you like a drink?	**¿Le gustaría una bebida?**	leh goos-tah-REE-ah OO-nah beh-BEE-dah?
With pleasure.	**Con gusto.**	kohn GOOS-toh
Cheers!	**¡Salud!**	sah-LOOD!

No, thanks.	**No, gracias.**	noh, GRAH-syahs

Note: Gracias (Thank you) is sometimes used alone to accept or decline something. In doing so, it is usually accompanied by a slight nod or shake of the head.

Would you like to go with us	**¿Le gustaría acompañarnos**	leh goos-tah-REE-ah ah-kohm-pah-NYAHR-nohs
• to the theater?	• **al teatro?**	• ahl teh-AH-troh?
• to the movies?	• **al cine?**	• ahl SEE-neh?
• to a restaurant?	• **a un restaurante?**	• ah oon rrehs-tow-RAHN-teh?
Gladly.	**Con mucho gusto.**	kohn MOO-choh GOOS-toh
Can I bring a friend?	**¿Puedo llevar a un amigo?**	PWEH-doh yeh-VAHR ah oon ah-MEE-goh?
Do you mind if I smoke?	**¿Le importa si fumo?**	leh eem-POHR-tah see FOO-moh?
Not at all.	**Claro que no.**	KLAH-roh keh noh
May I telephone you?	**¿Puedo llamarle por teléfono?**	PWEH-doh yah-MAHR-leh pohr teh-LEH-foh-noh?
What is your phone number?	**¿Cuál es su número de teléfono?**	KWAHL ehs soo NOO-meh-roh deh teh-LEH-foh-noh?
What is your address?	**¿Cuál es su dirección?**	KWAHL ehs soo dee-rehk-SYOHN?
Are you married?	**¿Es usted casado(-a)?**	ehs oos-TEHD kah-SAH-doh(-dah)?
No, I'm	**No, soy**	noh, soy
• single.	• **soltero(-a).**	• sohl-TEH-roh(-rah)
• divorced.	• **divorciado(-a).**	• dee-vohr-SYAH-doh(-dah)
• a widower (widow)	• **viudo(-a)**	• vyoo-doh(-dah)
I'm traveling with a friend.	**Estoy viajando con un amigo(-a).**	ehs-TOY vyah-HAHN-doh kohn oon ah-MEE-goh (-gah).

My family is with me.	**Mi familia está conmigo.**	mee fah-MEE-lyah es-TAH kohn-MEE-goh
Do you have any children?	**¿Tiene usted hijos?**	TYEH-neh oos-TEHD EE-hohs?
Yes, I have	**Sí, tengo**	see, TEHN-goh
• a child.	• **un hijo.**	• oon EE-hoh
• two children.	• **dos hijos.**	• dohs EE-hohs
• three children.	• **tres hijos.**	• trehs EE-hohs
• four children.	• **cuatro hijos.**	• KWAH-troh EE-hohs
• a son.	• **un hijo.**	• oon EE-hoh
• a daughter.	• **una hija.**	• OO-nah EE-hah
Here are pictures of my family.	**Aquí tengo fotografías de mi familia.**	ah-KEE TEHN-goh foh-toh-grah-FEE-ahs deh mee fah-MEE-lyah
It's getting late.	**Se hace tarde.**	seh AH seh TAHR deh
It's time to get back.	**Es hora de regresar.**	ehs OH-rah deh rreh-greh-SAHR
We're leaving tomorrow.	**Nos vamos mañana.**	nohs VAH-mohs mah-NYAH-nah
Thanks for everything.	**Gracias por todo.**	GRAH-syahs pohr TOH-doh
I had a very good time.	**Lo pasé muy bien.**	loh pah-SEH mwee byehn
We're going to miss you.	**Vamos a extrañarle.**	VAH-mohs ah eks-trah-NYAHR-leh
It was nice to have met you.	**Gusto en conocerle.**	GOOS-toh ehn koh-noh-SEHR-leh
Give my best to	**Mis saludos a**	mees sah-LOO-dohs ah
• your fiancé(e).	• **su novio(-a).**	• soo NOH-vyoh (-vyah)
• your boyfriend (girlfriend).	• **su amigo(-a).**	• soo ah-MEE-goh (-gah)
• your family.	• **su familia.**	• soo fah-MEE-lyah
• your husband.	• **su esposo.**	• soo ehs-POH-soh
• your wife.	• **su esposa.**	• soo ehs-POH-sah

47

Can I give you a ride?	**¿Puedo llevarlo?**	PWEH-doh yeh-VAHR-loh?
Don't bother, thank you.	**No se moleste, gracias.**	noh seh moh-LES-teh, GRAH-syahs
I can take a taxi.	**Puedo tomar un taxi.**	PWEH-doh toh-MAHR oon TAHK-see
Bye.	**Hasta luego.**	AHS-tah LWEH-goh

THE FAMILY

I'm traveling	**Viajo**	VYA-hoh
• with my family.	• **con mi familia.**	• kohn mee fah-MEE-lyah
• without my family.	• **sin mi familia.**	• seen mee fah-MEE-lyah
My family lives in New York.	**Mi familia vive en Nueva York.**	mee fah-MEE-lyah VEE veh ehn NWEH-vah yohrk
My family is spread out.	**Mi familia vive en diferentes lugares.**	mee fah-MEE-lya VEE-veh ehn dee-feh-REHN-tehs loo-GAH-rehs
I have a . . . family.	**Tengo una familia**	TEHN-goh OO-nah fah-MEE-lyah
• big.	• **grande.**	• GRAHN-deh
• small.	• **pequeña.**	• peh-KEH-nyah
I have . . .	**Tengo . . .**	TEHN-goh . . .
• many relatives.	• **muchos parientes.**	• MOO-chohs pah-RYEHN-tehs
• a baby.	• **un bebé.**	• oon beh-BEH
• a father.	• **un padre.**	• oon PAH-dreh
• a mother.	• **una madre.**	• OO-nah MAH-dreh
• a grandmother.	• **una abuela.**	• OO-nah ah-BWEH-lah
• a grandfather.	• **un abuelo.**	• oon ah-BWEH-loh
• a grandson.	• **un nieto.**	• oon NYEH-toh
• a granddaughter.	• **una nieta.**	• OO-nah NYEH-tah

• a cousin (*female*).	• **una prima.**	• OO-nah PREE-mah
• a cousin (*male*).	• **un primo.**	• oon PREE-moh
• an aunt.	• **una tía.**	• OO-nah TEE-ah
• an uncle.	• **un tío.**	• oon TEE-oh
• a sister.	• **una hermana.**	• OO-nah ehr-MAH-nah
• a brother.	• **un hermano.**	• oon ehr-MAH-noh
• in-laws.	• **suegros.**	• SWEH-grohs
• a father-in-law.	• **un suegro.**	• oon SWEH-groh
• a mother-in-law.	• **una suegra.**	• OO-nah SWEH-grah
• a sister-in-law	• **una cuñada.**	• OO-nah koo-NYAH-dah
• a brother-in-law.	• **un cuñado.**	• oon koo-NYAH-doh

How old are your children?	**¿Cuántos años tienen sus hijos?**	KWAHN-tohs AH-nyohs TYEH-nehn soos EE-hohs?
My children are	**Mis hijos son**	mees EE-hohs sohn
• very young.	• **muy jóvenes.**	• mwee HOH-vehn-ehs
• all grown up.	• **grandes.**	• GRAHN-dehs
Peter is three years old.	**Pedro tiene tres años.**	PEH-droh TYEH-neh trehs AH-nyohs
He is older than Paul.	**El es mayor que Pablo.**	ehl ehs mah-YOHR keh PAH-bloh
He is	**El es**	ehl ehs
• my eldest son.	• **mi hijo mayor.**	• mee EE-hoh mah-YOHR
• my youngest son.	• **mi hijo menor.**	• mee EE-hoh meh-nohr
She is	**Ella es**	ehl-yah ehs
• my eldest daughter.	• **mi hija mayor.**	• mee EE-hah mah-YOHR
• my youngest daughter.	• **mi hija menor.**	• mee EE-hah meh-NOHR
I am a widow.	**Soy viuda.**	soy VYOO-dah
I am a widower.	**Soy viudo.**	soy VYOO-doh

TALKING ABOUT LANGUAGE

Do you speak*	¿Habla usted	AH-blah oos-TEHD
• English?	• inglés?	• een-GLEHS?
• French?	• francés?	• frahn-SEHS?
• German?	• alemán?	• ah-leh-MAHN?

*For a more complete list of languages, see page 176.

I only speak English.	Hablo solamente inglés.	AH-bloh soh-lah-MEHN-teh een-GLEHS
I don't speak Spanish.	No hablo español.	noh AH-bloh ehs-pah-NYOHL
I speak very little.	Hablo muy poco.	AH-bloh mwee POH-koh
I speak a little Spanish.	Hablo un poco de español.	AH-bloh oon POH-koh deh ehs-pah-NYOHL
I want to learn Spanish.	Quiero aprender español.	KYEH-roh ah-prehn-DEHR ehs-pah-NYOHL
I understand.	Comprendo.	kohm-PREHN-doh
I don't understand.	No comprendo.	noh kohm-PREHN-doh
Can you understand me?	¿Me comprende?	meh kohm-PREHN-deh?
Please repeat that.	¿Puede repetir eso?	PWE-deh rreh-peh-teer EH-soh?
Speak more slowly.	Hable más despacio.	AH-bleh mahs dehs-PAH-syoh
Could you write that?	¿Me lo escribe?	meh loh ehs-KREE-beh?
How do you say . . .	¿Cómo se dice . . .	KOH-moh seh DEE-seh . . .
• in Spanish?	• en español?	• ehn ehs-pah-NYOHL?
• in English?	• en inglés?	• ehn een-GLES?
Is there anyone who speaks English here?	¿Hay alguien que habla inglés aquí?	ahy AHL-gyehn keh HAH-blah een-GLEHS ah-KEE?

Could you translate this?	¿Puede traducir esto?	PWEH-deh trah-doo-SEER EHS-toh?
Spanish is a beautiful language.	El español es una lengua hermosa.	ehl ehs-pah-NYOHL ehs OO-nah LEHN-gwah ehr-MOH-sah
I like Spanish a lot.	Me gusta mucho el español.	meh GOOS tah MOO-choh ehl ehs-pah-NYOHL

IN THE HOME

Make yourself at home.	Está en su casa.	ehs-TAH ehn soo KAH-sah
You may sit here.	Puede sentarse aquí.	PWEH-deh sehn-TAHR-seh ah-KEE
What a pretty house!	¡Qué casa tan bonita!	keh KAH-sah tahn boh-NEE-tah!
I really like this neighborhood.	Me gusta mucho este barrio.	meh GOOS-tah MOO-choh EHS-teh BAH-rryoh

Here is	Aquí está	ah-KEE ehs-TAH
• the kitchen.	• la cocina.	• lah koh-SEE-nah
• the living room.	• la sala.	• lah SAH-lah
• the dining room.	• el comedor.	• ehl koh-meh-DOHR
• the bedroom.	• el dormitorio.	• ehl dohr-mee-TOH-ryoh
• the bathroom.	• el baño.	• ehl BAH-nyoh
• the study.	• el estudio.	• ehl ehs-TOO-dyoh
• the attic.	• el desván.	• ehl dehs-VAHN
• the cellar.	• el sótano.	• ehl SOH-tah-noh
• the couch.	• el sofá.	• ehl soh-FAH
• the armchair.	• el sillón.	• ehl see-YOHN
• the table.	• la mesa.	• lah MEH-sah
• the chair.	• la silla.	• lah SEE-yah
• the lamp.	• la lámpara.	• lah LAHM-pah-rah
• the door.	• la puerta.	• lah PWEHR-tah

It's	Es	ehs
• a house.	• **una casa.**	• OO-nah KAH-sah
• an apartment.	• **un apartamento**	• oon deh-pahr-tah-MEHN-toh
• a mansion.	• **una mansión.**	• OO-nah mahn-SYOHN
• a ranch.	• **una hacienda.**	• OO-nah ah-SYEHN-dah
Thanks for having invited us to your home.	**Gracias por habernos invitado a su casa.**	GRAH-syahs pohr ah-BEHR-nohs een-vee-TAH-doh ah soo KAH-sah
Please come to visit us sometime.	**Debe venir a visitarnos también.**	DEH-beh veh-NEER ah vee-see-TAHR-nos tahm-BYEHN

6/DINING OUT

Spain and Mexico—as well as most other areas where you might travel in Latin America—offer rich and varied cuisines. Spanish cuisine spread throughout Latin America, where it often mixed with native dishes, resulting in many exotic combinations.

Can you recommend a good restaurant?	**¿Puede recomendarme un buen restaurante?**	PWEH-deh rrleh-koh-mehn-DAHR-me oon bwehn rrehs-tow-RAHN-tch?
I want a(n) . . . restaurant.	**Quiero un restaurante**	KYEH-roh oon rrehs-tow-RAHN-teh
• Typical	• **típico.**	• TEE-pee-koh
• international	• **internacional.**	• een-tehr-nah-syoh-NAHL
• inexpensive	• **no muy caro.**	• noh muee KAH-roh
• very good	• **muy bueno.**	• muee BWEH-noh
Is that restaurant expensive?	**¿Es caro esé restaurante?**	ehs KAH-roh eh-seh rrehs-tow-RAHN-teh?
What's the name of the restaurant?	**¿Cómo se llama el restaurante?**	KOH-moh seh YAH-mah ehl rrehs-tow-RAHN-teh?
Where is it located?	**¿Dónde está situado?**	DOHN-deh ehs-TAH see-TWAH-doh?
Do I need reservations?	**¿Se necesita una reservación?**	seh neh-seh-SEE-tah OO-nah rreh-sehr-vah-SYOHN?
	(*or*) . . . **una reserva?** (*Spain*)	. . . OO-nah rreh-SEHR-vah
I'd like to reserve a table	**Quisiera reservar una mesa**	kee-SYEH-rah rreh-sehr-VAHR OO-nah MEH-sah
• for two people.	• **para dos personas.**	• PAH-rah dohs pehr-SOH-nahs
• for this evening.	• **para esta noche.**	• PAH-rah EHS-tah NOH-cheh

53

• for 8:00 P.M.	• **para las ocho de la noche.**	• PAH-rah lahs OH-choh deh lah NOH-cheh
• for tomorrow evening.	• **para mañana en la noche.**	• PAH-rah mah-NYAH-nah ehn lah NOH-cheh
• on the terrace.	• **en la terraza.**	• ehn lah teh-RRAH-sah
• by the window.	• **cerca de la ventana.**	• SEHR-kah deh lah vehn-TAH-nah
• outside.	• **afuera.**	• ah-FWEH-rah
• inside.	• **adentro.**	• ah-DEHN-troh

DIALOGUE: AT THE RESTAURANT (EN EL RESTAURANTE)

Mesero*:	**¿Puedo tomar su pedido?**	PWEH-doh toh-MAHR soo peh-DEE-doh?
Cliente:	**No sé. ¿Cuál es la especialidad?**	noh seh, kwal ehs lah ehs-peh-syah-lee-dad?
Mesero:	**Hoy le recomiendo la paella.**	ohy leh rreh-koh-MYEHN-doh lah pah-EH-ya
Cliente:	**Bien. Me trae eso, por favor.**	byehn. meh TRAH-eh EH-soh, pohr fah-VOHR
Mesero:	**¿Algo para tomar?**	AHL-goh PAH-rah to-MAHR?
Cliente:	**Sí, por favor. Quisiera una botella de agua mineral.**	see, pohr fah-VOHR kee-SYEH-rah OO-nah boh-TEH yah deh AH-gwah mee-neh-RAHL

Mesero is used in Mexico for "waiter," whereas *mozo* and *camarero* are used in Spain.

. . . .

Waiter: May I take your order?

Customer: I don't know. What's the specialty?

> Waiter: I would recommend the *paella* today.
>
> Customer: Fine. I'll take that.
>
> Waiter: Something to drink?
>
> Customer: Yes, please.
> Bring me a bottle of mineral water.

GOING TO A RESTAURANT

Waiter!	**¡Mesero! (*Mexico*)**	meh-SEH-roh!
	(*or*) ¡Mozo! (*Spain*)	MOH-soh!
	(*or*) ¡Camarero! (*Spain*)	cah-mah-REH-roh!
Waitress!	**¡Mesera!**	meh-SEH-rah!
Miss!	**¡Señorita!**	seh-nyoh-REE-tah!
Can you bring	**¿Puede traer**	PWEH-deh trah-EHR
• the menu?	• **la carta?**	• lah KAHR-tah?
• the wine list?	• **la lista de vinos?**	• lah LEES-tah deh VEE-nohs?
• an appetizer?	• **un aperitivo?**	• oon ah-peh-ree-TEE-voh?
Do you serve local dishes?	**¿Tiene algún plato regional?**	TYEH-neh ahl-GOON PLAH-toh rreh-hyoh-NAHL?
I'd like	**Quisiera**	kee-SYEH-rah
• something light.	• **algo ligero.**	• AHL-goh lee-HEH-roh
• a full meal.	• **una comida completa.**	• OO-nah koh-MEE-dah kohm-PLEH-tah
• the meal of the day.	• **la comida corrida.** (*Mexico*)	• lah koh-MEE-dah ko-RREE-dah
Do you have children's portions?	**¿Tiene raciones para niños?**	TYEH-neh rrah-SYOH-nehs PAH-rah NEE-nyohs?

55

I'm ready to order.	**Estoy listo(-a) para pedir.**	ehs-TOY LEES-toh(-tah) PAH-rah peh-DEER
Could I have . . .	**Quisiera**	kee-SYEH-rah . . .
To begin . . .	**Para comenzar . . .**	PAH-rah koh-mehn-SAHR . . .
Next . . .	**Después . . .**	dehs-PWEHS . . .
Finally . . .	**Para terminar . . .**	PAH-rah tehr-mee-NAHR . . .
That's all.	**Es todo.**	ehs TOH-doh
Is the dish	**¿Este plato es**	EHS-teh PLAH-toh ehs
• baked?	• **al horno?**	• ahl OHR-noh?
• boiled?	• **hervido?**	• ehr-VEE-doh?
• braised?	• **estofado?**	• ehs-toh-FAH-doh?
• broiled?	• **a la parrilla?**	• ah lah pah-RREE-yah?
• fried?	• **frito?**	• FREE-toh?
I prefer the meat	**Prefiero la carne**	preh-FYEH-roh lah KAHR-neh
• well done.	• **bien cocida.**	• byehn koh-SEE-dah
• medium.	• **en un término medio.**	• ehn oon TEHR-mee-noh MEH-dyoh
• rare.	• **poco cocida.**	• POH-koh koh-SEE-dah
The soup is cold.	**La sopa está fría.**	lah SOH-pah ehs-TAH FREE-ah
I'd like another dish.	**Quisiera otro plato.**	kee-SYEH-rah OH-troh PLAH-toh
More water, please.	**Más agua, por favor.**	mahs AH-gwah, pohr fah-VOHR
I'm on a special diet.	**Estoy en una dieta especial.**	ehs-TOY ehn OO-nah DYEH-tah ehs-peh-SYAHL
Is it very spicy (hot)?	**¿Es muy picante?**	ehs mwee pee-KAHN-teh?

	(or) . . . picoso? (Mexico)	. . . pee-KOH-soh?
I'm diabetic.	**Soy diabético(-a).**	soy dee-ah-BEH-tee-koh(-kah)
I can't eat	**No puedo comer**	noh PWEH-doh koh-MEHR
• salt.	• **sal.**	• sahl
• fat.	• **grasas.**	• GRAH-sahs
• sugar.	• **azúcar.**	• ah-SOO-kahr
• flour.	• **harina.**	• ah-REE-nah
I don't eat pork.	**No como puerco.**	noh KOH-moh PWEHR-koh
I want to lose weight.	**Quiero perder peso.**	KYEH-roh pehr-DEHR PEH-soh
Where's the toilet?	**¿Dónde está el servicio? (Mexico) (or) . . . el aseo? (Spain)**	DOHN-deh es-TAH ehl ser-VEE-syoh? ehl ah-SAY-yoh?

RESTAURANT ITEMS

silverware	**cubiertos**	koo-BYEHR-tohs
a fork	**un tenedor**	oon teh-neh-DOHR
a knife	**un cuchillo**	oon koo-CHEE-yoh
a spoon	**una cuchara**	OO-nah koo-CHAH-rah
a napkin	**una servilleta**	OO-nah sehr-vee-YEH-tah
a cup	**una taza**	OO-nah TAH-sah
a saucer	**un platillo**	oon plah-TEE-yoh
a plate	**un plato**	oon PLAH-toh
a glass	**un vaso**	oon VAH-soh
some bread	**un poco de pan**	oon POH-koh deh pahn

some butter	**un poco de mantequilla**	oon POH-koh deh mahn-teh-KEE-yah
water	**agua natural**	AH-gwah nah-too-RAHL
the salt	**la sal**	lah sahl
the pepper	**la pimienta**	lah pee-MYEHN-tah
the mustard	**la mostaza**	lah mohs-TAH-sah
the ketchup	**la salsa de tomate**	lah SAHL-sah deh toh-MAH-teh
the mayonnaise	**la mayonesa**	lah mah-yoh-NEH-sah
some coffee	**café**	kah-FEH
some tea	**té**	teh
some lemon	**un poco de limón**	oon POH-koh deh lee-MOHN
the sugar	**el azúcar**	ehl ah-SOO-kahr
some saccharine	**un poco de sacarina**	oon POH-koh deh sah-kah-REE-nah
an ashtray	**un cenicero**	oon seh-nee-SEH-roh
a toothpick	**un palillo** (*Mexico*) (*or*) **un mondadientes**	oon pah-LEE-yoh oon mohn-dah-DYEHN-tehs
a beer	**una cerveza**	OO-nah sehr-VEH-sah

What the Waiter Says

¿Cuántas per-sonas son?	KWAHN-tahs pehr-SOH-nahs sohn?	How many people?
¿Está bien esta mesa?	ehs-TAH byehn EHS-tah MEH-sah?	Is this table all right?
¿Quiere una silla para niños?	KYEH-reh OO-nah SEE-yah PAH-rah NEE-nyohs?	Do you want a high chair?

58

¿Quieren pedir ahora?	KYEH-rehn peh-DEER ah-OH-rah?	Do you want to order now?
¿Quieren más agua?	KYEH-rehn mahs AH-gwah?	Do you want more water?
¿Desean algo más?	deh-SEH-ahn AHL-goh mahs?	Do you want anything else?
¿Todo va bien?	TOH-doh vah byehn?	Is everything all right?
¿Todo en una cuenta?	TOH-doh ehn OO-nah KWEHN-tah?	All on one bill?

THE BILL

May I have the check, please?	¿Me da la cuenta, por favor?	meh dah lah KWEHN-tah, pohr fah-VOHR?
Only one check, please.	Sólo una cuenta, por favor.	SOH-loh OO-nah KWEHN-tah, pohr fah-VOHR
Please give us separate checks.	Nos da cuentas separadas, por favor.	nohs dah KWEN-tahs seh-pah-RAH-dahs, pohr fah-VOHR
Is service included?	¿Está incluido el servicio?	ehs-TAH een-KLUEE-doh ehl sehr-VEE-syoh?
I think there's a mistake.	Creo que hay un error.	KREH-oh keh ahy oon eh-RROHR
Do you accept	¿Aceptan	ah-SEHP-tahn
• credit cards?	• tarjetas de crédito?	• tahr-HEH-tahs deh CREH-dee-toh?
• traveler's checks?	• cheques de viajero?	• CHEH-kehs deh vyah-HEH-roh?
• dollars?	• dólares?	• DOH-lah-rehs?
This is for you.	Esto es para usted.	EHS-toh ehs PAH-rah oos-TEHD

59

Keep the change.*	**Guarde el cambio.**	GWAHR-deh ehl KAHM-byoh
The meal was excellent.	**La comida estuvo deliciosa.**	lah koh-MEE-dah ehs-TOO-voh deh-lee-SYOH-sah
And the service was very good.	**Y el servicio estuvo muy bien.**	ee ehl sehr-VEE-syoh ehs-TOO-voh MUEE byehn

*For information on tipping, see page 13.

ABOUT SPANISH FOOD

Spanish cuisine varies greatly from region to region. It reflects the influence of both the Arabs, who were in the south of Spain for nearly 700 years, and of Latin America.

Spanish meals normally consist of several courses. Foods commonly served are beef, pork, rabbit, and many different kinds of fish (especially in the coastal regions) as well as beans, vegetables, rice, and fruit. Sweet desserts are not common at the end of the meal, but wonderful pastries are always obtainable in pastry shops.

Some typical Spanish dishes are: *callos a la andaluza* and *gazpacho* (Andalucía), *cordero asado* (Castilla), *migas* (Extremadura), *paella valenciana* (Levante), *lentejas a la babia* (León), *cabrito asado* (Aragón), *fabada asturiana* (Asturias), *caldo gallego* (Galicia), *merluza a la riojana* (Rioja and Navarra), and *bacalao a la vizcaína* (Vascongadas).

Depending on the town, you will find either a great variety of restaurants or perhaps just one or two local places. Local restaurants or *bares* (bars) in small towns tend to be family operated. Food is prepared for local tastes. Prices vary according to the type of restaurant. For breakfast you might try a *café* (kah-FEH) or *churrería* (choo-rreh-REE-ah). *Combinados* (kohm-bee-NAH-dohs), or combination dishes, are popular and inexpensive. A great variety of prepared dishes may be ordered à la carte by *raciones* (rrah-SYOH-nehs) or *medias raciones* (MEH-dyahs rrah-SYOH-nehs)—i.e., full or half portions—so you can try different kinds of food.

A very popular custom in many parts of Spain is that of *tapas* (TAH-pahs), or snacks. Going out for a glass of wine accompanied by *tapas* is also an occasion to meet friends and to socialize. Bars are usually lined with an amazing variety of dishes—shrimp, olives, diced omelettes, artichokes, cheese, and salami, to name a few. When you're ready to leave, count up the items you've eaten and pay. In Granada, *tapas* are often served free, courtesy of the house.

Spanish restaurants, like hotels, often display a rating scale outside—from one to five "forks" reflecting the number of dishes in specific categories.

Eating hours, except in the case of breakfast (*desayuno*/deh-sah-YOO-noh/), are usually quite late. Restaurants and bars usually serve lunch between 1:30 P.M. and 3:00 P.M. Dinner (*cena*/SE-nah/) is served from 8:30 to midnight. Menus are posted outside most restaurants, so you can make your choices before you enter.

SPANISH RESTAURANTS

café
(kah-FEH)

A small locale for alcoholic and non-alcoholic drinks, plus simple snacks.

cafetería
(kah-fe-teh-REE-ah)

A café-type place, specializing in foods such as sandwiches, snacks, and sweets (not self-service).

bar
(bahr)

Typical bars which serve wine, *tapas,* and other light snacks.

fonda/posada/hosteria
(FOHN-dah/poh-SAH-dah/ohs-teh-REE-ah)

Small restaurants, sometimes part of an inn, which specialize in regional dishes.

merendero
(meh-rehn-DEH-roh)

Outdoor cafés, usually found near parks or on the coast, which serve seafood, soft drinks, ice cream, and so forth.

restaurante
(rrehs-tow-RAHN-teh)

Restaurant, offering varied menus and prices. Most restaurants post menus outside showing the range of dishes and prices; many offer both local and international fare.

TYPICAL SPANISH DISHES

Tapas	TAH-pahs	Appetizers
alcachofas	ahl-kah-CHOH-fahs	artichokes
almejas	ahl-MEH-hahs	clams
anguilas	ahn-GHEE-lahs	eel
calamares	kah-lah-MAH-rehs	squid
caracoles	kah-rah-KOH-lehs	snails
chorizo	choh-REE-soh	sausage
gambas	GAHM-bahs	shrimp
huevos	WEH-vohs	eggs
jamón	hah-MOHN	ham
ostras	OHS-trahs	oysters
sardinas	sahr-DEE-nahs	sardines

Sopas (SOH-pahs)	Soups
caldo gallego (KAHL-doh gah-YEH-goh)	white bean, turnip green, and potato soup

62

fabada asturiana (fah-BAH-dah ahs-too-RYAN-nah) — bean soup with sausage

sopa de ajo (SOH-pah deh AH-hoh) — spicy garlic soup

gazpacho (gahs-PAH-choh) — cold fresh vegetable soup

Mariscos (mah-REES-kohs)	Seafood
almejas a la marinera (ahl-MEH-hahs ah lah mah-ree-NEH-rah)	clams in white wine sauce with garlic, onion, and tomatoes
bacalao al ajo arriero (bah-kah-LAH-oh ahl AH-hoh ah-RRY-eh-roh)	salt cod with tomatoes, onion, and garlic
besugo al horno (beh-SOO-goh ahl OHR-noh)	red snapper baked with potatoes
calamares en su tinta (kah-lah-MAH-rehs ehn soo TEEN-tah)	squid in its ink
merluza a la gallega (mehr-LOO-sah ah lah gah-YEH-gah)	poached hake with potatoes and tomato sauce
paella (pah-EH-yah)	saffron rice with seafood and chicken
zarzuela de mariscos (sahr-SWEH-lah deh mah-REES-kohs)	Catalonian shellfish stew

Carnes (KAHR-nehs)	Meats
callos a la madrileña (KAH-yohs ah lah mah-dree-LEH-nyah)	tripe stew with calves' feet, ham, and sausages
cocido madrileño (koh-SEE-doh mah-dree-LEH-nyoh)	boiled chicken, meats, and vegetables
riñones al jerez (rree-NYOH-nehs ahl heh-REHS)	sautéed kidneys with sherry sauce

63

ternera a la sevillana (tehr-NEH-rah ah lah seh-vee-YAH-nah) — sautéed veal with sherry and green olives

Aves (AH-vehs) — Poultry

arroz con pollo (ah-RROHS kohn POH-yoh) — chicken with saffron rice and peas

empanada gallega (ehm-pah-NAH-dah gah-YEH-gah) — chicken-filled bread pie

pollo a la chilindrón (POH-yoh ah lah chee-leen-DROHN) — sautéed chicken with peppers, tomatoes, and olives

Huevos (WEH-vohs) — Eggs

tortilla de patata (tohr-TEE-yah deh pah-TAH-tah) — potato and onion omelet

huevos a la flamenca (WEH-vohs ah lah flah-MEHN-kah) — baked eggs with vegetables and meat

huevos fritos (WEH-vohs FREE-tohs) — fried eggs

huevos duros (WEH-vohs DOO-rohs) — hard-boiled eggs

huevos revueltos (WEH-vohs rreh-VWEHL-tohs) — scrambled eggs

huevos pasados por agua (WEH-vohs pah-SAH-dohs pohr AH-gwah) — poached eggs

Vegetales, arroz, ensaladas y salsas (beh-heh-TAH-lehs, ah-RROHS, ehn-sah-LAH-dahs ee SAHL-sahs) — Vegetables, rice, salads, and sauces

alio-li (AH-lee-OH lee) — garlic mayonnaise

arroz con azafrán (ah-RROHS kohn ah-sah-FRAN) — saffron rice

espinacas con piñones y almendras (ehs-pee-NAH-kahs kohn pee-NYOH-nehs ee ahl-MEHN-drahs) — spinach with pine nuts and almonds

habas a la catalana (AH-bahs ah lah kah-tah-LAH-nah) — fava beans with sausages and mint

judías verdes con salsa de tomate (hoo-DEE-ahs VEHR-dehs kohn SAHL-sah deh toh-MAH-teh) — green beans in tomato sauce

patatas en salsa verde (pah-TAH-tahs ehn SAHL-sah VEHR-deh) — potatoes in parsley sauce

Panes y dulces (PAH-nehs ee DOOL-sehs) — Breads and Sweets

---

churros (CHOO-rrohs) — crisp fried crullers

tortas de aceite (TOHR-tahs deh ah-SAY-teh) — anise and sesame-seed cookies

Postres y bebidas (POHS-trehs ee be-BEE-dahs) — Desserts and Drinks

---

Brazo gitano (BRAH-soh hee-TAH-noh) — sponge-cake roll with rum cream filling

flan de naranja (flahn deh nah-RAHN-hah) — orange caramel custard

leche frita (LEH-cheh FREE-tah) — fried custard squares

natillas (nah-TEE-yahs) — soft custard

torta moca (TOHR-tah MOH-kah) — mocha layer cake with rum

sangría (sahn-GREE-ah) — red wine and fruit punch

ABOUT MEXICAN FOOD

Mexico's restaurants come in all styles and sizes, from elegant dining rooms serving imaginative international cuisine to simple stands selling snacks and family-operated restaurants in smaller towns, where food is prepared for local tastes. Although you will find Spanish dishes in Mexico, the roots of the nation's cuisine can be traced to the Aztecs, the Maya, and other indigenous cultures. The blend of flavors, spices, and styles of preparation is among the most unusual in the world.

Generally, the staples are corn, rice, and beans, often served with beef, pork, lamb, or fish, depending on the region. A standard feature of typical meals is the *tortilla* (tohr-TEE-yah), made of specially prepared cornmeal, which is used to create *enchiladas* (ehn-chee-LAH-dahs), *tostadas* (tohs-TAH-dahs), *chilaquiles* (chee-lah-KEE-lehs), *garnachas* (gahr-NAH-chahs), *flautas* (FLOW-tahs), *sopes* (SOH-pehs), and *tacos* (TAH-kohs; eaten at any time of day). Cornmeal is also used in *tamales* (tah-MAH-lehs), which consist of a stewlike mixture stuffed inside dough that is wrapped in corn husks or banana leaves.

Mexican food uses many special ingredients and sauces. The popular *mole* (MOH-leh) sauce is based on peanuts (*mole de cacahuate*), squash seeds (*pipián*), sunflower seeds, sesame seeds, or other ingredients; *mole poblano* (MOH-leh poh-BLAH-noh), from the state of Puebla, contains almonds, peanuts, and pine nuts as well as tomato, chocolate, and hot pepper. Because its preparation is complicated and laborious, *mole* is often served on special occasions, such as christenings, weddings, and birthdays.

Frijoles (free-HOH-lehs), beans, are part of the Mexican diet every day, beginning with breakfast. Sometimes, a small dish of *frijoles* signals the end of a meal. Many types of *frijoles* are used; especially common are pinto beans and black beans. There is an even greater variety of *chiles* (CHEE-lehs), hot peppers—some twenty different kinds.

Meat is usually eaten at least once a day, as a simple *barba-*

coa (barhr-bah-KOH-ah), barbecue, or *carnitas* (kahr-NEE-tahs), shredded meat; pork and beef show up in *adobo* (ah-DOH-boh), a mixture of *achiote* and *chile. Carnes y quesos al carbón* (grilled meats over coals and melted cheese), usually accompanied by wheat flour tortillas, is a favorite. Also try *parrillada* (pah-rree-YAH-dah), an assortment of grilled meats. Some dishes combine several kinds of meat. *Pozole* (poh-SOH-leh), a soup that originated in the state of Guerrero, is made from hulled corn, chicken, pork, and beef, and topped with oregano, radishes, lettuce, and hot pepper.

Vegetables are used mainly as garnish or in cooked soups. Peppers are probably the most widely consumed vegetable. *Chiles rellenos* (CHEE-lehs rreh-YEH-nohs), stuffed hot peppers, is based on a special big green *chile* that is not too hot once the seeds have been removed; the *chiles* are filled with cheese or ground meat, covered with an egg batter, fried, and sometimes served with a red sauce and rice. In August, you may well find *chiles en nogada* (CHEE-lehs ehn noh-GAH-dah), another Puebla specialty—*chile* stuffed with dried fruits, meat, and nuts, and covered with a white sauce made of walnuts and sprinkled with pomegranate seeds.

Every region has its specialties. In the state of Veracruz, for example, fish and seafood dishes stand out, including *huachinango a la veracruzana* (wah-chee-NAHN-goh ah lah veh-rah-kroo-SAH-nah), red snapper Veracruz-style, and *ceviche* (seh-VEE-cheh), raw fish or seafood marinated in lemon and lime juice. Other special dishes require a more adventurous palate. You might try the famous *maguey* (mah-GAY) worms, often one of the most expensive dishes on the menu; these are taken from the *maguey* plant, put into a sauce, and eaten in a *taco*. Or sample the purple corn fungus, *huitlacoche* (ueet-lah-KOH-cheh), or squash blossoms, which come either fried or in soups. In Acapulco, local *iguana* (ee-GWAH-nah) cooked with coconut milk is a favorite.

Mexicans are also fond of Spanish cuisine, and dishes such as *paella* (pah-EH-yah), *gazpacho* (gahs-PAH-choh), and *sopa de mariscos* (SOH-pah deh mah-REES-kohs) are commonly served in restaurants and homes. Note that some of the "Mexican" dishes so well known in the United States—such as *chile con carne, burritos,* and *nachos*—are actually more typical of Texas and New Mexico and not often found in Mexico proper.

Mexico offers a great variety of regional drinks, both alcoholic and non-alcoholic. Beer, *cerveza* (sehr-VEH-sah), comes in many styles. And there are always the indigenous liquors—including *tequila* (teh-KEE-lah), *pulque* (POOL-keh), and *mezcal* (mehs-KAHL), all unique to Mexico.

Delicious and quite common are fruit-based drinks, *licuados* (lee-KWAH-dohs), made from practically every fruit: *papaya* (pah-PAH-yah), pineapple, strawberries, melon, watermelon, banana, *guanábana* (gwah-NAH-bah-nah), *zapote* (sah-POH-teh), tamarind, and guava. They are made with either milk or water, often with sugar added.

Water—*agua* (AH-gwah)—is used for another popular drink, a watered-down version of fruit juice mixed with sugar. Try the *agua de limón* (AH-gwah-deh lee-MOHN), "lemon water" or lemonade; *de papaya* (pah-PAH-yah); *de melón* (meh-LOHN); *de sandía* (sahn-DEE-ah), made of rice; and *atole* (ah-TOH-leh), made of cornstarch, water, cinnamon, sugar, and various flavorings.

When ordering plain water, you need to specify the kind you want; for mineral water, ask for *agua mineral* (AH-gwah mee-neh-RAHL). And speaking of water, a word of caution: Avoid unboiled tap water wherever you go; in restaurants and homes, always request bottled mineral water. In addition, make sure that any drinks you order are made from boiled, purified, or bottled water, and that the ice they contain is, too. Similarly, avoid fresh vegetables or any uncooked food.

When visiting restaurants, look for the *comida corrida* (koh-MEE-dah koh-RREE-dah), the fixed menu of the day, offered at a set price. Usually it costs less than the same meal ordered à la carte. Expect to see a 15 percent I.V.A. *(Impuesto al Valor Adquirido)* added to restaurant checks at the bottom of the bill. Plan to tip 10 percent to 15 percent of the pretax cost of the meal—in other words, roughly the same amount as the tax.

MEXICAN RESTAURANTS

bar
(bahr)

For drinks and *botana* (boh-TAH-nah), or snacks.

cantina
(kahn-TEE-nah)

Bars, for men only. They also serve *botana* and sometimes prepare special soups for that after-the-party hangover.

hacienda
(ah-SYEHN-dah)

An old ranch turned restaurant that preserves some of the patios, gardens, and atmosphere; they serve indoors or outdoors, usually offering regional specialties.

**hostería/posada/
fonda**
(ohs-teh-REE-ah/poh-
SAH-dah/FOHN-dah)

Restaurants serving regional specialties or general Mexican food.

restaurante
(rrehs-tow-RAHN-teh)

Restaurants, varying in size, price, style and type of menu, some catering especially to tourists.

TYPICAL MEXICAN DISHES

Botana	boh-TAH-nah	Appetizers
guacamole	gwah-kah-MOH-leh	mashed avocado, seasoned with condiments
camarones	kah-mah-ROH-nehs	shrimp
taquitos	tah-KEE-tohs	miniature *tacos*
cacahuates	kah-kah-WAH-tehs	peanuts

Sopas (SOH-pahs)	Soups
consomé (kon-soh-MEH)	consommé/broth
caldo mexicano (KAHL-doh meh-hee-KAH-noh)	Mexican meat stock
sopa de frijol (SOH-pah deh free-HOHL)	black bean soup
sopa de aguacate (SOH-pah deh ah-gwah-KAH-teh)	avocado soup
sopa de elote (SOH-pah deh eh-LOH-teh)	corn soup
sopa de flor de calabaza (SOH-pah deh flohr deh kah-lah-BAH-sah)	squash blossom soup
sopa de tortilla (SOH-pah deh tohr-TEE-yah)	crisp tortilla soup
puchero a la mexicana (poo CHEH-roh ah lah meh-hee-KAH-nah)	Mexican boiled dinner, usually chicken or pork and vegetables in a soup
pozole (poh-SOH-leh)	hulled corn, chicken, beef, and pork soup
Arroz (ah-RROHS)	Rice
arroz a la mexicana (ah-RROHS ah lah meh-hee-KAH-nah)	rice with tomatoes
arroz verde (ah-RROHS VEHR-deh)	rice with green *chile* and green tomato
Huevos (WEH-vohs)	Eggs
huevos rancheros (WEH-vohs rrahn-CHEH-rohs)	fried eggs on tortilla topped with hot tomato sauce

huevos a la Mexicana
(WEH-vohs ah lah meh-hee-KAH nah)

scrambled eggs with onion and tomato sauce

Carnes (KAHR-nehs) | Meats

---

carne asada (KAHR-neh ah-SAH-dah)

roast meat

carne de puerco en adobo (KAHR-neh deh PWEHR-koh ehn ah-DOH-boh)

pork loin in achiote and *chile* sauce

pipián (pee-PYAHN)

pork meat in pumpkin-seed sauce

albóndigas (ahl-BOHN-dee-gahs)

meatballs

cecina a la mexicana (seh-SEE-nah ah lah meh-hee-KAH-nah)

Mexican hung beef

picadillo (pee-kah-DEE-yoh)

Mexican hash

cochinita pibil (koh-chee-NEE-tah pee-BEEL)

suckling pig stuffed with fruit, *chile*, and spices, baked in a pit

---

Aves (AH-vehs) | Poultry

---

mancha manteles (MAHN-chah mahn-TEH-lehs)

turkey, sausage, and *chile* stew seasoned with almonds, pineapple, apples, banana, and cinnamon

mole de guajolote (MOH-leh deh gwah-hoh-LOH-teh)

turkey in chocolate, tomato, and nut sauce

arroz con pollo (ah-RROHS kohn POH-yoh)

rice with chicken and tomato sauce

Antojitos mexicanos (ahn-toh-HEE-tohs meh-hee-KAH-nohs)	Mexican Specialties
enchiladas rojas (ehn-chee-LAH-dahs RROH-has)	rolled tortillas stuffed with chicken or meat and topped with tomato sauce
enchiladas verdes (ehn-chee-LAH-dahs VEHR-dehs)	rolled tortillas stuffed with chicken or cheese and topped with green tomato sauce
ceviche acapulqueño (seh-VEE-cheh ah-kah-pool-KEH-nyoh)	raw fish or shellfish marinated in lime and orange juice and seasoned with tomato, onion, and hot pepper
guacamole (gwah-kah-MOH-leh)	mashed avocado with chopped tomato, onion, and *chile*
quesadillas (keh-sah-DEE-yahs)	tortillas folded in half and stuffed with cheese, tomato, sausage, beans, etc.
sopes (SOH-pehs)	two tortillas put together with filling in the middle
chilaquiles (chee-lah-KEE-lehs)	a stew made of broken tortillas, mixed with tomato sauce and topped with cream and raw onion
Vegetales (veh-heh-TAH-lehs)	Vegetables
budín de elote (boo-DEEN deh eh-LOH-teh)	corn pudding

flores de calabaza rellenas (FLOH-rehs deh kah-lah-BAH-sah rreh-YEH-nahs)	stuffed squash blossoms
nopalitos rellenos (noh-pah-LEE-tohs rreh-YEH-nohs)	stuffed prickly-pear leaves
chiles rellenos (CHEE-lehs rreh-YEH-nohs)	stuffed *chiles*

Frijoles (free-HOH-lehs)	Beans
frijoles mexicanos (free-HOH-lehs meh-hee-KAH-nohs)	boiled beans seasoned with salt, garlic, and—usually—lard
frijoles charros (free-HOH-lehs CHAH-rrohs)	beans cooked with beer
frijoles refritos (free-HOH-lehs rreh-FREE-tohs)	refried beans

Postres (POHS-trehs)	Desserts
arroz con leche (ah-RROHS kohn LEH-cheh)	rice with milk and cinnamon
chongos zamoranos (CHOHN-gohs sah-moh-RAH-nohs)	egg yolks with milk and sugar, cooked with cinnamon and syrup
flan (flahn)	caramel custard
capirotada (kah-pee-roh-TAH-dah)	bread, cheese, brown sugar, and pine nuts in a cakelike form
ate (AH-teh)	jellied paste made of different fruit, such as guava, apple, and quince

GENERAL FOOD CATEGORIES

Carne	KAHR-neh	Meat
cabrito	kah-BREE-toh	goat
carnero	kahr-NEH-roh	mutton
conejo	koh-NEH-hoh	rabbit
cordero	kohr-DEH-roh	lamb
puerco (Mexico)	PWEHR-koh	pork
cerdo (Spain)	SEHR-doh	pork
res	rrehs	beef
ternera	tehr-NEH-rah	veal
venado	veh-NAH-doh	venison

Cortes de carne	KOHR-tehs deh KAHR-neh	Cuts of Meat
bistec	pees-TEHK	steak
carne picada	KAHR-neh pee-KAH-dah	chopped beef
carne molida	KAHR-neh moh-LEE-dah	ground beef
chuletas	choo-LEH-tahs	chops
churrasco	choo-RRAHS-koh	T-bone steak
costilla	kohs-TEE-yah	ribs
corazón	koh-rah-SOHN	heart
hígado	EE-gah-doh	liver
lengua	LEHN-gwah	tongue
riñones	rree-NYOH-nehs	kidneys
sesos	SEH-sohs	brains
tripas	TREE-pahs	tripe

74

Aves	AH-vehs	Poultry
capón	kah-POHN	capon
codorniz	koh-dohr-NEES	quail
ganso	GAHN-soh	goose
pato	PAH-toh	duck
pavo	PAH-voh	turkey
guajolote (Mexico)	gwa-hoh-LOH-teh	
perdiz	pehr-DEES	partridge
pollo	POH-yoh	chicken

Pescado y mariscos	pehs-KAH-doh ee mah-REES-kohs	Fish and Seafood

Names of fish and seafood vary greatly between Spain and Latin America, and even from country to country. Fish from tropical waters probably are the most varied in their names. Here are some of the more common.

almejas	ahl-MEH-hahs	clams
anchoas	ahn-CHOH-hahs	anchovies
arenque	ah-REHN-keh	herring
atún	ah-TOON	tuna
bacalao	bah-kah-LAH-oh	codfish
calamares	kah-lah-MAH-rehs	squid
cangrejos	kahn-GREH-hohs	crabs
gambas	GAHM-bahs	large shrimp
langostinos	lahn-gohs-TEE-nohs	crayfish
langosta	lahn-GOHS-tah	lobster
pulpo	POOL-poh	octopus
salmón	sahl-MOHN	salmon

75

sardinas	sahr-DEE-nahs	sardines
trucha	TROO-chah	trout

Vegetales	veh-HEH-tah-lehs	Vegetables
aceitunas	ah-say-TOO-nahs	olives
alcachofas	ahl-kah-CHOH-fahs	artichokes
apio	AH-pyoh	celery
berenjena	beh-rehn-HEH-nah	eggplant
calabaza	kah-lah-BAH-sah	squash
calabacín	kah-lah-bah-SEEN	zucchini
cebolla	seh-BOH-yah	onion
coliflor	koh-lee-FLOHR	cauliflower
champiñón	chahm-pee-NYOHN	mushroom
espárrago	ehs-PAH-rrah-goh	asparagus
espinaca	ehs-pee-NAH-kah	spinach
garbanzo	gahr-BAHN-soh	chickpea
guisante (*or*) **chícharo** (*Mexico*)	gee-SAHN-teh CHEE-chah-roh	pea
habas (*or*) **frijoles** (*Mexico*)	AH-bahs free-HOH-lehs	beans
judía (*or*) **ejote** (*Mexico*)	hoo-DEE-ah eh-HOH-teh	green bean
lechuga	leh-CHOO-gah	lettuce

maíz (*or*) **elote** (*Mexico*)	mah-EES eh-LOH-teh	corn
papa (*or*) **patata** (*Spain*)	PAH-pah pah-TAH-tah	potato
pepino	peh-PEE-noh	cucumber
pimiento	pee-MYEHN-toh	green/red pepper
puerro	PWEH-rroh	leek
repollo	rreh-POH-yoh	cabbage
tomate (*or*) **jitomate** (*Mexico*)	toh-MAH-teh hee-toh-MAH-teh	tomato
zanahoria	sah-nah-OH-ryah	carrot

Condimentos	kohn-dee-MEHN-tohs	Herbs and Spices
achiote	ah-CHYOH-teh	annatto, achiote (provides a red coloring for rice, etc.)
albahaca	ahl-bah-AH-kah	basil
azafrán	ah-sah-FRAHN	saffron
cilantro	see-LAHN-troh	coriander
comino	kohh-MEE-noh	cumin
orégano	oh-REH-gah-noh	oregano
pimienta (blanca/ negra)	pee-MYEHN-tah (BLAHN-kah/NEH-grah)	(white/black) pepper
romero	rroh-MEH-roh	rosemary

Frutas	FROO-tahs	Fruits
albaricoque	ahl-bah-REE-koh-keh	apricots
ciruela	see-RWEH-lah	plum
durazno (*or*) **melocotón** (*Spain*)	doo-RAHS-noh me-loh-koh-TOHN	peach
frambuesa	frahm-BWEH-sah	raspberry
fresa	FREH-sah	strawberry
higo	EE-goh	fig
lima	LEE-mah	lime
limón	lee-MOHN	lemon
mandarina	mahn-dah-REE-nah	tangerine
manzana	mahn-SAH-nah	apple
melón	meh-LOHN	melon
naranja	nah-RAHN-hah	orange
pera	PEH-rah	pear
piña	PEE-nyah	pineapple
sandía	sahn-DEE-ah	watermelon
uva	OO-vah	grape

Frutas tropicales	FROO-tahs troh-pee-kahlehs	Tropical Fruits
plátano	PLAH-tah-noh	banana
guayaba	gwah-YAH-bah	guava
mango	MAHN-goh	mango
tuna	TOO-nah	prickly pear
zapote	sah-POH-teh	sapodilla

Digestivos y licores	dee-hehs-TEE-vohs ee lee-KOH-rehs	After-dinner Drinks (Liqueurs)
crema de menta	KREH-mah deh MEHN-tah	creme de menthe
Kahlúa (*Mexico*)	kah-LOO-ah	coffee liqueur
coñac	koh-NYAHK	brandy

7/PERSONAL CARE
DIALOGUE: GETTING A HAIRCUT (CORTARSE EL PELO)

Peluquera:	**¿De quién es el turno?**	de kyehn ehs ehl TOOR-noh?
Cliente:	**Mío. Quisiera un corte de pelo, por favor.**	MEE-oh. kee-syeh-rah oon KOHR-teh deh PEH-loh, pohr fah-VOHR
Peluquera:	**¿Cómo lo quiere?**	KOH-moh loh KYEH-reh?
Cliente:	**Largo de atrás y más corto de los lados.**	LAHR-goh deh ah-TRAHS ee mahs KOHR-toh deh lohs LAH-dohs
Peluquera:	**¡Cómo no! ¿Quiere un champú, también?**	KOH-moh noh! KYEH-reh oon chahm-POO, tahm-BYEHN?
Cliente:	**No. Solamente el corte. Gracias.**	noh. soh-lah-MEHN-teh ehl KOHR-teh. GRAH-syahs
Peluquera:	**Está bien.**	ehs-TAH byehnK

- -

Hairdresser:	Whose turn is it?
Client:	Mine. I'd like a haircut, please.
Hairdresser:	How would you like it?
Client:	Long in the back, but shorter on the sides.
Hairdresser:	Fine. Do you want a shampoo as well?
Client:	No. Just the haircut. Thank you.
Hairdresser:	Fine.

AT THE BARBERSHOP

I'd like a • haircut	**Quisiera** • **un corte de pelo.**	kee-SYEH-rah • oon KOHR-teh deh PEH-loh

• shampoo.	• un lavado. (or) un champú.	• oon lah-VAH-doh oon chahm-POO
Leave it a little longer	Déjelo un poquito más largo	DEH-heh-loh oon poh-KEE-toh mahs LAR-goh
• in the front.	• adelante.	• ah-deh-LAHN-teh
• on the sides.	• a los lados.	• ah lohs LAH-dohs
• in the back.	• atrás.	• ah-TRAHS
• on the top.	• arriba.	• ah-RREE-bah
Cut it short.	Déjelo corto.	DEH-heh-loh KOHR-toh
Cut it a little shorter.	Córtelo un poquito más corto.	KOHR-teh-loh oon poh-KEE-toh mahs KOHR-toh
I'd like the part	Quiero la raya	KYEH-roh lah RRAH-yah
• on the right.	• a la derecha.	• ah lah deh-REH-chah
• on the left.	• a la izquierda.	• ah lah ees-KYEHR-dah
• down the middle.	• al medio.	• ahl MEH-dyoh
Also trim my	También córteme	tahm-BYEHN KOHR-teh-meh
• beard.	• la barba.	• lah BAHR-bah
• mustache.	• los bigotes.	• lohs bee-GOH-tehs
• sideburns.	• las patillas.	• lahs pah-TEE-yahs
Cut a bit more right here	Corte un poco más aquí	KOHR-teh oon POH-koh mahs ah-KEE
• with the razor.	• con la navaja.	• kohn lah nah-VAH-hah
• with the scissors.	• con las tijeras.	• kohn lahs tee-HEH-rahs
It's fine like that.	Está bien así.	ehs-TAH BYEHN ah-SEE

AT THE BEAUTY PARLOR

I need to go to a hairdresser.	Debo ir a una peluquería.	DEH-boh eer ah OO-nah peh-LOO-keh-REE-ah

81

Is there a beauty salon in this hotel?	¿Hay un salón de belleza en este hotel?	ahy oon sah-LOHN deh beh-YEH-sah ehn EHS-teh oh-TEHL?
Is there a long wait?	¿Debo esperar mucho?	DEH-boh ehs-peh-RARR MOO-choh?
Do I need an appointment?	¿Necesito una cita?	neh-seh-SEE-toh OO-nah SEE-tah?
Can I make an appointment for	¿Puedo hacer una cita para	PWEH-doh ah-SEHR OO-nah SEE-tah PAH-rah
• later?	• más tarde?	• mahs TAHR-deh?
• this afternoon?	• esta tarde?	• EHS-tah TAHR-deh?
• three o'clock?	• las tres?	• lahs trehs?
• tomorrow?	• mañana?	• mah-NYAH-nah?
I'd like	Quisiera	kee-SYEH-rah
• a shampoo.	• un lavado.	• oon lah-VAH-doh
• a blowdry.	• un modelado.	• oon moh-deh-LAH-doh
• a set.	• un peinado.	• oon pay-NAH-doh
• a permanent.	• una permanente.	• OO-nah pehr-mah-NEHN-teh
• a manicure.	• hacerme la manicura.	• ah-SEHR-meh lah mah-nee-KOO-rah
• a touch-up.	• un retoque.	• oon rreh-TOH-keh
• a color rinse.	• un enjuague con color.	• oon ehn-HWAH-geh kohn koh-LOHR
Could I see a color chart?	¿Puedo ver una muestra de colores?	PWEH-doh vehr OO-nah MWEHS-trah deh koh-LOH-rehs?
I prefer	Prefiero	preh-FYEH-roh
• auburn.	• castaño.	• kahs-TAH-nyoh
• ash blond.	• rubio ceniza.	• RROO-byoh seh-NEE-sah
• light blond.	• rubio claro.	• RROO-byoh KLAH-roh
• a darker shade.	• un tono más os-curo.	• oon TOH-noh mahs ohs-KOO-roh

82

• a lighter shade.	• un tono más claro.	• oon TOH-noh mahs KLAH-roh
Please use hairspray.	Con laca, por favor.	kohn LAH-kah, pohr fah-VOHR
No hairspray, please.	Sin laca, por favor.	seen LAH-kah, pohr fah-VOHR
That's perfect!	¡Está perfecto!	ehs-TAH pehr-FEK-toh!

LAUNDRY AND DRY CLEANING

I'm looking for	Estoy buscando	ehs-TOY boos-KAHN-doh
• a laundry.	• una lavandería.	• OO-nah lah-vahn-deh-REE-ah
• a dry cleaner.	• una tintorería.	• OO-nah teen-toh-reh-REE-ah
• a laundromat.	• una lavandería automática.	• OO-nah lah-vahn-deh-REE-ah ow-toh-MAH-tee-kah
I have a dress to be	Tengo un vestido para	TEHN-goh oon vehs-TEE-doh PAH-rah
• washed.	• lavar.	• lah-VAHR
• ironed.	• planchar.	• plahn-CHAHR
• dry-cleaned.	• limpiar en seco.	• leem-PYAHR ehn SEH-koh
• mended.	• zurcir.	• soor-SEER
These clothes are dirty.	Esta es ropa sucia.	EHS-tah ehs RROH-pah SOO-syah
Can they be cleaned today?	La puede limpiar hoy?	lah PWEH-deh leem-PYAR oy?
When will they be ready?	¿Cuando va a estar lista?	KWAHN-doh vahn ah ehs-TAHR LEES-tah?
I need them	Las necesito	lahs neh-seh-SEE-toh
• tomorrow.	• mañana	• mah-NYAH-nah
• the day after tomorrow.	• pasado mañana.	• pah-SAH-doh mah-NYAH-nah
• in a week.	• en una semana.	• ehn OO-nah seh-MAH-nah

83

• as soon as possible.	• **lo más pronto posible.**	• loh mahs PROHN-toh poh-SEE-bleh
I'm leaving tomorrow.	**Me voy mañana.**	meh voy mah-NYAH-nah
Can you get this stain out?	**¿Puede sacar esta mancha?**	PWEH-deh sah-KAHR EHS-tah MAHN-chah?
Can you sew on this button?	**¿Puede coser este botón?**	PWEH-deh KOH-sehr EHS-teh boh-TOHN?
This isn't mine.	**Esto no es mío.**	EHS-toh noh ehs MEE-oh
There's an item missing.	**Falta algo aquí.**	FAHL-tah AHL-goh ah-KEE
Here is my list.	**Aquí está mi lista.**	ah-KEE ehs-TAH mee LEES-tah
• 2 shirts	• **dos camisas**	• dohs kah-MEE-sahs
• 5 pairs of men's undershorts	• **cinco calzones**	• SEEN-koh kahl-SOH-nehs
• a suit	• **un traje**	• oon TRAH-heh
• 8 pairs of socks	• **ocho pares de calcetines**	• OH-choh PAH-rehs deh kahl-seh-TEE-nehs
• several handkerchiefs	• **varios pañuelos**	• VAH-ryohs pah-NYWEH-lohs
• 2 ties	• **dos corbatas**	• dohs kohr-BAH-tahs
• a sweater	• **un suéter**	• oon SWEH-tehr
• 2 pairs of pants	• **dos pantalones**	• dohs pahn-tah-LOH-nehs
• a jacket	• **un saco**	• oon SAH-koh
• a bathing suit	• **un traje de baño**	• oon TRAH-heh deh BAH-nyoh
• 3 blouses	• **tres blusas**	• trehs BLOO-sahs
• a skirt	• **una falda**	• OO-nah FAHL-dah
• a bra	• **un sostén**	• oon sohs-TEHN
• 4 panties	• **cuatro pantaletas (or) bragas (Spain)**	• KWAH-troh pahn-tah-LEH-tahs BRAH-gahs
• a dress	• **un vestido**	• oon vehs-TEE-doh

8/HEALTH CARE

You can usually locate English-speaking doctors in Spain and Mexico, especially in the big cities. Your embassy or consulate can help.

You should carry basic medicine, such as aspirin, and any prescription drugs you are currently using. Be sure to keep the prescription or label handy on your return trip, so that you can show it to the customs authorities, thus avoiding any problems.

The major health risk in Mexico is posed by consuming contaminated drinking water, fresh fruit, and vegetables. So watch what you eat and drink. Avoid unpasteurized milk, milk products, and uncooked food, such as salads and even uncooked garnishes on cooked food. Stay away from fruits that you don't peel yourself. Drink only bottled water or water that has been boiled for at least 20 minutes. At establishments not frequented by tourists, ask for drinks without ice, *sin hielo* (sin hee-EH-lo). You can usually identify ice made commercially from purified water by its uniform shape and the hole in the center. Hotels with water purification systems post signs to that effect in the rooms.

If your precautions fail, take liquid Pepto-Bismol, Imodium, or Lomotil—all available throughout Mexico. Rest as much as possible and drink plenty of purified water. In severe cases, rehydrate yourself with a salt-sugar solution (1/2 tsp. salt and 4 Tbsp. sugar per quart of water).

DIALOGUE: FINDING A DOCTOR (ENCONTRAR UN DOCTOR)

Turista:	**No me siento bien.**	noh meh SYEHN-toh byehn
Recepcionista:	**¿Necesita un doctor?**	neh-seh-SEE-tah oon dohk-TORH?
Turista:	**Creo que sí, ¿Puede recomendar uno?**	KREH-oh keh see, PWEH-deh reh-koh-mehn-DAHR OO-noh?
Recepcionista:	**Sí. Hay un Centro Médico en la esquina.**	see. ahy oon SEHN-troh MEH-dee-koh ehn lah ehs-KEE-nah
Turista:	**¿Hay un doctor que habla inglés?**	ahy oon dohk-TOHR keh AH-blah een-GLEHS?
Recepcionista:	**No, pero la enfermera sí lo habla.**	noh, PEH-roh lah ehn-fehr-MEH-rah see loh AH-blah

- -

Tourist:	I don't feel well.
Hotel clerk:	Do you need a doctor?
Tourist:	I think so. Can you recommend one?
Hotel clerk:	Yes. There's a Medical Center on the corner.
Tourist:	Is there a doctor who speaks English?
Hotel clerk:	No, but the nurse does.

FINDING A DOCTOR

| Is there a doctor here? | **¿Hay un doctor aquí?** | ahy oon dohk-TOHR ah-KEE? |
| Could you call me a doctor? | **¿Puede llamarme a un doctor?** | PWEH-deh yah-MAHR-meh ah oon dohk-TOHR? |

86

Where is the doctor's office?	**¿Dónde está el consultorio del doctor?**	DOHN-deh ehs-TAH ehl kohn-sool-TOH-ryoh dehl dohk-TOHR?
I need a doctor who speaks English.	**Necesito un doctor que hable inglés.**	neh-seh-SEE-toh oon dohk-TOHR keh AH-bleh een-GLEHS
When can I see the doctor?	**¿Cuándo puedo ver al doctor?**	KWAHN-doh PWEH-doh vehr ahl dohk-TOHR?
Can the doctor see me now?	**¿Puede verme el doctor ahora?**	PWEH-deh VEHR-meh ehl dohk-TOHR ah-OH-rah?
It's an emergency.	**Es una emergencia.**	ehs OO-nah eh-mehr-HEHN-syah
Do I need an appointment?	**¿Necesito una cita?**	neh-seh-SEE-toh OO-nah SEE-tah?
Can I have an appointment	**¿Puedo hacer una cita**	PWEH-doh ah-SEHR OO-nah SEE-tah
• as soon as possible?	• **la más pronto posible?**	• loh mahs PROHN-toh poh-SEE-bleh?
• for 2 o'clock?	• **para las dos?**	• PAH-rah lahs dohs?
What are the doctor's office hours?	**¿Cuáles son las horas de consulta?**	KWAH-lehs sohn lahs OH-rahs deh kohn-SOOL-tah?
I need	**Necesito**	neh-seh-SEE-toh
• a general practitioner.	• **un médico general.**	• oon MEH-dee-koh heh-neh-RAHL
• a pediatrician.	• **un pediatra.**	• oon peh-DYAH-trah
• a gynecologist.	• **un ginecólogo.**	• oon hee-neh-KOH-loh-goh
• an eye doctor.	• **un oftalmólogo.**	• oon ohf-tahl-MOH-loh-goh
• a dentist.	• **un dentista.**	• oon dehn-TEES-tah

87

TALKING TO THE DOCTOR

I don't feel well.	**No me siento bien.**	noh meh SYEHN-toh byehn
I'm sick.	**Estoy enfermo(-a).**	ehs-TOY ehn-FEHR-moh(-mah)
I don't know what I have.	**No sé lo que tengo.**	noh seh loh keh TEHN-goh
I feel	**Me siento**	meh SYEHN-toh
• weak.	• **débil.**	• DEH-beel
• dizzy.	• **mareado(-a).**	• mah-reh-AH-doh (-dah)
I have a fever.	**Tengo fiebre.**	TEHN-goh FYEH-breh
I don't have fever.	**No tengo fiebre.**	noh TEHN-goh FYEH-breh
I'm nauseated.	**Tengo náuseas.**	TEHN-goh NOW-seh-ahs
I can't sleep.	**No puedo dormir.**	noh PWEH-doh dohr-MEER
I threw up.	**Vomité.**	voh-mee-TEH
I have diarrhea.	**Tengo diarrea.**	TEHN-goh dyah-RREH-ah
I'm constipated.	**Estoy estreñido(-a).**	ehs-TOY ehs-treh-NYEE-doh(-dah)
I have	**Tengo**	TEHN-goh
• asthma.	• **asma.**	• AHS-mah
• a (animal) bite.	• **una mordida.**	• OO-nah mohr-DEE-dah
• bruises.	• **ematomas.**	• eh-mah-TOH-mahs
• a burn.	• **una quemadura.**	• OO-nah keh-mah-DOO-rah
• something in my eye.	• **algo en el ojo.**	• AHL-goh ehn ehl OH-hoh
• a cold.	• **un resfrío.**	• oon rrehs-FREE-oh
• a cough.	• **tos.**	• tohs

• cramps.	• **calambres.**	• kah-LAHM-brehs
• a cut.	• **una cortada.**	• OO-nah kohr-TAH-dah
• the flu.	• **gripe.**	• GREE-peh
• a headache.	• **dolor de cabeza.**	• doh-LOHR deh kah-BEH-sah
• a lump.	• **un bulto.**	• oon BOOL-toh
• a rash.	• **urticaria.**	• oor-tee-KAH-ryah
• rheumatism.	• **reumatismo.**	• rreu-mah-TEES-moh
• a sore throat.	• **dolor de garganta.**	• doh-LOHR deh gahr-GAHN-tah
• a sting.	• **una picadura.**	• OO-nah pee-kah-DOO-rah
• a stomach ache.	• **dolor de estómago.**	• doh-LOHR deh ehs-TOH-mah-goh
• sunstroke.	• **insolación.**	• een-soh-lah-SYOHN
• a swelling.	• **una hinchazón.**	• OO-nah een-chah-SOHN
• an upset stomach.	• **malestar en el estómago.**	• mah-lehs-TAHR ehn ehl ehs-TOH-mah-goh
My . . . hurts (hurt).	**Me duele (-n)***	meh DWEH-leh (-lehn)
• stomach	• **el estómago.**	• ehl ehs-TOH-mah-goh
• feet	• **los pies.**	• lohs pyehs
• head	• **la cabeza.**	• lah kah-BEH-sah
• nose	• **la nariz.**	• lah nah-REES
• (inner) ear	• **el oído.**	• ehl oh-EE-doh
• mouth	• **la boca.**	• lah BOH-kah
• eye	• **el ojo.**	• ehl OH-hoh
• throat	• **la garganta.**	• lah gahr-GAHN-tah
• tongue	• **la lengua.**	• lah LEHN-gwah
• tooth	• **el diente.**	• ehl DYEHN-teh
• torso	• **el torso.**	• ehl TOHR-soh
• neck	• **el cuello.**	• ehl KWEH-yoh
• shoulder	• **el hombro.**	• ehl OHM-broh
• arm	• **el brazo.**	• ehl BRAH-soh

89

• elbow	• **el codo.**	• ehl KOH-doh
• chest	• **el pecho.**	• ehl PEH-choh
• breast	• **el seno.**	• ehl SEH-noh
• back	• **la espalda.**	• lah ehs-PAHL-dah
• hand	• **la mano.**	• lah MAH-noh
• wrist	• **la muñeca.**	• lah moo-NYEH-kah
• waist	• **la cintura.**	• lah seen-TOO-rah
• hip	• **la cadera.**	• lah kah-DEH-rah
• leg	• **la pierna.**	• lah PYEHR-nah
• knee	• **la rodilla.**	• lah rroh-DEE-yah
• ankle	• **el tobillo.**	• ehl toh-BEE-yah
• foot	• **el pie.**	• ehl pyeh
• heart	• **el corazón.**	• ehl koh-rah-SOHN
• liver	• **el hígado.**	• ehl EE-gah-doh
• appendix	• **el apéndice.**	• ehl ah-PEHN-dee-seh
• lungs	• **los pulmones.**	• lohs pool-MOH-nehs
• bladder	• **la vejiga.**	• lah veh-HEE-gah
• glands	• **las glándulas.**	• lahs GLAHN-doo-lahs

*In Spanish, the verb adds an -n when its subject is plural.

I'm allergic to	**Soy alérgico(-a) a**	soy ah-LEHR-hee-koh (-kah) ah
• penicillin.	• **la penicilina.**	• lah peh-nee-see-LEE-nah
• sulfa.	• **la sulfa.**	• lah SOOL-fah
• certain medicines.	• **ciertas medicinas.**	• SYEHR-tahs meh-dee-SEE-nahs
Here is the medicine I take.	**Aquí está la medicina que tomo.**	ah-KEE ehs-TAH lah meh-dee-SEE-nah keh TOH-moh
I've had this pain for two days.	**He tenido este dolor por dos días.**	eh teh-NEE-doh EHS-teh doh-LOHR pohr dohs DEE-ahs

90

I had a heart attack four years ago.	**Tuve un infarto hace cuatro años.**	TOO-beh oon een-FAHR-toh AH-seh KWAH-troh AH-nyohs
I'm four months pregnant.	**Estoy embarazada de cuatro meses.**	ehs-TOY ehm-bah-rah-SAH-dah deh KWAH-troh MEH-sehs
I have menstrual pains.	**Tengo dolores menstruales.**	TEHN-goh doh-LOH-rehs mehns-TRWAH-lehs

What the Doctor Says

¿Dónde le duele?	DOHN-deh leh DWEH-leh?	Where does it hurt?
¿Qué síntomas tiene?	keh SEEN-toh-mahs TYEH-neh?	What symptoms do you have?
Desvístase.	dehs-VEES-tah-seh	Get undressed.
Desvístase hasta la cintura.	dehs-VEES-tah-seh AHS-tah lah seen-TOO-rah	Undress to the waist.
Acuéstese aquí.	ah-KWEHS-teh-seh ah-KEE	Lie down here.
Abra la boca.	AH-brah la BOH-kah	Open your mouth.
Tosa.	TOH-sah	Cough!
Respire a fondo.	rrehs-PEE-reh ah FOHN-doh	Breathe deeply.
Indíqueme donde le duele.	een-DEE-keh-meh DOHN-deh leh DWEH-leh	Show me where it hurts.
Saque la lengua.	SAH-keh lah LEHN-gwah	Stick out your tongue.
Vístase.	VEES-tah-seh	Get dressed.

91

Voy a tomarle la	voy ah toh-MAHR-leh lah	I'm going to take your
• **temperatura.**	• tehm-peh-rah-TOO-rah	• temperature.
• **presión.**	• preh-SYOHN	• blood pressure.
Necesito una muestra de	neh-seh-SEE-toh OO-nah MWEHS-trah deh	I need a sample of your
• **sangre.**	• SAHN-greh	• blood.
• **materia fecal.**	• mah-TEH-ryah feh-CAHL	• stool.
• **orina.**	• oh-REE-nah	• urine.
Le voy a dar un calmante.	leh voy ah dahr oon kahl-MAHN-teh	I'm going to give you a painkiller.
Usted necesita	oos-TEHD neh-seh-SEE-tah	You need
• **una radiografía.**	• OO-nah rrah-dyoh-grah-FEE-ah	• an X ray.
• **una inyección.**	• OO-nah een-yehk-SYOHN	• an injection.
• **ir al hospital.**	• eer ahl ohs-pee-TAHL	• to go to the hospital.
• **ver a un especialista.**	• vehr ah oon ehs-peh-syah-LEES-tah	• to see a specialist.
No es serio.	noh ehs SEH-ryoh	It's not serious.
No es grave.	noh ehs GRAH-veh	It's not serious.
Es	ehs	It's
• **serio.**	• SEH-ryoh	• serious.
• **un poco serio.**	• oon POH-koh SEH-ryoh	• somewhat serious.
Está	ehs-TAH	It's
• **dislocado.**	• dees-loh-KAH-doh	• dislocated.
• **roto.**	• RROH-toh	• broken.
• **luxado.**	• loo-KSAH-doh	• sprained.
• **infectado.**	• een-fehk-TAH-doh	• infected.

Usted tiene	oos-TEHD TYEH-neh	You have
• **apendicitis.**	• ah-pehn-dee-SEE-tees	• appendicitis.
• **una fractura.**	• OO-nah frahk-TOO-rah	• a fracture.
• **un hueso roto.**	• oon WEH-soh RROH-toh	• a broken bone.
• **gastritis.**	• gahs-TREE-tees	• gastritis.
• **gripe.**	• GREE-peh	• the flu.
• **una intoxi-cación.**	• OO-nah een-tohk-see-kah-SYOHN	• food poisoning.
• **pulmonía.**	• pool-moh-NEE-ah	• pneumonia.
• **viruela.**	• vee-RWEH-lah	• smallpox.
• **malaria.**	• mah-LAH-ryah	• malaria.

Patient's Questions

Is it serious?	**¿Es serio?**	ehs SEH-ryoh?
Is it contagious?	**¿Es contagioso?**	ehs kohn-tah-HYOH-soh?
How long should I stay in bed?	**¿Cuánto tiempo debo estar en cama?**	KWAHN-toh TYEHM-poh DEH-boh ehs-TAHR ehn KAH-mah?
What exactly is wrong with me?	**¿Qué es lo que tengo exactamente?**	keh ehs loh keh TEHN-goh ehk-sahk-tah-MEHN-teh?
How frequently should I take the medication?	**¿Cada cuanto tiempo debo tomar la medicina?**	KAH-dah KWAHN-toh TYEHM-poh DEH-boh toh-MAHR lah meh-dee-SEE-nah?
Do I need to see you again?	**¿Debo verlo otra vez? (or) . . . verle . . . (Spain)**	DEH-boh VEHR-loh OH-trah vehs? . . . VEHR-leh . . .
Do I need a prescription?	**¿Necesito una re-ceta?**	neh-seh-SEE-toh OO-nah rreh-SEH-tah?

When can I start traveling again?	¿Cuándo puedo empezar a viajar otra vez?	KWAHN-doh PWEH-doh ehm-peh-SAHR ah vyah-HAHR OH-trah vehs?
Can you give me a prescription for	¿Puede darme una receta para	PWEH-deh DAHR-meh OO-nah rreh-SEH-tah PAH-rah
• a painkiller?	• un calmante?	• oon kahl-MAHN-teh?
• a tranquilizer?	• un tranquilizante?	• oon trahn-kee-lee-SAHN-teh?
• a sleeping pill?	• una pastilla para dormir?	• OO-nah pahs-TEE-yah PAH-rah dohr-MEER?
Can I have a bill for my insurance?	¿Me puede dar un recibo para mi seguro?	meh PWEH-deh dahr oon rreh-SEE-boh PAH-rah mee seh-GOO-roh?
Could you fill out this medical form?	¿Puede llenar este formulario médico?	PWEH-deh yeh-NAHR EHS-teh fohr-moo-LAH-ryoh meh-DEE-koh?

AT THE HOSPITAL

Is there a hospital close by?	¿Hay un hospital por aquí?	ahy oon ohs-pee-TAHL pohr ah-KEE?
Call an ambulance!	¡Llame una ambulancia!	YAH-meh OO-nah ahm-boo-LAHN-syah!
Help me!	¡Ayúdeme!	ah-YOO-deh-meh!
Get me to the hospital!	¡Lléveme al hospital!	YEH-veh-meh ahl ohs-pee-TAHL!
I need first aid fast!	¡Necesito primeros auxilios rápido!	neh-seh-SEE-toh pree-MEH-rohs owk-SEE-lyohs RRAH-pee-doh!

I was in an accident!	¡Tuve un accidente!	TOO-veh oon ahk-see-DEHN-teh!
I cut my	Me corté	meh kohr-TEH
• hand.	• la mano.	• lah MAH-noh
• face.	• la cara.	• lah KAH-rah
• finger.	• el dedo.	• ehl DEH-doh
• leg.	• la pierna.	• lah PYEHR-nah
• neck.	• el cuello.	• ehl KWEH-yoh
I can't move.	No puedo moverme.	noh PWEH-doh moh-VEHR-meh
He hurt his head.	Se lastimó la cabeza.	seh lahs-tee MOH lah kah-BEH-sah
His ankle is	Tiene el tobillo	TYEH-neh ehl toh-BEE-yoh
• broken.	• roto.	• RROH-toh
• twisted.	• torcido.	• tohr-SEE-doh
• swollen.	• hinchado.	• een-CHAH-doh
She (he) is bleeding heavily.	Está sangrando mucho.	ehs-TAH sahn-GRAHN-doh MOO-choh
He's (she's) unconscious.	Está inconsciente.	ehs-TAH een-kohn-SYEHN-teh
I burned myself.	Me quemé.	meh keh-MEH
I ate something poisonous.	Comí algo venenoso.	koh-MEE AHL-goh veh-neh-NOH-soh
When can I leave?	¿Cuándo puedo salir?	KWAHN-doh PWEH-doh sah-LEER?
When will the doctor come?	¿Cuándo va a venir el doctor?	KWAHN-doh vah ah veh-NEER ehl dohk-TOHR?
Where is the nurse?	¿Dónde está la enfermera?	DOHN-deh ehs-TAH lah ehn-fehr-MEH-rah?

I can't	No puedo	noh PWEH-doh
• eat.	• comer.	• koh-MEHR
• drink.	• beber.	• beh-BEHR
• sleep.	• dormir.	• dohr-MEER
What are the visiting hours?	¿Cuáles son las horas de visita?	KWAH-lehs sohn lahs OH-rahs deh vee-SEE-tah?

THE DENTIST

I need to see a dentist.	Debo ver un dentista.	DEH-boh vehr oon dehn-TEES-tah
It's an emergency.	Es una emergencia.	ehs OO-nah eh-mehr-HEHN-syah
I'm in a lot of pain.	Tengo mucho dolor.	TEHN-goh MOO-choh doh-LOHR
I've lost a filling.	He perdido un arreglo.	eh pehr-DEE-doh oon ah-RREH-gloh
This tooth is broken.	Este diente está roto.	EHS-teh DYEHN-teh ehs-tah RROH-toh
This tooth hurts.	Me duele este diente.	meh DWEH-leh EHS-teh DYEHN-teh
I don't want to have it extracted.	No quiero que me lo saque.	noh KYEH-roh keh meh loh SAH-keh
Can you fill it	¿Puede rellenármelo	PWEH-deh reh-yeh-NAHR-meh-loh
• with gold?	• con oro?	• kohn OH-roh?
• with silver?	• con plata?	• kohn PLAH-tah?
• temporarily?	• temporalmente?	• tehm-poh-rahl-MEHN-teh?
I want a local anesthetic.	Quiero anestesia local.	KYEH-roh ah-nehs-TEH-syah loh-KAHL
My denture is broken.	Mi dentadura postiza está rota.	mee dehn-tah-DOO-rah pohs-TEE-sah ehs-TAH RROH-tah

What the Dentist Says

Usted tiene	oos-TEHD TYEH-neh	You have
• una infección.	• OO-nah een-fehk-SYOHN	• an infection.
• una carie.	• OO-nah KAH-ryeh	• a cavity.
• un abseso.	• oon ahb-SEH-soh	• an abscess.
¿Le duele esto?	leh DWEH-leh EHS-toh?	Does this hurt?
Debo sacarle esta muela.	DEH-boh sah-KAHR-leh EHS-tah MWEH-lah	This tooth must come out.
Puedo arreglar	PWEH-doh ah-rreh-GLAHR	I can fix
• este puente.	• EHS-teh PWEHN-teh	• this bridge.
• esta corona.	• EHS-tah koh-ROH-nah	• this crown.
Usted debe regresar	oos-TEHD DEH-beh rreh-greh-SAHR	You'll need to come back
• mañana.	• mah-NYAH-nah	• tomorrow.
• en unos días.	• ehn OO-nohs DEE-ahs	• in a few days.
• la próxima semana.	• lah PROK-see-mah seh-MAH-nah	• next week.

THE OPTICIAN

If you wear prescription glasses or contact lenses, be sure to bring an extra pair and a copy of your prescription. Note that in Mexico City, the smog may irritate your eyes if you wear contact lenses; don't forget your glasses.

I broke	**Rompí**	rrohm-PEE
• a lens.	• **un lente.**	• oon LEHN-teh
• the frame.	• **la montura.**	• lah mohn-TOO-rah

I lost a lens.	**Perdí un lente.**	pehr-DEE oon LEHN-teh
I've lost my • glasses. • contact lenses.	**He perdido mis** • **lentes.** • **lentes de contacto.**	eh pehr-DEE-doh mees • LEHN-tehs • LEHN-tehs deh kohn-TAHK-toh
Can you replace them right away?	**¿Puede reemplazarlos ahora?**	PWEH-deh rrehm-plah-SAHR-lohs ah-OH-rah?
When can I pick them up?	**¿Cuándo puedo recogerlos?**	KWAHN-doh PWEH-doh rreh-koh-HEHR-lohs?
Do you have sunglasses?	**¿Tiene lentes para el sol?**	TYE-neh LEHN-tehs PAH-rah ehl sohl?

AT THE PHARMACY

Pharmacies abound in Spain and Latin America, and are easy to find. Often they are identified by the prescription symbol outside the establishment. When a pharmacy in an area is closed, there is usually a sign indicating which one is "on duty" (*de turno*/deh TOOR-noh). Or you can check a local newspaper to see which one is open after regular hours.

Except for some unusual prescription drugs, you can find most medicines in pharmacies. Prescriptions are not needed for anything except sleeping pills, but you may feel more comfortable bringing medicine from home, as drug names vary from one country to another. Pharmacies in Spain tend to sell primarily medicinal products, and are called *droguerías* (droh-geh-REE-ahs); however, in Mexico the *farmacias* (fahr-MAH-syahs) usually sell other items, such as beauty products, baby food, and toilet paper.

| Is there a pharmacy nearby? | **¿Hay una farmacia por aquí?** | ahy OO-nah fahr-MAH-syah pohr ah-KEE? |

When does the pharmacy open?	¿Cuándo abre la farmacia?	KWAHN-doh AH-breh lah fahr-MAH-syah?
What pharmacy is open now?	¿Cuál es la farmacia de turno?	KWAHL ehs lah fahr-MAH-syah deh TOOR-noh?
I need something for	Necesito algo para	neh-seh-SEE-toh AHL-goh PAH-rra
• a cold.	• el resfrío.	• ehl rrehs-FREE-oh
• constipation.	• el estreñimiento.	• ehl ehs-treh-nyee-MYEHN-toh
• a cough.	• la tos.	• lah tohs
• diarrhea.	• la diarrea.	• lah dyah-RREH-ah
• fever.	• la fiebre.	• lah FYEH-breh
• hay fever.	• la alergia.	• lah ah-IFHR-hyah
• headache.	• el dolor de cabeza.	• ehl doh-LOHR deh kah-BEH-sah
• an insect bite.	• una picadura.	• OO-nah pee-kah-DOO-rah
• sunburn.	• la quemadura de sol.	• lah keh-mah-DOO-rah deh sohl
• motion sickness.	• el mareo.	• ehl mah-REH-oh
• an upset stomach.	• el malestar de estómago.	• ehl mah-lehs-TAHR deh ehs-TOH-mah-goh
Other items:	Otros productos:	OH-trohs proh-DOOK-tohs
• alcohol	• alcohol	• ahl-KOHL
• analgesic	• analgésico	• ah-nahl-HEH-see-koh
• antiseptic	• antiséptico	• ahn-tee-SEHP-tee-koh
• aspirin	• aspirina	• ahs-pee-REE-nah
• bandages	• vendas	• VEHN-dahs
• Band-Aids	• curitas	• koo-REE-tahs
• contact lens solution	• líquido para lentes de contacto	• LEE-kee-doh PAH-rah LEHN-tehs deh kohn-TAHK-toh
• contraceptives	• anticonceptivos	• ahn-tee-kohn-sehp-TEE-vohs

99

• cotton	**algodón**	• ahl-goh-DOHN
• cough drops	**pastillas para la tos**	• pahs-TEE-yahs-PAH-rah lah tohs
• disinfectant	**desinfectante**	• deh-seen-fehk-TAHN-teh
• eardrops	**gotas para el oído**	• GOH-tahs PAH-rah ehl oh-EE-doh
• gauze	**gaza**	• GAH-sah
• insect spray	**repelente**	• rreh-peh-LEHN-teh
• iodine	**yodo**	• YOH-doh
• laxative	**laxante**	• lahk-SAHN-teh
• nose drops	**gotas para la nariz**	• GOH-tahs PAH-rah lah nah-REES
• sanitary napkins	**toallas sanitarias**	• toh-AH-yahs sah-nee-TAH-ryahs
• sleeping pills	**pastillas para dormir**	• pahs-TEE-yahs PAH-rah dohr-MEER
• suppositories	**supositorios**	• soo-poh-see-TOH-ryohs
• tablets	**obleas**	• oh-BLEH-ahs
• tampons	**tapones sanitarios**	• tah-POH-nehs sah-nee-TAH-ryahs
• thermometer	**termómetro**	• tehr-MOH-meh-troh
• vitamins	**vitaminas**	• vee-tah-MEE-nahs
It's urgent!	**¡Es urgente!**	ehs oor-HEHN-teh!

9/ON THE ROAD
CAR RENTALS

Most major car rental agencies have offices in Spain and Mexico. To get the best deal, book through a travel agent and shop around.

When driving in Mexico, carry proof of Mexican auto liability insurance at all times. It is usually provided by car-rental agencies and included in the cost of the rental. If you don't have proof of insurance and happen to injure someone—whether it's your fault or not—you stand the risk of being jailed.

Obey speed limits, parking regulations, and all highway rules, even if others do not.

DIALOGUE: AT THE CAR-RENTAL AGENCY
(EN EL ALQUILER DE COCHES)

Turista:	**Necesito alquilar un automóvil.**	neh-seh-SEE-toh ahl-kee-LAHR oon ow-toh-MOH-veel
Empleado:	**¿Tiene usted una reservación*?**	TYEH-neh oos-TEHD OO-nah rreh-sehr-vah-SYOHN?
Turista:	**No, ¿pero tiene uno disponible?**	noh, PEH-roh TYEH-neh OO-noh dees-poh-NEE-ble?
Empleado:	**Sí, ¿por cuánto tiempo lo quiere?**	see, pohr KWAHN-to TYEHM-poh loh KYEH-reh?
Turista:	**¿Cuál es la tarifa por día?**	kwahl ehs lah tah-REE-fah pohr DEE-ah?

Empleado:	**Cuesta $200 al día, más el kilometraje.**	KWEHS-tah dose-YEN-toes PEH-sohs ahl DEE-ah, mahs ehl kee-loh-meh-TRAH-heh
Turista:	**¿Es más barato por semana?**	ehs mahs bah-RAH-toh pohr seh-MAH-nah?
Empleado:	**¡Por supuesto! ¿Lo quiere llevar hoy?**	pohr soo-PWEH-toh! loh KYEH-reh yeh-VAHR ohy?
Turista:	**Sí, por favor. Lo quiero por una semana.**	see, pohr fah-VOHR. loh KYEH-roh pohr OO-nah seh-MAH-nah

*In Spain, you would say, "*una reserva* (rreh-SEHR-vah)."

. . . .

Tourist: I need to rent a car.
Clerk: Do you have a reservation?
Tourist: No, but do you have one available?
Clerk: Yes, for how long do you want it?
Tourist: What's the rate per day?
Clerk: It's $30,000 (*pesos*) per day, plus mileage.
Tourist: Is it cheaper by the week?
Clerk: Of course! Do you want it today?
Tourist: Yes, please. I'd like it for a week.

I need to rent	**Necesito alquilar**	neh-seh-SEE-toh ahl-kee-LAHR
• a car.	• **un automóvil.**	• oon ow-toh-MOH-veel
• a compact car.	• **un automóvil pequeño.**	• oon ow-toh-MOH-veel peh-KEH-nyoh

102

• an automatic car.	• **un automóvil automático.**	• oon ow-toh-MOH-veel ow-toh-MAH-tee-koh
• a station wagon.	• **una camioneta.**	• OO-nah kah-myoh-NEH-tah
How much is it per • hour? • day? • week? • month? • kilometer?	**¿Cuánto es por** • **hora?** • **día?** • **semana?** • **mes?** • **kilómetro?**	KWAHN-toh ehs pohr • OH-rah? • DEE-ah? • seh-MAH-nah? • mehs? • kee-LOH-meh-troh?
How much is the insurance?	**¿Cuánto cuesta el seguro?**	KWAHN-toh KWEHS-tah ehl seh-GOO-roh?
Do you need • a deposit? • my driver's license?	**¿Necesita** • **un depósito?** • **mi licencia de conducir?**	neh-seh-SEE-tah • oon deh-POH-see-toh? • mee lee-SEHN-syah deh kohn-doo-SEER?
Do you accept credit cards?	**¿Aceptan tarjetas de crédito?**	ah-SEHP-tahn tahr-HEH-tahs deh KREH-dee-toh?
Can I leave the car in another city?	**¿Puedo dejar el automóvil en otra ciudad?**	PWEH-doh deh-HAR ehl ow-toh-MOH-veel ehn OH-trah syoo-DAHD?

DISTANCES AND LIQUID MEASURES

Distances in Spain, Mexico, and the rest of Latin America are expressed in kilometers, or *kilómetros* (kee-LOH-meh-trohs), and liquid measures (for gas and oil), in liters, or *litros* (LEE-trohs).

Miles/Kilometers

1 kilometer (km.) = .62 miles 1 mile = 1.61 km.	
Kilometers	**Miles**
1	0.62
5	3.1
8	5.0
10	6.2
15	9.3
20	12.4
50	31.0
75	46.6
100	62.1

Gallons/Liters

1 liter (l) = .26 gallon 1 gallon = 3.78 liters	
Liters	**Gallons**
10	2.6
15	4.0
20	5.3
30	7.9
40	10.6
50	13.2
60	15.8
70	18.5

THE SERVICE STATION

Unleaded gas is now available in Mexico, but you may not be able to find it at every station. Gasoline stations are owned and operated by the government and are few and far between, so don't let your tank run too low. The stations are called *Pemex,* and can usually be identified by their fluorescent orange signs.

Where is there a service station?	**¿Dónde hay una gasolinera?**	DOHN-deh ahy OO-nah gah-soh-lee-NEH-rah?
Fill it with	**Llénelo con**	YEH-neh-loh kohn
• regular.	• **regular.**	• rreh-goo-LAHR
• super.	• **super.**	• SOO-pehr
• diesel.	• **diesel.**	• DEE-sehl
Give me 40 liters of regular.	**Déme cuarenta litros de regular.**	DEH-meh kwa-REHN-tah LEE-trohs deh rreh-goo-LAHR
Please check the	**Por favor, revise**	pohr fah-VOHR, rreh-VEE-seh

104

- carburetor.
- **el carburador.**
- ehl kahr-boo-rah-DOHR

- break fluid.
- **el líquido de frenos.**
- ehl LEE-kee-doh deh FREH-nohs

- spark plugs.
- **las bujías.**
- lahs boo-HEE-ahs

- tire pressure.
- **la presión de las llantas.**
- lah preh-SYOHN deh lahs YAHN-tahs

- water.
- **el agua.**
- ehl AH-gwah

- oil.
- **el aceite.**
- ehl ah-SAY-teh

Change the oil.

Cambie el aceite.

KAHM-byeh ehl ah-SAY-teh

DRIVING

Before taking off on a car trip, ask for a map of the country at a tourist office. Tourist offices are usually found in airports as well as in central locations in major cities.

Main highways are called *carreteras* (kah-rreh-TEH-rahs) and *autopistas* (ow-toh-PEES-tahs). These should be clearly indicated on the country's road map, showing toll roads and freeways. In Spain, toll roads are called *autopistas de peaje* (ow-toh-PEES-tahs deh peh-AH-heh), and in Mexico, *carretera cuota* (kah-rreh-TEH-rah KWOH-tah). In general, both the national highways—*carreteras nacionales* (kah-rreh-TEH-rahs nah-syo-NAH-lehs)—of Spain, and the free highways—*carreteras libres* (kay-rreh-TEH-rahs LEE-breh)—of Mexico are good. Although speed limits vary by area, they are quite standard on major highways.

Highways	120 km/h	(75 m.p.h)
Double-lane highway	100 km/h	(62 m.p.h)
Most local roads	90 km/h	(55 m.p.h)
Urban areas	60 km/h	(37 m.p.h)

In Spain and Mexico, drivers tend not to pay much attention to speed limits. This is not to say that there is no control or enforcement. Radar control is common and if you are found exceeding the speed limit, you may get a ticket. Mexico's automobile association, affiliated with the AAA in the United States, is the Asociación Mexicana Automovilística (AMA; tel. 52-5-511-01-84 in Mexico City). There are branches throughout the country.

Is this the road to . . .	¿Es éste el camino a . . .	ehs EHS-teh ehl kah-MEE-noh a . . .
• Madrid?	• Madrid?	• mah-DREED?
• Granada?	• Granada?	• grah-NAH-dah?
Is there a better road?	¿Hay un camino mejor?	ahy oon kah-MEE-noh MEH-hohr?
Is there a less congested road?	Hay un camino menos transitado?	ahy oon kah-MEE-noh MEH-nohs trahn-see-TAH-doh?
Is there a shortcut?	¿Hay un atajo?	• ahy oon ah-TAH-hoh?
I think we are	Creo que estamos	KREH-oh keh ehs-TAH-mohs
• lost.	• perdidos.	• pehr-DEE-dohs
• in the outskirts.	• en las afueras.	• ehn lahs ah-FWEH-rahs
• in the wrong lane.	• en el carril equivocado.	• ehn ehl kah-RREEL eh-kee-voh-KAH-doh
• in the wrong exit.	• en la salida errada.	• ehn lah sah-LEE-dah eh-RRAH-dah
• in the center of town.	• en el centro de la ciudad.	• ehn ehl SEHN-troh deh lah syoo-DAHD
• arriving at the next town.	• llegando al próximo pueblo.	• yeh-GAHN-doh ahl PROK-see-moh PWEH-bloh
How do I get to	¿Cómo voy	KOH-moh voy
• the Rex Hotel?	• al hotel Rex?	• ahl oh-TEHL rrehks?
• the next town?	• al próximo pueblo?	• ahl PROHK-see-moh PWEH-bloh?

106

• the main highway?	• a la carretera principal?	• ah lah kah-rreh-TEH-rah preen-see-PAHL?
• the center of town?	• al centro de la ciudad?	• ahl SEHN-troh deh lah syoo-DAD?
Do I go	¿Voy	vohy?
• straight ahead?	• derecho?	• deh-REH-choh?
• to the right?	• a la derecha?	• ah lah deh-REH-chah?
• to the left?	• a la izquierda?	• ah lah ees-KYEHR-dah?
• two (three, etc.) more blocks?	• dos (tres, etc.) cuadras más?	• dohs (trehs) KWAH-drahs mahs?
Is it	¿Queda	KEH-dah
• nearby?	• cerca?	• SEHR-kah?
• far from here?	• lejos de aquí?	• LEH-hohs deh ah-KEE?
• near the hotel?	• cerca del hotel?	• SEHR-kah dehl oh-TEHL?
• far from the center?	• lejos del centro?	• LEH-hohs dehl SEHN-troh?
• close to the center?	• cerca del centro?	• SEHR-kah dehl SEHN-troh?
Are there any tourist services?	¿Hay servicios turísticos?	ahy sehr-VEE-syohs too-REES-tee-kohs?
May I park the car here?	¿Puedo estacionar el auto aquí?	PWEH-doh ehs-tah-syoh-NAHR ehl OW-toh ah-KEE?

EMERGENCIES AND CAR PROBLEMS

Sponsored by the Mexico Ministry of Tourism, the *Angeles Verdes* (Green Angels) patrol the highways daily from 8 A.M. to 8 P.M. in green-and-white cars. English-speaking car mechanics, they carry emergency gasoline and oil, and an assortment of spare parts; they do not charge for labor. They also have two-way radios and first-aid equipment, and are prepared to offer tourism information and advice on highway and weather conditions ahead.

My car won't start.	**Mi auto no arranca.**	mee OW-toh noh ah-RRAHN-kah
Something must be wrong.	**Debe tener algún problema.**	DEH-beh teh-NEHR ahl-GOON proh-BLEH-mah
I don't know what's wrong.	**No sé que tiene.**	noh seh keh TYEH-neh
I have a flat tire.	**Tengo una llanta ponchada.** (*Mexico*) (*or*) . . . **pinchada.** (*Spain*)	TEHN-goh OO-nah YAHN-tah pohn-CHAH-dah . . . peen-CHAH-dah
I'm out of gas.	**Se me terminó la gasolina.**	seh meh tehr-mee-NOH la gah-soh-LEE-nah
The battery's dead.	**No funciona la bactería.**	noh foon-SYOH-nah lah bah-teh-REE-ah
It's overheating.	**Se está calentando mucho.**	seh es-TAH kah-lehn-TAHN-doh MOO-choh
I left the keys inside the car.	**Olvidé las llaves adentro.**	ohl-vee-DEH lahs YAH-vehs ah-DEHN-troh
I don't have an extra key.	**No tengo una llave extra.**	noh TEHN-goh OO-nah YAH-veh EHKS-trah
I don't have any tools.	**No tengo herramientas.**	noh TEHN-goh eh-rrah-MYEHN-tahs
I need	**Necesito**	neh-seh-SEE-toh
• a flashlight.	• **una linterna.**	• OO-nah leen-TEHR-nah
• a hammer.	• **un martillo.**	• oon mahr-TEE-yoh
• a jack.	• **un gato.**	• oon GAH-toh

pliers.	**unas pinzas.** (*Mexico*) (*or*) **un alicate.** (*Spain*)	OO-nahs PEEN-sahs oon ah-lee KAH-teh
a bolt.	**un perno.**	oon PEHR-noh
a nut.	**una tuerca.**	OO-nah TWEHR-kah
a screwdriver.	**un destornillador.**	oon dehs-tohr-nee-yah-DOHR
Can you open the	**¿Puede abrir**	PWEH-deh ah-BREER
• hood?	• **el cofre?** (*Mexico*) (*or*) **el capó?** (*Spain*)	• ehl KOH-freh? ehl kah-POH?
• trunk?	• **la cajuela?** (*Mexico*) (*or*) **la maletera?** (*Spain*)	• lah kah-HWEH-lah? lah mah-leh-TEH-rah?
• gas tank?	• **el tanque de gasolina?**	• ehl TAHN-keh deh gah-soh-LEE-nah?
Can you	**¿Puede**	PWEH-deh
• charge my battery?	• **cargar la batería?**	• kahr-GAHR lah bah-teh-REE-ah?
• change the tire?	• **cambiar la llanta?**	• kahm-BYAHR la YAHN-tah?
• tow the car to a garage?	• **remolcar el auto a un garage?**	• rreh-mohl-KAHR ehl OW-toh ah oon gah-RAH-heh?

Car Repairs

When renting a car, be sure to ask for a list of authorized agencies and repair shops.

| There's something wrong with the | **Algo anda mal con** | AHL-goh AHN-dah mahl kohn |

• car.	• **el automóvil.**	• ehl ow-toh-MOH-veel
• brakes.	• **los frenos.**	• lohs FREH-nohs
• tires.	• **las llantas.**	• lahs YAHN-tahs
• spark plugs.	• **las bujías.**	• lahs boo-HEE-ahs
• motor.	• **el motor.**	• ehl moh-TOHR
Please check the	**Por favor revise**	pohr fah-VOHR rreh-VEE-seh
• oil.	• **el aceite.**	• ehl ah-SAY-teh
• water.	• **el agua.**	• ehl AH-gwah
• carburetor.	• **el carburador.**	• ehl kahr-boo-rah-DOHR
• battery.	• **la batería.**	• lah bah-teh-REE-ah
• radiator.	• **el agua del radiador.**	• ehl AH-gwah dehl rrah-dyah-DOHR
• brake fluid.	• **el líquido para los frenos.**	• ehl LEE-kee-doh PAH-rah lohs FREH-nohs
• tire pressure.	• **la presión de las llantas.**	• lah preh-SYOHN deh lahs YAHN-tahs
I have a problem with the	**Tengo un problema con**	TEHN-goh oon proh-BLEH-mah kohn
• gears.	• **los cambios.**	• lohs KAHM-byohs
• headlights.	• **las luces delanteras.**	• lahs LOO-sehs deh-lahn-TEH-rahs
• high beams.	• **las altas.**	• lahs AHL-tahs
• directional signals.	• **las luces direccionales.**	• lahs LOO-sehs dee-rehk-syo-NAH-lehs
• ignition.	• **el encendido.**	• ehl ehn-sehn-DEE-doh
• radiator.	• **el radiador.**	• ehl rrah-DYAH-dohr
• transmission	• **la transmisión.**	• la trahns-mee-SYOHN
• the windshield wipers.	• **los limpiaparabrisas.**	• lohs leem-pyah-pah-rah-BREE-sahs
Can you repair the	**Puede componer**	PWEH-deh kohm-poh-NEHR
• brakes?	• **los frenos?**	• lohs FREH-nohs?
• horn?	• **la bocina?**	• lah boh-SEE-nah?
• radio?	• **la radio?**	• lah RRAH-dyoh?

110

English	Spanish	Pronunciation
• starter?	• **el arranque?**	• ehl ah-RRAHN-keh?
• steering wheel?	• **el volante?**	• ehl voh-LAHN-teh?
• electrical system?	• **el sistema eléctrico?**	• ehl sees-TEH-mah eh-LEHK-tree-koh?
• door handle?	• **la manija de la puerta?**	• lah mah-NEE-hah deh lah PWEHR-tah?
• speedometer?	• **el velocímetro?**	• ehl veh-loh-SEE-meh-troh?
How long will this take?	**¿Cuánto tiempo va a demorar?**	KWAHN-toh TYEHM-poh vah ah deh-moh-RAHR?
How much will it cost?	**¿Cuánto va a costar?**	KWAHN-toh vah ah kohs-TAHR?

Other parts of the car	**Otras partes del automóvil**	OH-trahs PAHR-tehs dehl ow-toh-MOH-veel
the transmission	**la transmisión**	luh trahns-mee-SYOHN
the water pump	**la bomba de agua**	lah BOHM-bah deh AH-gwah
the directional signals	**las luces direccionales**	lahs LOO-sehs dee-rehk-syoh-NAH-lehs
the fuel pump	**la bomba de gasolina**	lah BOHM-bah deh gah-soh-LEE-nah
the distributor	**el distribuidor**	ehl dees-tree-BUEE-dohr
the gearshift	**el cambio de velocidad**	ehl KAHM-byoh deh veh-loh-see-DAHD
the headlights	**las luces delanteras**	lahs LOO-sehs deh-lahn-TEH-rahs
the taillights	**los faros traseros**	lohs FAH-rohs trah-SEH-rohs
the fan belt	**la correa del ventilador**	lah koh-RREH-ah dehl vehn-tee-lah-DOHR

111

ROAD SIGNS

CASETA DE COBRO	kah-SEH-tah deh KOH-broh	TOLL BOOTH
CAMBIO EXACTO	KAHM-byoh ehk-SAHK-toh	EXACT CHANGE
CARRIL (*Mexico*) (*or*) CANAL	kah-RREEL kah-NAHL	LANE
CARRIL DERECHO	kah-RREEL deh-REH-choh	RIGHT LANE
CARRIL IZ-QUIERDO	kah-RREEL ees-KYEHR-doh	LEFT LANE
CUENTA (*Mexico*) (*or*) HOMBRILLO	koo-NEH-tah ohm-BREE-yoh	SHOULDER
VELOCIDAD MAXIMA	veh-loh-see-DAHD MAHK-see-mah	MAXIMUM SPEED
VELOCIDAD MINIMA	veh-loh-see-DAHD MEE-nee-mah	MINIMUM SPEED
REDUCIR LA VELOCIDAD	rreh-doo-SEER lah veh-loh-see-DAHD	REDUCE SPEED
DESVIACION (*Mexico*) (*or*) DESVIO	dehs-vyah-SYOHN dehs-VEE-oh	DETOUR
PASO DE PEATONES	PAH-soh deh peh-ah-TOH-nehs	PEDESTRIAN CROSSING
CAMINO EN REPARACION	kah-MEE-noh ehn rreh-pah-rah-SYOHN	ROAD CONSTRUC-TION

NO ENTRY FOR MOTOR VEHICLES

DANGEROUS INTERSECTION AHEAD

STOP

NO ENTRY

MINIMUM SPEED (km/hr)

SPEED LIMIT (km/hr)

DIRECTION TO BE FOLLOWED

OVERHEAD CLEARANCE (meters)

ROTARY

NO PASSING

END OF NO PASSING ZONE

END OF RESTRICTION

NO LEFT TURN

NO U-TURN

NO PARKING

ONE WAY

MAIN ROAD

PARKING

SUPERHIGHWAY

YIELD

GAS
(10 km ahead)

**DANGER
AHEAD**

**DANGEROUS
DESCENT**

BUMPS

**ROAD
NARROWS**

**LEVEL
(RAILROAD)
CROSSING**

**TWO-WAY
TRAFFIC**

**SLIPPERY
ROAD**

**CAUTION—SHARP
CURVES**

**PEDESTRIAN
CROSSING**

TELEPHONES

Telephone systems are gradually being overhauled in both Spain and Mexico. To make international calls in Spain, go to a local telephone office; in Mexico, use the LADATEL phones found in many hotel lobbies. In both countries, pay phones are widely available. In Spain, they are bright green and use either special telephone credit cards, sold for 1,000 or 2,000 pesetas at *estancos* (ess-TAHN-kos), or coins, although not the new 5-, 10-, or 25-peseta coins. You need at least 15 pesetas for a local call, 50 pesetas to call another province. Older Mexican pay phones are black (and give free local calls); new models are blue or ivory. Some phones accept only old peso coins, and others have an additional slot where you can use LADATEL phone cards, sold by tourist offices and newsstands; still others have an extra slot where you can use Mexican bank cards and sometimes Visa or MasterCard.

A telephone booth in Spain is called a *cabina telefónica* (kah-BEE-nah teh-leh-FOH-nee-kah), and in Mexico, *caseta de teléfono* (kah-SEH-tah deh teh-LEH-foh-noh).

Is there a	¿Hay	ahy
• public telephone?	• **un teléfono público?**	• oon teh-LEH-foh-noh POO-blee-koh?
• telephone booth?	• **una cabina telefónica?**	• OO-nah kah-BEE-nah teh-leh-FOH-nee-kah?
• telephone directory?	• **una guía telefónica?**	• OO-nah GEE-ah teh-leh FOH-nee-kah?
Operator.	**Operadora.**	oh-peh-rah-DOH-rah
I'd like to call	**Quisiera llamar a**	kee-SYEH-rah yah-MAHR ah

115

• this number.	• **este número.**	• EHS-teh NOO-meh-roh
• information.	• **información.**	• een-fohr-mah-SYON
• the international operator.	• **la operadora internacional.**	• lah oh-peh-rah-DOH-rah een-tehr-nah-syoh-NAHL

I'd like to use my credit card.	**Quisiera usar mi tarjeta de crédito.**	kee-SYEH-rah oo-SAHR mee tahr-HEH-tah deh KREH-dee-toh
I'd like to make a	**Quisiera hacer una llamada**	kee-SYEH-rah ah-SEHR OO-nah yah-MAH-dah
• long-distance call.	• **de larga distancia.**	• deh LAHR-gah dees-TAHN-syah
• person-to-person call.	• **de persona a persona.**	• deh pehr-SOH-nah ah pehr-SOH-nah
• local call.	• **local.**	• loh-KAHL
• collect call.	• **por cobrar.**	• pohr KOH-brahr
• conference call.	• **por conferencia.**	• pohr kohn-feh-REHN-syah
• a call with time and charges.	• **con tiempo y costo.**	• kohn TYEM-poh ee KOHS-toh

What the Caller Says

Hello!	**¡Hola!**	OH-lah!
	¡Bueno!	BWEH-noh!
This is	**Habla**	AH-blah
• Mr. . . .	• **el señor . . .**	ehl seh-NYOHR
• Mrs. . . .	• **la señora . . .**	lah seh-NYOH-rah
• Miss/Ms. . . .	• **la señorita . . .**	lah seh-NYOH-REE-tah
May I speak to . . . ?	**¿Puedo hablar con . . . ?**	PWEH-doh ah-BLAHR kohn . . . ?

Can you repeat, please?	¿Puede repetir, por favor?	PWEH-deh rreh-peh-TEER, pohr fah-VOHR?
I can't hear very well.	No oigo muy bien.	noh OY-goh muee byehn
It's a bad connection.	Es una conexión mala.	ehs OO-nah koh-nehk-SYOHN MAH lah
Speak louder, please.	Hable más fuerte, por favor.	AH-bleh mahs FWEHR-teh, pohr fah-VOHR
I'd like to leave a message.	Quisiera dejar un mensaje.	kee-SYEH-rah deh-HAHR oon mehn-SAH-he
My number is . . .	Mi número es . . .	mee NOO-meh-roh ehs . . .

What the Operator Says

La línea está ocupada.	lah LEE-nyah ehs TAH oh-koo-PAH-dah	The line is busy.
No contestan.	noh kohn-TEHS-tahn	They don't answer.
¿Quiere que siga probando?	KYEH-reh keh SEE-gah proh-BAHN-doh?	Do you want me to keep trying?
¿Puede llamar más tarde?	PWEH-deh yah-MAHR mahs TAHR-deh?	Can you call later?
No cuelgue.	noh KWEHL-geh	Don't hang up.
Espere, por favor.	es-PEH-reh, pohr fah-VOHR	Please wait a moment.
Se interrumpió su llamada.	seh een-teh-rroom-PYOH soo yah-MAH-dah	Your call was disconnected.
¿Con quién desea hablar?	kohn kyen de-SEH-ah ah-BLAR?	Who do you want to speak to?

¿Quiere dejar un mensaje?	KYEH-reh deh-HAHR oon men-SAH-heh?	Do you want to leave a message?
¿Tiene otro número?	TYEH-neh OH-troh NOO-meh-roh?	Do you have another number?
Repita eso, por favor.	rreh-PEE-tah EH-soh, pohr fah-VOHR	Please repeat that.

THE POST OFFICE

Letters from Spain to the United States usually take from about one week to ten days. Look for stamps at the *estancos* (es-TAHN-kohs) as well as in the post office. *Estancos* can be found on almost every block in major cities.

In Mexico, stamps can be purchased only at a post office. Occasionally some stores and hotels that sell postcards also have a limited supply of stamps. But do not expect to find stamps there for other types of mail.

In both countries post offices are generally open from 9:00 A.M. to noon, and reopen again from 4:00 to 7:00 P.M., Monday to Friday. Post offices are also open until noon on Saturdays. In Mexico, mail to the United States may take about five days to a week from major cities, up to three weeks from smaller towns.

Is this the post office?	¿Es el correo?	ehs ehl koh-RREH-oh?
I would like to send	Quisiera mandar	kee-SYEH-rah mahn-DAHR
• a letter.	• una carta.	• OO-nah KAHR-tah
• a postcard.	• una tarjeta postal.	• OO-nah tahr-HEH-tah pohs-TAHL
• a registered letter.	• una carta registrada.	• OO-nah KAHR-tah rreh-hees-TRAH-dah
• a special-delivery letter	• una carta con entrega inmediata.	• OO-nah KAHR-tah kohn ehn-TREH-gah een-meh-DYAH-tah

118

• a certified letter.	• **una carta certificada.**	• OO-nah KAHR-tah sehr-tee-fee-KAH-dah
• a package.	• **un paquete.**	• oon pah-KEH-teh
• a money order.	• **un giro postal.**	• oon HEE-roh pohs-TAHL

How many stamps do I need for	**¿Cuántos timbres (or, sellos [Spain]) necesito para**	KWAHN-tohs TEEM-brehs (SEH-yohs) neh-seh-SEE-toh PAH-rah
• surface mail?	• **vía normal?**	• VEE-ah nohr-MAHL?
• airmail?	• **vía aérea?**	• VEE-ah ah-EH-reh-ah?
• a postcard?	• **una tarjeta postal?**	• OO-nah tahr-HEH-tah pohs-TAHL?
• a letter to the United States?	• **una carta a los Estados Unidos?**	• OO-nah KAHR-tah ah lohs ehs-TAH-dos oo-NEE-dohs?

I'd also like to buy	**También quisiera**	tahm-BYEHN kee-SYEH-rah
• airmail envelopes.	• **sobres aéreos.**	• SOH-brehs ah-EH-reh-ohs
• aerograms.	• **aerogramas.**	• ah-eh roh-GRAH-mahs
• airmail paper.	• **papel aéreo.**	• pah-PEHL ah-EH-reh-oh
• a collection of stamps.	• **una colección de estampillas.**	• OO-nah koh-lehk-SYOHN deh ehs-tahm-PEE-yahs

Where is the	**¿Dónde está**	DOHN-deh ehs-TAH
• letterbox?	• **el buzón?**	• ehl boo-SOHN?
• stamp machine?	• **la máquina de estampillas?**	• lah MAH-kee-nah deh ehs-tahm-PEE-yahs?
• the window for certified mail?	• **la ventanilla para correo certificado?**	• lah vehn-tah-NEE-yah PAH-rah koh-RREH-oh sehr-tee-fee-KAH-doh?

119

TELEGRAMS AND FAXES

Telegrams, used in Spain largely for congratulatory messages, are still used in Mexico for all kinds of short messages. Telegraph offices are usually located near a post office and sometimes in the same building. Some hotels conveniently provide telegram service as well. Faxes are a fixture in Spain and common in larger businesses in Mexican cities.

May I send . . . to New York?	**Puedo mandar . . . a Nueva York?**	PWEH-doh mahn-DAHR . . . ah NWEH-vah yohrk?
• a telegram	• **un telegrama**	• oon teh-leh-GRAH-mah
• a telex	• **un telex**	• oon TEH-lehks
• a cable	• **un cable**	• oon KAH-bleh
• a night letter	• **una carta nocturna**	• OO-nah KAHR-tah nohk-TOOR-nah
• a fax	• **un fax**	• oon-FAHKS
I would like to wire some money.	**Quisiera mandar dinero por cable.**	kee-SYEH-rah mahn-DAHR dee-NEH-roh pohr KAH-bleh
How much is it per word?	**¿Cuánto cuesta por palabra?**	KWAHN-toh KWEHS-tah pohr pah-LAH-brah?
Will it arrive tomorrow morning?	**¿Llegará mañana por la mañana?**	yeh-gah-RAH mah-NYAH-nah pohr lah mah-NYAH-nah?

THE MEDIA

In Madrid you can get newspapers and magazines from all over the world. Among the English-language newspapers, look for the *London Times* and the *New York Times* (international editions), the *International Herald Tribune,* and the *Wall Street Journal.* In Mexico City you can also find a variety of English-language publications, especially at the airport and in Sanborns (a department store). Several bookstores specialize in English-language magazines and books. The *News* is a special English-language newspaper sold all over the country.

In Madrid, you can listen to the BBC radio from London. In Mexico, CBS affiliates feature syndicated news programs on a regular basis and there is also an English-speaking radio station. Thanks to Cablevisión (kah-bleh-vee-SYOHN) you can now see TV programs directly from the United States in Mexico. Spain also carries various foreign programs from other parts of Europe via satellite.

Books and Newspapers	Libros y periódicos	LEE-brohs ee peh-RYOH-dee-kohs
Do you have	¿Tienen	TYEH-nehn
• newspapers in English?	• periódicos en inglés?	• peh-RYOH-dee-kohs ehn een-GLEHS?
• magazines in English?	• revistas en inglés?	• rreh-VEES-tahs ehn een-GLEHS?
• books in English?	• libros en inglés?	• LEE-brohs ehn een-GLEHS?
• any publications in English?	• alguna publicación en inglés?	• ahl-GOO-nah poo-blee-kah-SYOHN ehn een-GLEHS?
Radio and Television	Radio y televisión	RRAH-dyoh ee teh-leh-vee-SYOHN
Is there a(an)	¿Hay una	ahy OO-nah
• English-speaking station?	• estación en inglés?	• ehs-tah-SYOHN ehn een-GLEHS?
• music station?	• estación con música?	• ehs-tah-SYOHN kohn MOO-see-kah?
• news station?	• estación que da noticias?	• ehs-tah-SYOHN keh dah noh-TEE-syahs?
• weather station?	• estación que da el tiempo?	• ehs-tah-SYOHN keh dah ehl TYEHM-poh?
What number is it on the dial?	¿En qué número se sintoniza?	ehn keh NOO-meh-roh seh seen-toh-NEE-sah?

121

What time is the program?	¿A qué hora es el programa?	ah ke OH-rah ehs ehl proh-GRAH-mah?
Is there an English-speaking channel?	¿Hay un canal en inglés?	ahy oon kah-NAHL ehn een-GLEHS?
Do you have a television guide?	¿Tiene un programa de televisión?	TYEH-neh oon proh-GRAH-mah deh teh-leh-vee-SYOHN?
Do they have international news in English?	¿Tienen las noticias internacionales en inglés?	TYEH-nehn lahs noh-TEE-syahs een-tehr-nah-syoh-NAH-lehs ehn een-GLEHS?
When is the weather forecast?	¿Cuándo es el pronóstico del tiempo?	KWAHN-doh ehs ehl proh-NOHS-tee-koh dehl TYEHM-poh?

11/SIGHT-SEEING

You can obtain information about what to see and do from national and local tourist offices and from guidebooks. At your destination, ask your hotel for a guide to the city and activities of the week. You may also be able to obtain information about bus tours and places of interest to visit.

DIALOGUE: TOURING THE CITY (VISITAR LA CIUDAD)

Turista:	**¿Cuáles son algunos de los lugares para visitar?**	KWAH-lehs sohn ahl-GOO-nohs deh lohs loo-GAH-rehs PAH-rah vee-see-TAHR?
Empleado del hotel:	**Hay muchas cosas interesantes en esta ciudad.**	ahy MOO-chas KOH-sahs een-teh-reh-SAHN-tehs en ES-tah syoo-DAHD.
Turista:	**¿Es fácil ir al distrito histórico?**	ehs FAH-seel eer ahl dees-TREE-toh ees-TOH-ree-koh?
Empleado:	**Sí, puede tomar un autobús en la esquina. Llega hasta la parte vieja de la ciudad.**	see, PWEH-deh toh-MAHR oon ow-toh-BOOS ehn lah ehs-KEE-nah. YEH-gah AHS-tah lah PAHR-teh VYEH-hah deh lah syoo-DAHD
Turista:	**¿Hay muchas iglesias allí?**	ahy MOO-chahs ee-GLEH-syahs ah-YEE?
Empleado:	**Sí, y también varios museos.**	see, ee tahm-BYEHN VAH-ryohs moo-SEH-ohs
Turista:	**Gracias por la información.**	GRAH-syahs pohr lah een-fohr-mah-SYOHN

```
. . . . . . . . . . . . . . . . . . . . . . . . . . . . .
```

Tourist:	What are some places to visit?
Hotel clerk:	There are many interesting things to see in this city.
Tourist:	Is it easy to get to the historic district?
Hotel clerk:	Yes, you can take a bus at the corner. It goes right to the old part of town.
Tourist:	Are there many churches there?
Hotel clerk:	Yes, and also several museums.
Tourist:	Thanks for the information.

FINDING THE SIGHTS

I want to go to the	Quiero ir a	KYEH-roh eer ah
• cathedral.	• la catedral.	• lah kah-teh-DRAHL
• main market.	• el mercado central.	• ehl mehr-KAH-doh sehn-TRAHL
• art museum.	• el museo de arte.	• ehl moo-SEH-oh deh AHR-teh
• natural science museum.	• el museo de ciencias naturales.	• ehl moo-SEH-oh deh SYEHN-syahs nah-too-RAH-lehs
• folk-art museum.	• el museo de arte folklórico.	• ehl moo-SEH-oh deh AHR-teh fohl-KLOH-ree-koh
• national theater.	• el teatro nacional.	• ehl teh-AH-troh nah-syoh-NAHL
• business district.	• el sector comercial.	• ehl sehk-TOHR koh-mehr-SYAHL
• library.	• la biblioteca.	• lah bee-blyoh-TEH-kah
• government palace.	• el palacio de gobierno.	• ehl pah-LAH-syoh deh goh-BYEHR-noh
• botanical gardens.	• el jardín botánico.	• ehl hahr-DEEN boh-TAH-nee-koh
• zoo.	• el zoológico.	• ehl soh-LOH-hee-koh

Note: When "a" is followed by the indefinite masculine article "el," it becomes "al." For example, you say *Quiero ir al mercado* rather than *Quiero ir a el* mercado.

At what time do they open (close)?	¿A qué hora abren (cierran)?	ah keh OH-rah AH-brehn (SYEH-rrahn)?
Is it open today?	¿Está abierto hoy?	ehs-TAH ah-BYEHR-toh ohy?
How much is the admission?	¿Cuánto es la entrada?	KWAHN-toh ehs lah ehn-TRAH-dah?
How much is it for	¿Cuánto pagan	KWAHN-toh PAH-gahn
• children?	• los niños?	• lohs NEE-nyohs?
• students?	• los estudiantes?	• lohs ehs-too-DYAHN-tehs?
How much is it for a group?	¿Cuánto es para un grupo?	KWAHN-toh ehs PAH-rah oon GROO-poh?

AT THE MUSEUM

Where can I get an English-speaking guide?	¿Dónde hay un guía que habla inglés?	DOHN-deh ahy oon GEEH-ah keh AH-blah een-GLEHS?
How long does a tour take?	¿Cuánto demora una gira?	KWAHN-toh deh-MOH-rah OO-nah HEE-rah?
Where is the gift shop?	¿Dónde está la tienda del museo?	DOHN-deh ehs-TAH lah TYEHN-dah dehl moo-SEH-oh?
Do they sell prints?	¿Venden reproducciones?	VEHN-dehn rreh-proh-dook-SYOH-nehs?
Do they sell postcards?	¿Venden tarjetas postales?	VEHN-dehn tahr-HEH-tahs pohs-TAH-lehs?
Is there a restaurant here?	¿Hay un restaurante aquí?	ahy oon rrehs-tow-RAHN-teh ah-KEE?

IN THE OLD PART OF TOWN

Which are the historic sites?	¿Cuáles son los sitios históricos?	KWAH-leh sohn lohs SEE-tyohs ees-TOH-ree-kohs?

How many churches are there here?	¿Cuántas iglesias hay aquí?	KWAHN-tahs ee-GLEH-syahs ahy ah-KEE?
Is that church old?	¿Es vieja esa iglesia?	ehs VYEH-hah EH-sah ee-GLEH-syah?
What religion is it?	¿De qué religión es?	deh keh rreh-lee-HYOHN ehs?
Are there any monuments nearby?	¿Hay algún monumento por aquí?	ahy ahl-GOON moh-noo-MEHN-toh pohr ah-KEE?
What does that one commemorate?	¿Qué conmemora ése?	keh kohn-meh-MOH-rah EH-seh?
When was that built?	¿Cuándo fue construído eso?	KWAHN-doh fweh kohns-TRUEE-doh EH-soh?
How old is that building?	¿Es viejo ese edificio?	ehs VYEH-hoh EH-seh eh-dee-FEE-syoh?
Are there many statues here?	¿Hay muchas estatuas aquí?	ahy MOO-chahs ehs-TAH-twahs ah-KEE?
Whose statue is that?	¿De quién es esa estatua?	deh kyehn ehs EH-sah ehs-TAH-twah?
Who was he (she)?	¿Quién fue esa persona?	KYEHN fweh EH-sah pehr-SOH-nah?

IN THE BUSINESS DISTRICT

At what time are businesses open?	¿A qué hora abren los negocios?	ah keh OH-rah AH-brehn lohs neh-GOH-syohs?
Which are the department stores?	¿Cuáles son las tiendas grandes?	KWAH-lehs sohn lahs TYEHN-dahs GRAHN-dehs?
Are they open on weekends?	¿Abren los fines de semana?	AH-brehn lohs FEE-nes deh seh-MAH-nah?

Where is a souvenir shop?	¿Dónde hay una tienda de recuerdos?	DOHN-deh ahy OO-nah TYEHN-dah deh rreh-KWEHR-dohs?
Which is the main bank?	¿Cuál es el banco principal?	KWAHL ehs ehl BAHN-koh preen-see-PAHL?
Where is the money exchange?	¿Dónde hay una casa de cambio? (*Mexico*)	DOHN-deh ahy OO-nah KAH-sah deh KAHM-byoh?

IN THE COUNTRY

What is the best way to get to the country?	¿Cuál es la mejor manera de ir al campo?	kwahl ehs lah meh-HOHR mah-NEH-rah deh eer ahl KAHM-poh?
Is there a bus from here?	¿Hay un autobús desde aquí?	ahy oon ow-toh-BOOS DEHS-deh ah-KEE?
How long does it take?	¿Cuánto demora?	KWAHN-toh deh-MOH-rah?
Is there any place to eat there?	¿Hay algún lugar para comer allí?	ahy ahl-GOON loo-GAHR PAH-rah koh-MEHR ah-YEE?
Should we take some food?	¿Debemos llevar comida?	deh-BEH-mohs yeh-VAHR koh-MEE-dah?
Are there re-strooms?	¿Hay baños públicos?	ahy BAH-nyohs POO-blee-kohs?
I like (the)	**Me gustan**	meh GOOS-tahn
• mountains.	• **las montañas.**	• lahs mohn-TAH-nyahs
• plants.	• **las plantas.**	• lahs PLAHN-tahs
• flowers.	• **las flores.**	• lahs FLOH-rehs
• fields.	• **los campos.**	• lohs KAHM-pohs
• hills.	• **las colinas.**	• lahs koh-LEE-nahs
• woods.	• **los bosques.**	• lohs BOHS-kehs
• birds.	• **los pájaros.**	• lohs PAH-ha-rohs
• wild animals.	• **los animales silvestres.**	• lohs ah-nee-MAH-lehs seel-VEHS-trehs

• farms.	• las granjas.	• lahs GRAHN-hahs
• houses.	• las casas.	• lahs KAH-sahs
• cottages.	• las cabañas.	• lahs kah-BAH-nyahs
• villages.	• los pueblitos.	• lohs pweh-BLEE-tohs

Look! There's a	¡Mire! Ahí hay	MEE-reh! ah-EE ahy
• barn.	• un granero.	• oon grah-NEH-roh
• bridge.	• un puente.	• oon PWEHN-teh
• castle.	• un castillo.	• oon kahs-TEE-yoh
• waterfall.	• una catarata.	• OO-nah kah-tah-RAH-tah
• stream.	• un arroyo.	• oon ah-RROH-yoh
• lake.	• un lago.	• oon LAH-goh
• beach.	• una playa.	• OO-nah PLAH-yah
• pond.	• un estanque.	• oon ehs-TAHN-keh
• village.	• un pueblo.	• oon PWEH-bloh

The view is	La vista es	lah VEES-tah ehs
• breathtaking.	• impresionante.	• eem-preh-syoh-NAHN-teh
• magnificent.	• magnífica.	• mahg-NEE-fee-kah

This place is	Este lugar es	EHS-teh loo-GAHR ehs
• beautiful.	• hermoso.	• ehr-MOH-soh
• very pretty.	• muy bonito.	• muee boh-NEE-toh
• very touristy.	• muy turístico.	• muee too-REES-tee-koh

What is a typical souvenir from here?	¿Cuál es un recuerdo típico de aquí?	kwahl ehs oon rreh-KWEHR-doh TEE-pee-koh deh ah-KEE?
Do you tip the guide?	¿Se da propina al guía?	seh dah proh-PEE-nah ahl GEE-ah?

PLACES TO SEE IN SPAIN

Some of the principal tourist attractions of the capital, Madrid, are listed below.

Plaza Mayor
(PLAH-sah mah-YOHR)

You can get to this main square through the famous Arco de Cuchilleros, which also takes you into old Madrid, a fascinating part of the city. The Plaza Mayor has many shops and outdoor cafés, and is one of the most visited places in the city.

Puerta del Sol
(PWEHR-tah dehl sohl)

This area is considered the center of the city. Most bus and metro lines start and end here. It is a good place to do your shopping since you will find both tourist shops and department stores here.

Calle Serrano
(KAH-ye seh-rrah-noh)

This street is famous for its fashionable stores and its many excellent restaurants.

Parque del Retiro
(PAHR-keh dehl rreh-TEE-roh)

Located in the middle of Madrid, the grounds of this park once belonged to a royal palace. Here you will find rose gardens, fountains, two nightclubs, many outdoor cafés, and a lake for boating.

Rastro
(RRAHS-troh)

This flea market on Ribera de Curtidores Street is open Sundays only. Here you will find trinkets, antiques, junk, toys, and artwork. As in other flea markets in Spain, it's a good place to use your bargaining skills.

Palacio Real
(pah-LAH-syoh rreh-AHL)

This palace is used only for important official events. It makes for an interesting visit and you will enjoy its treasure of fine arts—including porcelain, tapestries, crystal, and paintings.

Calle de Alcalá y la Gran Vía
(KAH-yeh deh ahl-kah-LAH ee lah grahn VEE-ah)

Two of Madrid's main thoroughfares, where you will find innumerable shops and outdoor cafés.

Museo del Prado
(moo-SEH-oh dehl PRAH-doh)

This museum has some of the most famous works of art in the world. It is particularly rich in works of Spanish, Flemish, and Italian artists.

129

Museo de las Américas (moo-SEH-oh deh lahs ah-MEH-ree-kahs)	This museum has collections of items brought from pre-Columbian America.
Museo Arqueológico (moo-SEH-oh ahr-keh-oh-LOH-hee-kah)	Here, the focal point is the collection of reproductions of the Altamira caves, paintings of Altamira, and some 2,000 archaeological objects.
Museo del Pueblo Español (moo-SEH-oh dehl PWEH-bloh ehs-pah-NYOHL)	Regional dress and household items in this museum come from all over Spain.
Teatro de la Zarzuela (teh-AH-troh deh lah sahr-SWEH-lah)	This theater, located behind Las Cortes (the Spanish Parliament), offers not only *zarzuela*—light opera—but also ballet and opera.
Plaza de España (PLAH-sah ehs-PAH-nyah)	Here you will see the statue of Cervantes accompanied by his two most famous literary characters, Don Quixote and Sancho Panza.

Another city worth visiting is Toledo, near Madrid, to the south. In this medieval city, you will be able to visit an impressive palace as well as the home of the famous painter El Greco. A museum there contains many of his works. Not far from Madrid you can also visit El Escorial (ehl ehs-koh-RYAHL), the enormous monastery, mausoleum, and palace that was built by King Felipe II, and Segovia, another medieval town, famous for its Roman aqueduct.

Other cities of interest, if you have time, are Granada, Seville, Córdoba, and Barcelona. The first three, in the south of Spain, offer prime examples of the Moorish influence in art and architecture.

PLACES TO SEE AROUND MEXICO CITY

Mexico City, with 18 million inhabitants in the greater metropolitan area, is a vibrant and lively place to visit.

Getting around the capital is not too difficult—there is an abundance of taxis, whose fares are quite reasonable, and a metro system that rivals any in the world.

Following are some of the city's principal attractions.

Plaza de la Constitución
(PLAH-sah deh lah kohns-tee-too-SYOHN)

The main public square of Mexico City, it is second only to the Red Square in size. It is known by most people as the *Zócalo* (SOH-kah-loh). Virtually every Mexican town has a *zócalo*, or main square, around which you will normally also find a church and a government building.

Catedral Metropolitana
(kah-teh-DRAHL me-troh-poh-lee-TAH-nah)

Also located at the Zócalo, it is said to be the largest in Latin America. This magnificent structure was started in 1573 and completed in 1813, 240 years later. It houses many works of art from the colonial era.

Palacio Nacional
(pah-LAH-syoh nah-syoh-NAHL)

The oldest building on the square, it covers about two city blocks, and was built on the site of Montezuma's opulent palace and constructed from its rubble. A series of Diego Rivera murals, painted over a period of 25 years, are exhibited here. These extensive murals impressively depict many episodes in the history of Mexico, from pre-Columbian myth, all the way up to the Revolution of 1910.

Monte de Piedad
(MOHN-teh deh pyeh-DAHD)

This is the national pawn shop, and is a popular tourist attraction. The massive structure stands on the site of Montezuma's brother's palace.

Museo de las Culturas
(moo-SEH-oh deh lahs kool-TOO-rahs)

This museum houses a rich collection of artifacts from all over the world.

Iglesia de Santo Domingo
(ee-GLEH-syah deh SAHN-toh doh-MEEN-goh)

A beautiful little church that played an important role in the days of the Inquisition, it is set on a plaza just north of the Zócalo. Today, scribes often work under the arches of this charming place, typing out business memos and love letters for the illiterate.

Bazar del Sábado
(bah-SAHR dehl SAH-bah-doh)

This bazaar in the old part of Mexico is held only on Saturdays, and offers samples of artifacts from practically all over the country. Prices range from the very reasonable—outside—to the very expensive—inside.

Xochimilco
(soh-chee-MEEL-koh)

Floating gardens, reminiscent of the Aztec era, when canals laced the city. You can ride in one of the flower-covered boats, be serenaded, and eat, all at the same time. On Sundays you will find the most activity, but it's also harder to get an empty boat then.

Bosque de Chapultepec
(BOHS-keh deh chah-pool-teh-PEHK)

Chapultepec Park—with acres of woods and open spaces, picnic areas, restaurants, a children's zoo, pony rides, and boats for rent—is a popular place for recreation and leisure. In addition, Chapultepec is the site of several important museums, including the renowned Museo de Antropología.

Museo de Antropología
(moo-SEH-oh deh ahn-troh-poh-loh-HEE-ah)

Located in Chapultepec Park, this museum, with its massive architecture and spectacular display of archaeological artifacts—among them the 27-ton Aztec Calendar stone—is one of the great museums of the world.

Palacio de Bellas Artes
(pah-LAH-syoh deh BEH-yahs AHR-tehs)

It contains many of the most famous murals of Rivera, Orozco, Siqueiros, and Tamayo, and also houses the auditorium where the famous Ballet Folklórico de México performs.

Torre Latinoamericana
(TOH-reh lah-tee-noh-ah-meh-ree-KAH-nah)

Once the tallest building in Mexico, it offers an impressive bird's-eye view of the entire city.

Mercado de San Juan
(mehr-KAH-doh deh sahn kwahn)

A market that has possibly the best display of artifacts from around the country. Be sure to shop around for the best buys and bargains, as many vendors carry the same items.

Ciudad Universitaria
(syoo-DAHD oo-nee-vehr-see-TAH-ryah)

The grounds and buildings of this, the National University, are worth a visit. The many mosaic-covered buildings are in themselves works of art.

Basílica de Guadalupe
(bah-SEE-lee-kah deh gwah-dah-LOO-peh)

A church built in honor of Our Lady of Guadalupe, the Patron Saint of Mexico and the Americas. The original basilica was closed to visitors, as it is slowly sinking into the ground. The modern church built next to it is visited by thousands of pilgrims each year.

Teotihuacán
(teh-oh-tee-wah-KAHN)

Famous Toltec ruins outside Mexico City. Climb the pyramids dedicated to the moon and the sun, and walk the streets of this ancient city. Be sure not to miss the temple of Quetzalcóatl.

Zona Rosa
(SOH-nah RROH-sah)

The fashionable business district in Mexico City. Many four- and five-star hotels are located here, as well as both international and Mexican designer boutiques. You will also find some of the city's best restaurants.

From Mexico City, it's a short bus trip to many other places. Cuernavaca, about two hours away, is known for its excellent climate (it is called the City of Eternal Spring). Two hours beyond Cuernavaca is the silver capital of Mexico, Taxco, a colonial gem well worth seeing. Taxco is also the midpoint between Mexico City and Acapulco. You can also fly to Mérida in Yucatán, on the Gulf side of Mexico. There you can visit the famous Maya ruins in Chichen Itzá or Uxmal. Oaxaca, on the western side, offers other archaeological sites such as Mitla and Monte Albán.

12/SHOPPING
SHOPPING IN SPAIN

Spain is a wonderful place to shop. You may find prices lower than in many other European countries. Also, there is a great variety of things to buy: small handicrafts, pottery, embroidery, and leather goods, to name just a few. Wooden sculptures of saints—both old and new—are typical. Antiques can be found fairly easily along major streets in Madrid like the Paseo del Prado and Carrera de San Jerónimo, as well as in the famous flea market, the Rastro.

Special stores called Artespaña (ahr-tehs-PAH-nyah) carry wares from the various regions of Spain. Department stores are good sources for fine merchandise. The main department store in Madrid is El Corte Inglés, which has several locations throughout the city. Note that bargaining is customary only at flea markets.

SHOPPING IN MEXICO

Each region of Mexico offers its own array of crafts. Look for embroidered dresses in Cuernavaca, Taxco, and Oaxaca; the fashionable *guayabera* shirts (gwah-yah-BEH-rahs) in Yucatán and Veracruz. *Sarapes, guaraches,* leather goods, and hand-knitted sweaters are found all over Mexico. But other items—like silver and opal jewelry and certain heavy wool sweaters—are found primarily in certain regions.

If you decide to buy silver in Mexico make sure you are buying the real thing. Look for the engraved seal indicating 900—i.e., pure silver and not an alloy. Certain silver items may be marked "Taxco," indicating not only that it is silver but also that it comes from Taxco, the silver capital of Mexico.

Certain names in the world of merchandising carry special significance for the cognoscenti—for example, Tane silver shops, Aca Joe sportswear, Víctor (known for his handicrafts), and Sergio Bustamante (famous for his papier-mâché). There are also numerous copper and bronze artists, and their items are available in many places. Also look for Fonart, a government store with fixed prices, and Sanborns, a department store that carries handicrafts at reasonable prices.

For a fine selection of Mexican artifacts, the Bazar del Sábado in San Angel is a must. Prices are generally higher, but they have the largest selections of pottery, paper flowers, jewelry, bark paintings, *sarapes,* baskets, and leather goods. The smaller regional markets may have similar items at more economical prices. (See next page for a glossary of folk art.)

DIALOGUE: AT THE GIFT SHOP (EN LA TIENDA DE REGALOS)

Turista:	**¿Tiene cosas típicas del país?**	TYEH-neh KOH-sahs TEE-pee-kahs dehl pah-EES?
Vendedor:	**Sí, tenemos muchos objetos típicos.**	see, teh-NEH-mohs MOO-chohs ohb-HEH-tohs TEE-pee-kohs
Turista:	**¿Puedo ver algo en cuero?**	PWEH-doh vehr AHL-goh ehn KWEH-roh?
Vendedor:	**Claro. Hay bolsas, carteras y muchas otras cosas.**	KLAH-roh. ahy BOHL-sahs, kahr-TEH-rahs, ee MOO-chahs OH-trahs KOH-sahs
Turista:	**Muy bien. ¿Me muestra una bolsa?**	mwee byehn. meh MWEHS-trah OO-nah BOHL-sah?
Vendedor:	**¿De qué color la quiere?**	deh keh koh-LOHR lah KYEH-reh?
Turista:	**Negra, creo.**	NEH-grah, KREH-oh

Vendedor:	**Un momento, por favor.**	oon moh-MEHN-toh, pohr fah-VOHR
Turista:	**Gracias.**	GRAH-syahs

Tourist:	Do you have handicrafts from the country?
Vendor:	Yes, we have many typical items.
Tourist:	May I see something in leather?
Vendor:	Of course. We have bags, billfolds, and many other things.
Tourist:	Fine. Would you show me a bag?
Vendor:	What color would you like?
Tourist:	In black, I think.
Vendor:	One moment, please.
Tourist:	Thank you.

TYPES OF FOLK ART

basketwork	**cestería**	ses-teh-REE-ah
blanket	**sarape**	sah-RAH-peh
ceramics	**cerámica**	seh-RAH-mee-kah
clay	**barro**	BAH-rroh
copper	**cobre**	KOH-breh
embroidery	**bordados**	bohr-DAH-dohs
feather decorators	**adornos de plumas**	ah-DOHR-nohs de PLOO-mahs

137

glass	**vidrio**	VEE-dryoh
blown glass	**vidrio soplado**	VEE-dryoh soh-PLAH-doh
gold	**oro**	OH-roh
jade	**jade**	HAH-deh
lacquerware	**lacas**	LAH-kahs
leather	**cuero**	KWEH-roh
tooled leather	**cuero labrado**	KWEH-roh lah-BRAH-doh
embossed leather	**cuero repujado**	KWEH-roh rreh-poo-HAH-doh
marble	**mármol**	MAHR-mohl
mask	**máscara**	MAHS-kah-rah
musical instrument	**instrumento musical**	eens-troo-MEHN-toh moo-see-KAHL
onyx	**onix**	OH-neeks
paper cutouts	**papel recortado**	pah-PEHL rreh-kohr-TAH-doh
paper toys	**juguetes de cartón**	hoo-GEH-tehs deh kahr-TOHN
pottery	**cerámica**	seh-RAH-mee-kah
saddle	**montura**	mohn-TOO-rah
shawl	**rebozo**	rre-BOH-soh
silver	**plata**	PLAH-tah
thread	**hilo**	EE-loh
toy	**juguete**	hoo-GEH-teh
weaving	**tejidos**	teh-HEE-dohs
wood carvings	**madera tallada**	mah-DEH-rah tah-YAH-dah
wool	**lana**	LAH-nah
yarn	**hilo**	EE-loh

BARGAINING

In Spain, bargaining is acceptable in only a few places, such as the Rastro flea market in Madrid. In some places that sell regional souvenirs in cities like Granada and Seville, you might ask for a discount. In Latin America, bargaining is far more common. But even there, it is done primarily in markets and with street vendors.

Many people consider bargaining an art. To get the best price, you should first go from one vendor to another inquiring about prices for the same item in order to establish a range. Then return to the booth that asked for the lowest price and begin bargaining. Remember not to show too much interest: Act casual, mildly curious. If you seem uncommitted, you will have a better chance of obtaining a lower price. But remember that no matter how well you bargain, there is a limit below which the vendor cannot make a profit. The price may be lowered more significantly for costly items than for less expensive ones.

What the Shopper Says

Excuse me.	**Perdón.**	pehr-DOHN
I'm interested in this.	**Me interesa esto.**	meh een-teh-REH-sah EHS-toh
How much is it?	**¿Cuánto cuesta?**	KWAHN-toh KWEHS-tah?
It's very expensive!	**¡Es muy caro!**	ehs muee KAH-roh!
It's overpriced. (It's not worth so much.)	**No vale tanto.**	noh VAH-leh TAHN-toh
Do you have a cheaper one?	**¿Tiene uno más barato?**	TYEH-neh OO-noh mahs bah-RAH-toh?
This is damaged— do you have another one?	**Está dañado, ¿hay otro?**	ehs-TAH dah-NYAH-doh, ahy OH-troh?

139

What is the lowest price?	¿Cuál es el precio mínimo?	KWAHL ehs ehl PREH-syoh MEE-nee-moh?
Is that the final price?	¿Es el último precio?	ehs ehl OOL-tee-moh PREH-syoh?
Can't you give me a discount?	¿No me da una rebaja?	noh meh dah OO-nah rreh-BAH-hah?
I'll give you . . .	Le doy . . .	leh doy . . .
I won't pay more than . . .	No pago más de . . .	noh PAH-goh mahs deh . . .
I'll look somewhere else.	Voy a ver en otro sitio.	voy ah vehr ehn OH-troh SEE-tyoh
No, thank you.	No, gracias.	noh, GRAH-syahs

What the Vendor Says

¡Marchanta!	mahr-CHAHN-tah!	Customer!
¿Qué se le ofrece?	keh seh leh oh-FREH-seh?	What would you like? (What can I offer you?)
¿Qué se lleva?	keh seh YEH-vah?	What will you buy?
¡Lléveselo!	YEH-veh-seh-loh!	Buy it!
Se lo vendo en . . .	seh loh VEHN-doh ehn . . .	I'll sell it to you for . . .
Se lo dejo en . . .	seh loh DEH-hoh ehn . . .	I'll let you have it for . . .
Es lo mínimo.	ehs loh MEE-nee-moh.	That's the lowest price.
No se puede.	noh seh PWEH-deh	It's not possible.
¿Se lo lleva?	seh loh YEH-vah?	Will you take it?
Gracias. Que le vaya bien.	GRAH-syahs. keh leh VAH-yah, byehn	Thank you. Have a good day.

GENERAL SHOPPING LIST

I need to buy	**Necesito comprar**	neh-seh-SEE-toh kohm-PRAHR
• books.	• **libros.**	• LEE-brohs
• a roll of film.	• **un rollo de película.**	• oon RROH-yoh deh peh-LEE-koo-lah
• some food.	• **comida.**	• koh-MEE-dah
• candy.	• **dulces.**	• DOOL-sehs
• shoes.	• **zapatos.**	• sah-PAH-tohs
• clothes.	• **ropa.**	• RROH-pah
• medicine.	• **una medicina.**	• OO-nah meh-dee-SEE-nah
• jewelry.	• **joyas.**	• HOH-yahs
• cigarettes.	• **cigarillos.**	• see-gah-REE-yohs
• gifts.	• **regalos.**	• rreh-GAH-lohs
• souvenirs.	• **recuerdos.**	• rreh-KWEHR-dohs
• postcards.	• **tarjetas postales.**	• tahr-HEH-tahs pohs-TAH-lehs

TYPES OF STORES

shop	**tienda**	TYEHN-dah
bookstore	**librería**	lee-breh-REE-ah
camera shop	**tienda de artículos fotográficos**	TYEHN-dah deh ahr-TEE-koo-lohs foh-toh-GRAH-fee-kohs
grocery store	**tienda de comestibles**	TYEHN-dah deh koh-mehs-TEE-blehs
bakery	**panadería**	pah-nah-deh-REE-ah
candy store	**confitería**	kohn-fee-teh-REE-ah
shoe store	**zapatería**	sah-pah-teh-REE-ah
clothing store	**tienda de ropa**	TYEHN-dah deh RROH-pah
jewelry store	**joyería**	hoh-yeh-REE-ah
local market	**mercado**	mehr-KAH-doh
butcher shop	**carnicería**	kahr-nee-seh-REE-ah

141

department store	**tienda por departamentos**	TYEHN-dah pohr deh-pahr-tah-MEHN-tohs
flower shop	**florería**	floh-reh-REE-ah
fruit stand	**frutería**	froo-teh-REE-ah
gift shop	**tienda de regalos**	TYEHN-dah deh rreh-GAH-lohs
liquor store	**licorería**	lee-koh-reh-REE-ah
hardware store	**ferretería**	feh-rreh-teh-REE-ah
record store	**tienda de discos**	TYEHN-dah deh DEES-kohs
tobacco shop	**tabaquería**	tah-bah-keh-REE-ah
newsstand	**puesto de periódicos**	PWEHS-toh deh peh-RYOH-dee-kohs
supermarket	**supermercado**	soo-pehr-mehr-KAH-doh

CLOTHING

I want to buy	**Quiero comprar**	KYEH-roh kohm-PRAHR
• a blouse.	• **una blusa.**	• oo-nah BLOO-sah
• a sweater.	• **un suéter.**	• oon SWEH-tehr
• a dress.	• **un vestido.**	• oon vehs-TEE-doh
• a skirt.	• **una falda.**	• OO-nah FAHL-dah
• stockings.	• **medias.**	• MEH-dyahs
• an evening gown.	• **un traje de noche.**	• oon TRAH-heh deh NOH-cheh
• a tie.	• **una corbata.**	• OO-nah kohr-BAH-tah
• a shirt.	• **una camisa.**	• OO-nah kah-MEE-sah
• a belt.	• **un cinturón.**	• oon seen-too-RHON
• a hat.	• **un sombrero.**	• oon sohm-BREH-roh
• a robe.	• **una bata.**	• OO-nah BAH-tah
• an overcoat.	• **un abrigo.**	• oon ah-BREE-goh
• handkerchiefs.	• **pañuelos.**	• pah-NYWEH-lohs

My size is	**Mi talla es**	mee TAH-yah ehs
• small.	• **pequeña.**	• peh-KEH-nyah
• medium.	• **mediana.**	• meh-DYAH-nah
• large.	• **grande.**	• GRAHN-deh
• extra-large.	• **extra-grande.**	• EHKS-trah GRAHN-deh
• 10.	• **diez.**	• dyehs
• 12.	• **doce.**	• DOH-seh
• 14.	• **catorce.**	• kah-TOHR-seh

Note: See pages 144–145 for a complete chart of size equivalents.

Do you have it in	**¿Lo tiene en**	loh TYEH-neh ehn
• black?	• **negro?**	• NEH-groh?
• blue?	• **azul?**	• ah SOOL?
• brown?	• **marrón?**	• mah-RROHN?
• gray?	• **gris?**	• grees?
• white?	• **blanco?**	• BLAHN-koh?
• red?	• **rojo?**	• RROH-hoh?
• green?	• **verde?**	• VEHR-deh?
• yellow?	• **amarillo?**	• ah-mah-REE-yoh?
• orange?	• **anaranjado?**	• ah-nah-rahn-HAH-doh?

I prefer something in	**Prefiero algo en**	preh-FYEH-roh AHL-goh ehn
• cotton.	• **algodón**	• ahl-goh-DOHN
• silk.	• **seda.**	• SEH-dah
• corduroy.	• **pana.**	• PAH-nah
• denim.	• **dril de algodón.**	• dreel deh ahl-goh-DOHN
• gabardine.	• **gabardina.**	• gah-bahr-DEE-nah
• lace.	• **encaje.**	• ehn-KAH-heh
• linen.	• **hilo.**	• EE-loh
• leather.	• **cuero.**	• KWEH-roh
• nylon.	• **nilón.**	• nee-LOHN
• rayon.	• **rayón.**	• rrah-YOHN
• satin.	• **raso.**	• RRAH-soh
• suede.	• **gamuza.**	• gah-MOO-sah
• synthetic.	• **sintético.**	• seen-TEH-tee-koh
• taffeta.	• **tafetán.**	• tah-feh-TAHN

143

• terrycloth.	• **tela de toalla.**	• TE-lah deh TWAH-yah
• velvet.	• **terciopelo.**	• tehr-syoh-PEH-loh
• wool.	• **lana.**	• LAH-nah
• worsted.	• **estambre.**	• ehs-TAHM-breh
I'd like to try it on.	**Quiero probármelo.**	KYEH-roh proh-BAHR-meh-loh
It does not fit me.	**No me queda bien.**	noh meh KEH-dah byehn
It fits well.	**Me queda bien.**	meh KEH-dah byehn
I'll take it.	**Me lo llevo.**	meh loh YEH-voh

WOMEN'S CLOTHING SIZES

We recommend trying on all clothing before buying because sizes vary and do not always correlate exactly with U.S. sizes. Also, returning clothing that you have purchased is unusual in Spain and Latin America, except at the large department stores in major cities.

In Mexico, many clothing companies use U.S. sizes.

Suits/Dresses

U.S.	6,8	8,10	10,12	12,14	14,16
Mexico	30,32	32,34	34,36	36,38	38,40
Spain	36,37,38	40	42	44	46

Blouses/Sweaters

U.S.	small	medium	large
Mexico	*chico(-a)*	*mediano(-a)*	*grande*
Spain	same as Mexico		

Shoes

U.S.	5	6	7	8	9
Mexico	2–3	3–4	4–5	5–6	6–7
Spain	38	39	41	42	43

MEN'S CLOTHING SIZES

Suits/Coats					
U.S.	36	38	40	42	44
Mexico	36	38	40	42	44
Spain	46	48	50	52	54

Dress Shirts							
U.S.	14	14¼	15	15½	16	16½	17	17½
Mexico	may be same as U.S. or Europe						
Spain	36	37	38	40	41	42	43

Sleeve Lengths		
corto	(KOHR-toh)	= short
mediano	(me-DYAH-noh)	= medium
largo	(LAHR-goh)	= long

Shoes						
U.S.	7	8	9	10	11	12
Mexico	6	7	8	9	10	11
Spain	41	42	43	44	46	47

THE JEWELRY STORE

I'd like to see some **Quisiera ver** kee-SYEHR-ah vehr

- rings.
  - **unos anillos.**
  - OO-nohs ah-NEE-yohs

- necklaces.
  - **unos collares.**
  - OO-nohs koh-YAH-res

- chains.
  - **unas cadenas.**
  - OO-nahs kah-DEH-nahs

- bracelets.
  - **unas pulseras.**
  - OO-nahs pool-SEH-rahs

- brooches.
  - **unos broches.**
  - OO-nohs BROH-chehs

- earrings.
  - **unos aretes.**
  - OO-nohs ah-REH-tehs

145

• pins.	• **unos alfileres.**	• OO-nohs ahl-fee-LEH-rehs
• wristwatches.	• **unos relojes pulsera.**	• OO-nohs rreh-LOH-hes pool-SEHR-ah
Do you have this in	**¿Lo tiene en**	loh TYEH-neh ehn
• gold?	• **oro?**	• OH-roh?
• white gold?	• **oro blanco?**	• OH-roh BLAHN-koh?
• silver?	• **plata?**	• PLAH-tah?
• stainless steel?	• **acero inoxidable?**	• ah-SEH-roh ee-noh-ksee-DAH-bleh?
• platinum?	• **platino?**	• plah-TEE-noh?
I would like it with	**Lo quisiera con**	loh kee-SYEH-rah kohn
• jade.	• **jade.**	• HAH-deh
• onyx.	• **onix.**	• OH-neeks
• a pearl.	• **una perla.**	• OO-nah PEHR-lah
• ivory.	• **marfil.**	• marh-FEEL
• a diamond.	• **un diamante.**	• oon dyah-MAHN-teh
• an emerald.	• **una esmeralda.**	• OO-nah ehs-meh-RAHL-dah
• an aquamarine.	• **una aquamarina.**	• OO-nah ah-gwah-mah-REE-nah
• an amethyst.	• **una amatista.**	• OO-nah ah-mah-TEES-tah

THE PHOTO SHOP

Film is expensive in Spain and Mexico, so it's a good idea to bring it from home. Wait until you return home to have film developed, as this, too, is expensive.

I would like a roll of film	**Quisiera un rollo de película.**	kee-SYEHR-ah oon RROH-yoh deh pe-LEE-koo-lah

146

Do you have	¿Tiene película	TYEH-neh peh-LEE-koo-lah
• film for prints?	• **para fotografías?**	• PAH-rah foh-toh-grah-FEE-ahs?
• film for slides?	• **para diapositivas?**	• PAH-rah dy-ah-poh-see-TEE-vahs?
• movie film?	• **de cine?**	• deh SEE-neh?
• color film?	• **en colores?**	• ehn koh-LOH-rehs?
• black-and-white film?	• **en blanco y negro?**	• ehn BLAHN-koh ee NEH-groh?
• 35 mm film, 36 exposures?	• **de treinta y cinco milímetros con treinta y seis fotografías?**	• deh TRAYN-tah ee SEEN-koh kohn TRAYN-tah ee says foh-toh-grah-FEE-ahs?

Do you develop film here?	**¿Revelan películas aquí?**	rreh-VEH-lahn peh-LEE-koo-lahs ah-KEE?
How much does it cost?	**¿Cuánto cuesta?**	KWAHN-toh KWEHS-tah?
How long does it take?	**¿Cuánto tiempo demora?**	KWAHN-toh TYEHM-poh deh-MOH-rah?
When can I pick up the pictures?	**¿Cuándo puedo recoger las fotografías?**	KWAHN-doh PWEH-doh rreh-koh-HEHR lahs foh-toh-grah-FEE-ahs?

THE RECORD STORE

Do you have	¿Tiene	TYEH-neh
• records?	• **discos?**	• DEES-kohs?
• cassettes?	• **cassettes?**	• kah-SEHTS?

• tapes?	• **cintas?**	• SEEN-tahs?
• compact disks?	• **compact disks?**	• com-pahct deesk
Where is the . . . music?	**¿Dónde está la música**	DOHN-deh ehs-TAH lah MOO-see-kah
• classical	• **clásica?**	• KLAH-see-kah?
• folk	• **folklórica?**	• fohl-KLOH-ree-kah?
• popular	• **popular?**	• poh-poo-LAHR?
• Spanish	• **española?**	• ehs-pah-NYOH-lah?
• Latin American	• **latinoamericana?**	• lah-tee-noh-ah-meh-ree-KAH-nah?
• rock 'n' roll	• **rocanrol?**	• roh-kahn-ROHL?
Do you sell	**¿Vende**	VEHN-deh
• maracas?	• **maracas?**	• mah-RAH-kahs?
• castanets?	• **castañuelas?**	• kahs-tah-NYWEH-lahs?
• other musical instruments?	• **otros instrumentos musicales?**	• OH-trohs eens-troo-MEHN-tohs MOO-see-kah-lehs?

BOOKS, MAGAZINES, AND PAPER GOODS

Where is there a bookstore?	**¿Dónde hay una librería?**	DOHN-deh ay OO-nah lee-breh-REE-ah?
Is there a bookstore that carries English books?	**¿Hay una librería que vende libros en inglés?**	ay oo-nah lee-breh-REE-ah keh VEHN-deh LEE-brohs ehn een-GLEHS?
Do you have the book . . . ?	**¿Tiene el libro . . . ?**	TYEH-neh ehl LEE-broh . . . ?
Do you have this guide book in English?	**¿Tiene esta guía en inglés?**	TYEH-neh EHS-tah GEE-ah ehn een-GLEHS?
Do you have a Spanish-English dictionary?	**¿Tiene un diccionario español-inglés?**	TYEH-neh oon deek-syoh-NAH-ryoh ehs-pah-NYOHL-een-GLEHS?

148

Do you have	¿Tiene	TYEH-neh
• novels?	• novelas?	• noh-VEH-lahs?
• books?	• libros?	• LEE-brohs?
• magazines?	• revistas?	• rreh-VEES-tahs?
• a guide book?	• una guía?	• OO-nah GEE-ah?
• a map of the city?	• un mapa de la ciudad?	• oon MAH-pah deh lah syoo-DAHD?
• a pocket dictionary?	• un diccionario de bolsillo?	• oon deek-syoh-NAH-ryoh deh buhl-SEE-yoh?
a ball-point pen	un bolígrafo	oon boh-LEE-grah-foh
envelopes	sobres	SOH-brehs
a notebook	un cuaderno	oon kwah-DEHR-noh
posters	carteles	kahr-TEH-lehs
ribbon	cinta	SEEN-tah
Scotch tape	cinta adhesiva	SEEN-tah ah-deh-SEE-vah
stamps	timbres (*Mexico*) (or) sellos (*Spain*)	TEEM-brehs SEH-yohs
stationery	papel de correspondencia	pah-PEHL deh koh-rrehs-pohn-DEHN-syah
string	hilo	EE-loh
wrapping paper	papel de envolver	pah-PEHL deh ehn-vohl-VEHR
a writing pad	un bloc de papel	oon blohk deh pah-PEHL

TOILETRIES

a brush	un cepillo	oon seh-PEE-yoh
cologne	colonia	koh-LOH-nyah
a comb	un peine	oon PAY-neh

149

deodorant	**desodorante**	deh-soh-doh-RAHN-teh
disposable diapers	**pañales desechables**	pah-NYAH-lehs deh-seh-CHAH-blehs
hairspray	**laca**	LAH-kah
a mirror	**un espejo**	oon ehs-PEH-hoh
moisturizing lotion	**loción humectante**	loh-SYOHN oo-mehk-TAHN-teh
mouthwash	**enjuague bucal**	ehn-HWAH-geh boo-KAHL
nail clippers	**cortauñas**	kohr-ta-OO-nyahs
nail polish	**esmalte de uñas**	ehs-MAHL-teh deh OO-nyahs
nail polish remover	**quitaesmalte**	kee-tah-ehs-MAHL-teh
perfume	**perfume**	pehr-FOO-meh
sanitary napkins	**toallas sanitarias**	toh-AH-yahs sah-nee-TAH-ryahs
shampoo	**champú**	chahm-POO
shaving cream	**crema de afeitar**	KREH-mah deh ah-fay-TAHR
soap	**jabón**	hah-BOHN
a sponge	**una esponja**	OO-nah ehs-POHN-hah
tampons	**tampones**	tahm-POH-nehs
tissues	**pañuelos de papel**	pah-NYWEH-lohs deh pah-PEHL
toilet paper	**papel higiénico**	pah-PEHL ee-HYEH-ee-koh
a toothbrush	**un cepillo de dientes**	oon seh-PEE-yoh deh DYEHN-tehs

| toothpaste | **pasta de dientes** | PAHS-tah deh DYEHN-tehs |
| tweezers | **pinzas** | PEEN-sahs |

FOOD SHOPPING

I would like a	**Me gustaría**	meh goos-tah-REE-ah
• bottle of juice.	• **una botella de jugo.**	• oo-nah boh-TEH-yah deh HOO-goh
• bottle of milk.	• **una botella de leche.**	• OO-nah boh-TEH-yah deh LEH-cheh
• box of cereal.	• **una caja de cereales.**	• OO-nah KAH-hah deh seh-reh-AH-lehs
• box of cookies.	• **una caja de galletas.**	• OO-nah KAH-hah deh gah-YEH-tahs
• can of tomato sauce.	• **una lata de salsa de to-mate.**	• OO-nah LAH-tah deh SAHL-sah deh toh-MAH-teh
• dozen eggs.	• **una docena de huevos.**	• OO-nah doh SEH-nah deh WEH-vohs
• package of candies.	• **un paquete de dulces.**	• oon pah-KEH-teh deh dool-sehs
Do you have	**¿Tiene**	TYEH-neh
• cold cuts?	• **carnes frías?**	• KAHR-nehs FREE-ahs?
• cheese?	• **queso?**	• KEH-soh?
• soft drinks?	• **refrescos?**	• rreh-FREHS-kohs?
• cigarettes?	• **cigarrillos?**	• see gah-RREE-yohs?
• matches?	• **fósforos?**	• FOHS-foh-rohs?

151

WEIGHTS AND MEASURES

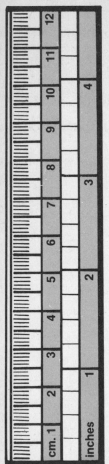

Metric Weight	**U.S.**
1 gram (g)	0.035 ounce
28.35 grams	1 ounce
100 grams	3.5 ounces
454 grams	1 pound
1 kilogram (kilo)	2.2 pounds

Liquids	**U.S.**
1 liter (l)	4.226 cups
1 liter	2.113 pints
1 liter	1.056 quarts
3.785 liters	1 gallon

Dry Measures	**U.S.**
1 litre	0.908 quart
1 decalitre	1.135 pecks
1 hectolitre	2.837 bushels

One inch = 2.54 centimeters
One centimeter = .39 inch

	in.	feet	yards
1 mm.	0.039	0.003	0.001
1 cm.	0.39	0.03	0.01
1 dm.	3.94	0.32	0.10
1 m.	39.40	3.28	1.09

.39 (# of centimeters) = (# of inches)
2.54 (# of inches) = (# of centimeters)

	mm.	cm.	m.
1 in.	25.4	2.54	0.025
1 ft.	304.8	30.48	0.304
1 yd.	914.4	91.44	0.914

13/ACTIVITIES AND ENTERTAINMENT

In Spain and Mexico, you will see people sitting in parks and cafés reading a magazine or newspaper, talking, or just doing nothing. There are also many movies, theater, operas, concerts, sports events (primarily soccer), bullfights, and beaches.

DIALOGUE: SWIMMING (NATACION)

Juan:	¡Hace tanto calor!	ah-seh TAHN-toh kah-LOHR!
María:	Sí, ¿qué tal si nos vamos a nadar?	see, keh tahl see nohs VAH-mohs ah nah-DAHR?
Juan:	Buena idea. ¿Vamos a la playa o a la piscina?	BWEH-nah ee-DEH-ah. VAH-mohs ah lah PLAH-yah oh ah lah pee-SEE-nah?
María:	¡Me encanta el mar! ¿Pero no es peligroso por aquí?	meh ehn-KAHN-tah ehl mahr! PEH-roh noh ehs peh-lee-GROH-soh pohr ah-KEE?
Juan:	No. El mar aquí es muy calmado.	noh. ehl mahr ah-KEE ehs muee kahl-MAH-doh
María:	¡Que bien! Entonces nos vemos en la playa en cinco minutos.	key byehn! ehn-TOHN-sehs nohs VEH-mohs ehn lah PLAH-yah ehn SEEN-koh mee-NOO-tohs
Juan:	¡Perfecto! No te olvides la loción bronceadora. El sol está muy fuerte.	pehr-FEHK-toh! noh teh ohl-VEE-dehs lah loh-SYOHN brohn-sehy-ah-DOH-rah. ehl sohl ehs-TAH muee FWEHR-teh

John:	It's so hot out!
Mary:	Yes. Why don't we go swimming?
John:	Good idea! Shall we go to the beach or the pool?

Mary:	I love the sea. But isn't it dangerous around here?
John:	No! The sea here is very calm.
Mary:	Good. Then I'll see you on the beach in five minutes.
John:	Right. And don't forget the suntan lotion! The sun is very strong.

Where are the best beaches?	¿Dónde están las mejores playas?	DOH-deh ehs-TAHN lahs meh-HOH-rehs PLAH-yahs?
How do we get there?	¿Cómo se puede ir allí?	KOH-moh seh PWEH-deh eer ah-YEE?
Is it a private or a public beach?	¿Es una playa privada o pública?	ehs OO-nah PLAH-yah pree-VAH-dah o POO-blee-kah?
Is there a lifeguard?	¿Hay un salvavidas?	ahy oon sahl-vah-VEE-dahs?
Is it dangerous for children?	¿Es peligroso para niños?	ehs peh-lee-GROH-soh PAH-rah NEE-nyohs?
Are there dangerous currents?	¿Hay corrientes peligrosas?	ahy koh-RRYEHN-tehs peh-lee-GROH-sahs?
When is • high tide?	¿Cuándo hay • marea alta?	KWAHN-doh ahy • mah-REH-ah AHL-tah?
• low tide?	• marea baja?	• mah-REH-ah BAH-hah?
We need • some beach chairs.	Necesitamos • unas sillas de playa.	neh-seh-see-TAH-mohs • OO-nahs SEE-yahs deh PLAH-yah
• some beach towels.	• unas toallas de playa.	• OO-nahs TWAH-yahs deh PLAH-yah

154

CAMPING

Can we camp here?	**¿Podemos acampar aquí?**	poh-DEH-mohs ah-kahm-PAHR ah-KEE?
Is there room for a trailer?	**¿Hay lugar para un trailer?**	ahy loo-GAHR PAH-rah oon TRY-lehr?
What does it cost for one night?	**¿Cuánto cuesta por una noche?**	KWAHN-toh KWEHS-tah pohr OO-nah NOH-cheh?
Is/Are there	**¿Hay**	ahy
• drinking water?	• **agua potable?**	• AH-gwah poh-TAH-bleh?
• electricity?	• **electricidad?**	• eh-lehk-tree-see-DAHD?
• showers?	• **duchas?**	• DOO-chahs?
• a grocery store?	• **una tienda de comestibles?**	• OO-nah TYEHN-dah deh koh-mehs-TEE-blehs?
• butane gas?	• **gas?**	• gahs?

MOVIES

Check the entertainment page of local newspapers to find out what's playing at the movies. Many English-speaking films are dubbed into Spanish, but occasionally Spanish subtitles are added instead. Watching locally produced movies can help improve your language skills, even if you don't understand everything you hear. Note that theaters can be crowded on weekends; some sell numbered tickets in advance.

Let's go to the movies.	**Vamos al cine.**	VAH-mohs ahl SEE-neh
What's playing?	**¿Qué presentan?**	keh preh-SEHN-tahn?
Is it in Spanish or English?	**¿Es en español o en inglés?**	ehs ehn ehs-pah-NYOHL oh ehn een-GLEHS?

155

With subtitles?	¿Con subtítulos?	kohn soob-TEE-too-lohs?
Is it dubbed?	¿Está doblada?	ehs-TAH doh-BLAH-dah?
What kind of film is it?	¿Qué tipo de película es?	keh TEE-poh deh peh-LEE-koo-lah ehs?
It's	Es	ehs
• a comedy.	• una comedia.	• OO-nah koh-MEH-dyah
• a drama.	• un drama.	• oon DRAH-mah
When does the show start?	¿Cuándo empieza la función?	KWAHN-doh ehm-PYEH-sah lah foon-SYOHN?
How much are the tickets?	¿Cuánto cuestan las entradas?	KWAHN-toh KWEHS-tahn lahs ehn-TRAH-dahs?
What theater is showing the new film	¿En qué teatro pasan la película nueva	ehn keh teh-AH-troh PAH-sahn lah peh-LEE-koo-lah NWEH-vah
• by . . . ?	• de . . . ?	• deh . . . ?
• with . . . ?	• con . . . ?	• kohn . . . ?

THEATER, CONCERTS, OPERA, AND BALLET

In Spain, you can get a *Guía del ocio* (GEE-ah dehl OH-syoh), a "leisure guide," from any newsstand. The guide provides information about schedules and admission fees for daily, weekly, and monthly events.

Madrid has many theaters. While most of them present some form of comedy or drama, the Teatro de la Zarzuela (teh-AH-troh deh lah sahr-SWEH-lah)is perhaps the most typical of all. *Zarzuela* is light opera, combining drama, comedy, singing, and dance, all in one choreographed piece. In the summer, *zarzuelas* are performed open-air at the Plaza Colón, free of charge. Many musical groups, including some major conductors, perform at the Teatro Real. Whereas most Spanish cities offer some form of theatrical activities, be prepared for other options in smaller towns.

In Mexico, the major theater companies are in the capital city. In the provinces, local universities and other cultural centers often mount productions. In Mexico City some theaters have translated Broadway musicals into Spanish.

There are several dance companies, specializing in different forms of dance. There are two major companies that specialize in folk repertoires. The best-known is the Ballet Folklórico de México (bah-LEHT fohl-KLOH-ree-koh deh MEH-hee-koh), or the Mexican Folkloric Ballet Company, which performs at the famous Museo de Bellas Artes (moo-SEH-oh deh BEH-yahs AHR-tehs), or Fine Arts Museum. The other is the Ballet de la Ciudad de México (bah-LEHT deh lah syoo-DAHD deh MEH-hee-koh), or the Mexico City Ballet Company, which offers another interpretation of Mexican folk dances. You will also find classical ballet companies. Many local universities have their own ballet company, performing primarily Mexican pieces. (*Note:* It is not unusual to give a small tip to ushers in theaters.)

What's playing at the theater?	¿Qué dan en el teatro?	keh dahn ehn ehl teh-AH-troh?
I'd like to go to	Me gustaría ir a	meh goos-tah-REE-ah eer ah
• a play.	• un drama.	• oon DRAH-mah
• an opera.	• una ópera.	• OO-nah OH-peh-rah
• an operetta.	• una zarzuela.	• OO-nah sahr-SWEH-lah
• a ballet.	• un ballet.	• oon bah-LEHT
• a musical.	• una obra musical.	• OO-nah OH-brah moo-see-KAHL
• a concert.	• un concierto.	• oon kohn-SYEHR-toh
What kind of play is it?	¿Qué tipo de obra es?	keh TEE-poh deh OH-brah ehs?
Who wrote it?	¿Quién la escribió?	KYEHN lah ehs-kree-BYOH?

157

Are there tickets for today?	¿Hay entradas para hoy?	ahy ehn-TRAH-dahs PAH-ray oy?
How much are the tickets?	¿Cuánto cuestan las entradas?	KWAHN-toh KWEHS-tahn lahs ehn-TRAH-dahs?
Do we need a reservation?	¿Necesitamos una reservación?	neh-seh-see-TAH-mohs OO-nah rreh-sehr-vah-SYOHN?
	(or) . . . una reserva? (*Spain*)	. . . OO-nah rreh-SEHR-vah?
Please give me . . . tickets.	Me da . . . boletos, por favor.	meh dah . . . boh-LEH-tohs, pohr fah-VOHR
I'd like	Quisiera	kee-SYEH-rah
• an orchestra seat.	• un sitio en platea.	• oon SEE-tyoh ehn plah-TEH-ah
• seats in the balcony.	• asientos en el balcón.	• ah-SYEHN-tohs ehn ehl bahl-KOHN
• a mezzanine seat.	• un sitio en anfiteatro.	• oon SEE-tyoh ehn ahn-fee-teh-AH-troh
• seats up front.	• asientos adelante.	• ah-SYEHN-tos ah-deh-LAHN-teh
• seats in back.	• asientos atrás.	• ah-SYEHN-tos ah-TRAHS
• seats on the side.	• asientos a los lados.	• ah-SYEHN-tos ah los LAH-dohs
• good seats.	• buenos asientos.	• BWEH-nohs ah-SYEHN-tohs
• inexpensive tickets.	• entradas no muy caras.	• ehn-TRAH-dahs noh muee KAH-rahs
• tickets for the matinee.	• entradas para la matinée.	• ehn-TRAH-dahs PAH-rah lah mah-tee-NEH
• tickets for the evening.	• entradas para la tanda.	• ehn-TRAH-dahs PAH-rah lah TAHN-dah
A program, please.	Un programa, por favor.	oon proh-GRAH-mah, pohr fah-VOHR

Who's	¿Quién	kyehn
• playing?	• actúa?	• ahk-TOO-ah?
• singing?	• canta?	• KAHN-tah?
• dancing?	• baila?	• BAH-ee-lah?
• directing?	• dirige?	• dee-REE-heh?
• speaking?	• habla?	• AH-blah?
• announcing?	• anuncia?	• ah-NOON-syah?

CLUBS, DISCOS, AND CABARETS

In some restaurants in Spain you can both have dinner and see a show. In Madrid, which has many of these establishments, some feature *flamenco* (flah-MEHN-koh) dancing and singing. On weekends, it is customary to eat as late as midnight, enjoying regularly scheduled music performances. There are also innumerable discos, which play everything from American-style music to Europop. Cabarets and boîtes are concentrated in certain parts of town, and reservations are sometimes needed— as at Madrid's Café Chinitas (kah-FEH chee-NEE-tahs), one of the best-known places for *flamenco*. Most nightclubs are open from 7:00 P.M. till 3:00 A.M.

In Mexico City and Acapulco, as in Spain, many clubs offer dinner and a show; cabarets usually serve only drinks and snacks with the show. For information about nightlife, consult a *Guía turistica* (GEE-ah too-REES-tee-kah), distributed at no charge by the tourist office.

Why don't we go dancing tonight?	¿Por qué no vamos a bailar esta noche?	pohr keh noh VAH-mohs ah bah-ee-LAHR EHS-tah NOH-cheh?
Can you suggest a good nightclub?	¿Podría recomendar un buen club nocturno?	poh-DREE-ah rreh-koh-mehn-DAHR oon bwehn kloob nohk-TOOR-noh?
Do they serve dinner?	¿Sirven cena?	SEER-vehn SEH-nah?

159

What kind of show do they have?	**¿Qué clase de función tienen?**	keh-KLAH-seh deh foon-SYOHN TYEH-nehn?
Is there an entrance fee?	**¿Se cobra la entrada?**	seh KOH-brah lah ehn-TRAH-dah?
There's a minimum charge.	**Se cobra un consumo mínimo.**	seh KOH-brah oon kohn-SOO-moh MEE-nee-moh
What kind of dress is required? (*lit.,* How should one dress?)	**Cómo se debe vestir?**	KOH-moh seh DEH-beh vehs-TEER?
Is there a place to go after dinner?	**¿Hay algún lugar adonde ir después de cenar?**	ahy ahl-GOON loo-GAHR ah-DOHN-deh eer dehs-PWEHS deh seh-NAHR?
Good evening.	**Buenas noches.**	BWEH-nahs NOH-chehs
We would like a table	**Quisiéramos una mesa**	kee-SYEH-rah-mohs OO-nah MEH-sah
• near the stage.	• **cerca del escenario.**	• SEHR-kah dehl eh-se-NAH-ryoh
• near the dance floor.	• **cerca de la pista de baile.**	• SEHR-kah deh lah PEES-tah deh BAH-ee-leh
How much do you charge for drinks?	**¿Cuánto cuestan las bebidas?**	KWAHN-toh KWEHS-tahn lahs beh-BEE-dahs?
Do you have any special drinks? (drinks of the house)	**¿Tienen alguna bebida de la casa?**	TYEH-nehn ahl-GOO-nah beh-BEE-dah deh lah KAH-sah?
What kind of non-alcoholic beverages do you serve?	**¿Qué tipo de bebidas sin alcohol tienen?**	keh TEE-poh deh beh-BEE-dahs seen ahl-KOHL TYEH-nehn?

160

Could we see the menu?	¿Podemos ver el menú?	poh-DEH-mohs vehr ehl meh-NOO?
At what time is the show?	¿A qué hora es el espectáculo?	ah keh OH-rah ehs ehl ehs-pehk-TAH-koo-loh?
How many shows are there?	¿Cuántas veces se da el espectáculo?	KWAHN-tahs VEH-sehs seh dah ehl ehs-pehk-TAH-koo-loh?

SPORTS

Soccer is the most popular sport in Spain and Latin America. In Mexico, soccer is played nearly year-round, while in Spain the season is primarily from September through June. There are many teams, and both Spanish and Mexican fans are passionate about their favorite.

I would like to see a soccer match.	Quisiera ver un partido de fútbol.	kee-SYEH-rah vehr oon pahr-TEE-doh deh FOOT-bohl
Who is playing?	¿Quiénes juegan?	KYEH-nehs HWEH-gahn?
Which is the best team?	¿Cuál es el mejor equipo?	kwahl ehs ehl meh-HOHR eh-KEE-poh?
Is the stadium near here?	¿Está cerca de aquí el estadio?	ehs-TAH SEHR-kah deh ah-KEE ehl ehs-TAH-dyoh?
How much are the tickets?	¿Cuánto cuestan las entradas?	KWAHN-toh KWEHS-tahn lahs ehn-TRAH-dahs?
Are there better seats?	¿Hay asientos mejores?	ahy ah-SYEHN-tohs meh-HOH-rehs?
What is the score?	¿Cuál es la anotación?	KWAHL ehs lah ah-noh-tah-SYOHN?
Who is winning?	¿Quién gana?	KYEHN GAH-nah?

161

BULLFIGHTS

The popularity of this ceremonial contest between man and beast, long a fixture of life in the Spanish-speaking world, has seen some decline with the protests of animal rights activists and the rise of soccer and other modern games. However, bullfighting is considered an art, not a sport, and likened to a ballet in which the *matador* acts out a series of poses and gracious steps, cape in hand, as he confronts the bull. Part of the art revolves around a series of classical positions, each with a specific name, some more daring and dangerous than others.

The *matador* is the primary bullfighter or *torero,* and the names of *matadores* are well known throughout the Spanish-speaking world. They are the principal actors, masters in the art of capework, expert in a variety of positions, through which they demonstrate their courage as they confront their adversary. After an initial performance with the cape, the bull is then weakened, first by the *picador* on horseback who strikes at the bull's massive neck muscles with a long lance. He is followed by the *banderilleros,* who insert pairs of *banderillas* (bahn-deh-REE yahs), or sharp spikes, into the bull's neck and back muscles. This is usually an extremely dangerous maneuver, accomplished while the bull is charging, and without the cape to help distract and confuse the animal.

The last segment of a bullfight is called the *faena* (fah-EH-nah). Here, the *matador* holds in his left hand a red, heart-shaped cloth, the *muleta* (moo-LEH-tah), and in his right hand a sword, which he will eventually use to kill the bull. The accomplishment of a good *faena* requires an extremely skilled *torero.* Such *toreros* gain fame throughout Spain and Latin America and often travel from one country to another at different times of the year.

Most bullfights, or *corridas de toros* (koh-RREE-dahs deh TOH-rohs), feature six bulls and three principal bullfighters.

Each bullfighter kills one bull in each of the two segments of the afternoon's event. Following are some of the principal figures in a bullfight.

el torero
(ehl toh-REH-roh)

A bullfighter. The *matador,* the *picador,* and the *banderillero* are all *toreros.* However, common usage often refers only to the *matador* as the *torero,* and to the others by their specific titles.

el matador
(ehl mah-tah-DOHR)

The principal bullfighter, the one who kills the bull.

el picador
(ehl pee-kah-DOHR)

Assistant on horseback who helps to weaken the bull by using a *pica* (PEE-kah), or lance.

el banderillero
(ehl bahn-deh-ree-YEH-roh)

Often the *matador* himself—or an assistant he may designate—who places pairs of *banderillas* (bahn-deh-REE-yahs) on the bull's back and neck.

la cuadrilla
(lah kwah-DREE-yah)

The team of bullfighters under the orders of the *matador.*

el monosabio
(ehl moh-noh-SAH-byoh)

An assistant who does various jobs in the *ruedo* (RWEH-doh) or bullfight ring.

Is there a bullfight today?	**¿Hay una corrida hoy?**	ahy OO-nah koh-RREE-dah oy?
Where is the bull-ring?	**¿Dónde está la plaza de toros?**	DOHN-deh ehs-TAH lah PLAH-sah deh TOH-rohs?
Who is the main bullfighter?	**¿Quién es el torero principal?**	KYEHN ehs ehl toh-REH-roh preen-SEE-pahl?

163

Do you have seats in the	¿Tiene asientos en	TYEH-neh ah-SYEHN-tohs ehn
• shade?	• la sombra?	• lah SOHM-brah?
• sun?	• el sol?	• ehl sohl?
Bravo!	¡Olé!	oh-LEH!

164

14/GENERAL INFORMATION
EXPRESSIONS OF TIME

now	**ahora**	ah-OH-rah
earlier	**más temprano**	mahs tehm-PRAH-noh
later	**más tarde**	mahs TAHR-deh
before	**antes**	AHN-tehs
after/afterward	**después**	dehs-PWEHS
soon	**pronto**	PROHN-toh
morning	**mañana**	mah-NYAH-nah
afternoon	**tarde**	TAHR-deh
night	**noche**	NOH-cheh
in the morning	**en la mañana**	ehn lah mah-NYAH-nah
in the afternoon	**en la tarde**	en lah TAHR-deh
at night	**en la noche**	en lah NOH-cheh
tomorrow morning	**mañana por la mañana**	mah-NYAH-nah por lah mah-NYAH-nah
the day after tomorrow	**pasado mañana**	pah-SAH-doh mah-NYAH-nah
yesterday	**ayer**	ah-YER
the day before yesterday	**anteayer**	ahn-teh-ah-YEHR
in a week	**en una semana**	ehn OO-nah seh-MAH-nah
next week	**la semana próxima**	lah seh-MAH-nah PROHK-see-mah
last week	**la semana pasada**	lah seh-MAH-nah pah-SAH-dah

next month	**el mes próximo**	ehl mehs PROHK-see-moh
last month	**el mes pasado**	ehl mehs pah-SAH-doh
next year	**el año próximo**	ehl AH-nyoh PROHK-see-moh
last year	**el año pasado**	ehl AH-nyoh pah-SAH-doh
five years ago	**hace cinco años**	AH-seh SEEN-koh AH-nyohs
during the eighties	**durante los años ochenta**	doo-RAHN-teh los AH-nyohs oh-CHEHN-tah

DAYS, MONTHS, AND SEASONS

Days of the Week	**Días de la semana**	DEE-ahs deh lah seh-MAH-nah
What day is it?	**¿Qué día es hoy?**	keh DEE-ah ehs oy?
Today is	**Hoy es**	oy ehs
• Monday.	• **lunes.**	• LOO-nehs
• Tuesday.	• **martes.**	• MAHR-tehs
• Wednesday.	• **miércoles.**	• MYEHR-koh-lehs
• Thursday.	• **jueves.**	• HWEH-vehs
• Friday.	• **viernes.**	• VYEHR-nehs
• Saturday.	• **sábado.**	• SAH-bah-doh
• Sunday.	• **domingo.**	• doh-MEEN-goh

Months of the Year	**Meses del año**	MEH-sehs dehl AH-nyoh
January	**enero**	eh-NEH-roh
February	**febrero**	feh-BREH-roh
March	**marzo**	MAHR-soh
April	**abril**	ah-BREEL
May	**mayo**	MAH-yoh
June	**junio**	HOO-nyoh

166

July	**julio**	HOO-lyoh
August	**agosto**	ah-GOHS-toh
September	**septiembre**	sohp-TYEHM-breh
October	**octubre**	ohk-TOO-breh
November	**noviembre**	noh-VYEHM-breh
December	**diciembre**	dee-SYEHM-breh
Seasons	**Estaciones**	ehs-tah-SYOH-nehs

spring	**la primavera**	lah pree-mah-VEHR-rah
summer	**el verano**	ehl veh-RAH-noh
autumn	**el otoño**	ehl oh-TOH-nyoh
winter	**el invierno**	ehl een-VYEHR-noh

THE DATE

What is today's date?	**¿Cuál es la fecha de hoy?**	kwahl ehs lah FEH-chah deh oy?
Today is	**Hoy es**	oy ehs
• June 1, 1989.	• **el primero* de junio, de mil novecientos ochenta y nueve.**	• ehl pree-MEH-roh deh HOO-nyoh deh meel noh-veh-SYEHN-tohs oh-CHEHN-tah ee NWEH-veh
• April 12, 1995.	• **el doce de abril, de mil novecientos noventa y cinco.**	• ehl DOH-seh deh ah-BREEL, deh meel noh-veh-SYEHN-tohs noh-VEHN-tah ee SEEN-koh
Her birthday is December 2, 1956.	**Su cumpleaños es el dos de diciembre de mil novecientos cincuenta y seis.**	soo coom-pleh-AH-nyohs ehs ehl dohs deh dee-SYEHM-breh deh mil noh-veh-SYEHN-tohs seen-KWEHN-tah ee says

*El primero ("the first") is used for the first day of each month. Otherwise, regular cardinal numbers are used for dates.

AGE

| How old are you? | **¿Cuantos años tiene usted?** | KWAHN-tohs AH-nyohs TYEH-neh oo-STEHD? |
| I'm 36. | **Tengo treinta y seis años.** | TEHN-goh TRAYHN-tah ee seh-ees AH-nyohs |

WEATHER

In Spain, summers are hot and winters are mild and rainy along the coast and bitterly cold elsewhere, with snow in the mountains. In Mexico, coasts and low-lying sections of the interior are often hot if not actually tropical in winter, even steamier in summer. But the high central plateau on which Mexico City, Guadalajara, and many colonial cities are located is springlike year-round. October and May are generally the driest months, but even during rainy season, June through September, it may rain for only a few hours every day.

What's the weather like?	**¿Qué tiempo hace?**	keh TYEHM-poh AH-seh?
It's nice today.	**Hace buen tiempo hoy.**	AH-seh bwehn TYEHM-poh oy
The day's not too nice.	**El día no está muy bueno.**	ehl DEE-ah noh ehs-TAH muee BWEH-noh
It's	**Hace**	AH-seh
• windy.	• **viento.**	• VYEHN-toh
• hot.	• **calor.**	• kah-LOHR
• cold	• **frío.**	• FREE-oh
• sunny.	• **sol.**	• sohl
It's cloudy.	**Está nublado.**	ehs-TAH noo-BLAH-doh
It's rainy.	**Llueve.**	YWEH-veh
It's not snowing now.	**No nieva ahora.**	noh NYEH-vah ah-OH-rah

TEMPERATURE CONVERSIONS

In both Spain and Mexico, temperature is measured in degrees Celsius, or centigrade. To convert degrees Celsius into degrees Fahrenheit, use this formula:

To Convert Centigrade to Fahrenheit

$$\left(\frac{9}{5}\right)C° + 32 = F°$$

1. Divide by 5
2. Multiply by 9
3. Add 32

To Convert Fahrenheit to Centigrade

$$(F° - 32)\frac{5}{9} = C°$$

1. Subtract 32
2. Divide by 9
3. Multiply by 5

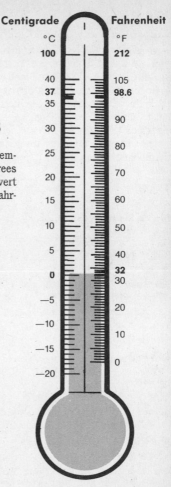

HOLIDAYS

In addition to celebrating familiar holidays like Christmas and New Year's, Spain and Latin America celebrate many holidays that are unique to specific areas. Most of these holidays are religious or national in origin. Small towns often hold celebrations to honor their patron saint or namesake (San José, San Luis, etc.). Keep holidays in mind when planning your trip, because most public offices and banks, and some museums, will be closed on these dates.

The following holidays are generally celebrated throughout the Spanish-speaking world.

Año Nuevo (AH-nyoh NWEH-voh)	New Year's Day	January 1
Día de los Reyes (DEE-ah deh lohs RREH-yehs) **(or) Epifanía** (eh-pee-fah-NEE-ah)	Epiphany	January 6
San José (sahn hoh-SEH)	St. Joseph's Day	March 19
Día del Trabajo (DEE-ah dehl trah- BAH-hoh)	Labor Day	May 1
San Pedro y San Pablo (sahn PEH-droh ee sahn PAH-bloh)	Saint Peter's and Saint Paul's Day	June 29
Santiago (Sahn-TYAH-goh)	Saint James' Day	July 25
Asunción (ah-soon-SYOHN)	Assumption Day	August 15
Día de la Raza (DEE-ah deh lah RRAH-sah)	Columbus Day	October 12

170

Todos los Santos   All Saints' Day   November 1
(TOH-dohs lohs SAHN-
tohs)

Immaculada Con-   Immaculate Concep-   December 8
cepción   tion
(een-mah-koo-LAH-
dah kohn-sehp-
SYOHN)

Navidad   Christmas   December 25
(nah-vee-DAHD)

Some religious holidays change dates according to the calendar. These include:

Viernes Santo   Good Friday
(VYER-nehs SAHN-
toh)

Pascua Florida   Easter
(PAHS-kwah floh-REE-
dah)
**(Pascua de
Ressurección)**
(PAHS-kwah deh rreh-
soo-rrehk-SYOHN)

Corpus Christi   Corpus Christi
(KOHR-poos KREES-
tee)

Other holidays which have different dates in accordance with the country are:

Día de la Madre   Mother's Day
(DEE-ah deh lah MAH-
dreh)

Día del Padre   Father's Day
(DEE-ah dehl PAH-
dreh)

Día del Maestro   Teacher's Day
(DEE-ah dehl mah-
EHS-troh)

171

Mexico

Most businesses in Mexico close on the following holidays as well as those listed above.

Día de la Constitución (DEE-ah deh lah kohns-tee-too-SYOHN)	Constitution Day (marks the signing of the constitutions of 1917 and 1957)	February 5
Benito Juárez (beh-NEE-toh HWAH-rehs)	Birthday of Benito Juárez (former President of Mexico)	March 21
Cinco de Mayo (SEEN-koh deh MAH-yoh)	Fifth of May (commemorates Mexico's victory over the French at the Battle of Puebla in 1862)	May 5
Apertura del Congreso (ah-pehr-TOO-rah dehl kohn-GREH-soh)	Opening Session of Congress (President's State of the Union Address)	September 1
Día de la Independencia (DEE-ah deh lah een-deh-pehn-DEHN-syah)	Independence Day (officially begins at 11:00 P.M. the night before, with El Grito (ehl GREE-toh) re-enacting Father Hidalgo's cry for independence from Spain in 1810)	September 16
Día de la Revolución (DEE-ah deh lah rreh-voh-loo-SYOHN)	Anniversary of the Revolution (parades and fireworks mark the anniversary of the Mexican Revolution of 1910)	November 20

		December 1
Inauguración del Presidente (ee-naw-goo-rah-SYOHN dehl preh-see-DEHN-teh)	President's inauguration (held every six years)	
Nuestra Señora de Guadalupe (NWEHS-trah seh-NYOH-rah deh gwah-dah-LOO-peh)	Our Lady of Guadalupe (day of the patron saint of Mexico; colorful processions and parades are held, especially at the Basilica in Mexico City)	December 12

COUNTRIES AND NATIONALITIES

Note: In common usage, the names of certain countries always take the article.

Country	**País** (pah-EES)	**Nationality/ Nacionalidad** (nah-syoh-nah-lee-DAHD)
Argentina	**la Argentina** (lah ahr-hen-TEE-nah)	**argentino(-a)** (ahr-hehn-TEE-noh[-nah])
Bolivia	**Bolivia** (boh-LEE-vyah)	**boliviano(-a)** (boh-lee-VYAH-noh[-nah])
Brazil	**el Brasil** (ehl brah-SEEL)	**brasileño(-a)** (brah-see-LEH-nyoh[-nyah])
Canada	**Canadá** (kah-nah-DAH)	**canadiense** (kah-nah-DYEHN-seh)
Chile	**Chile** (CHEE-leh)	**chileno(-a)** (chee-LEH-noh[-nah])
China	**la China** (lah CHEE-nah)	**chino(-a)** (CHEE-noh[-nah])

173

Colombia	**Colombia** (koh-LOHM-byah)	**colombiano(-a)** (koh-lohm-BYAH-noh[-nah])
Costa Rica	**Costa Rica** (KOHS-tah RREE-kah)	**costarricense** (kohs-tah-rree-SEHN-seh)
Cuba	**Cuba** (KOO-bah)	**cubano(-a)** (koo-BAH-noh[-nah])
Denmark	**Dinamarca** (dee-nah-MAHR-kah)	**danés(a)** (dah-NEHS[NEH-sah])
Dominican Republic	**la República Dominicana** (lah rreh-POO-blee-kah doh-mee-nee-KAH-nah)	**dominicano(-a)** (doh-mee-nee-KAH-noh [-nah])
Ecuador	**Ecuador** (eh-kwah-DOHR)	**ecuatoriano(-a)** (eh-kwah-toh-RYAH-noh [-nah])
Egypt	**Egipto** (eh-HEEP-toh)	**egipcio(-a)** (eh-HEEP-syoh[-syah])
El Salvador	**El Salvador** (ehl sahl-vah-DOHR)	**salvadoreño(-a)** (sahl-vah-doh-REH-nyoh [-nyah])
England	**Inglaterra** (een-glah-TEH-rrah)	**inglés(-glesa)** (een-GLEHS[-GLEH-sah])
Finland	**Finlandia** (feen-LAHN-dyah)	**finlandés(-désa)** (feen-lahn-DEHS[-DEH-sah])
France	**Francia** (FRAHN-syah)	**francés(-cesa)** (frahn-SEHS[-SEH-sah])
Germany	**Alemania** (ah-leh-MAH-nyah)	**alemán(-mana)** (ah-leh-MAHN[-MAH-nah])
Greece	**Grecia** (GRE-syah)	**griego(-a)** (GRYEH-goh[-gah])
Guatemala	**Guatemala** (gwah-teh-MAH-lah)	**guatemalteco(-a)** (gwah-teh-mahl-TEH-koh [-kah])

174

Holland	**Holanda** (oh-LAHN-dah)	**holandés(-desa)** (oh-lahn-DEHS[-DEH-sah])
Honduras	**Honduras** (ohn-DOO-rahs)	**hondureño(-a)** (ohn-doo-REH-nyoh[-nyah])
Iceland	**Islandia** (ees-LAHN-dyah)	**islandés(-desa)** (ees-lahn-DEHS[-DEH-sah])
Ireland	**Irlanda** (eer-LAHN-dah)	**irlandés(-desa)** (eer-lahn-DEHS[-DEH-sah])
Israel	**Israel** (ees-rah-EHL)	**israelí** (ees-rah-eh-LEE)
Italy	**Italia** (ee-TAH-lyah)	**italiano(-a)** (ee-tah-LYAH-noh[-nah])
Japan	**el Japón** (ehl hah-POHN)	**japonés(-nesa)** (hah-poh-NEHS[-NEH-sah])
Mexico	**México** (MEH-hee-koh)	**mexicano(-a)** (meh-hee-KAH-noh[-nah])
Nicaragua	**Nicaragua** (nee-kah-RAH-gwah)	**nicaragüense** (nee-kah-rah-GWEHN-seh)
Norway	**Noruega** (noh-RWEH-gah)	**noruego(-a)** (noh-RWEH-goh[-gah])
Panama	**Panamá** (pah-nah-MAH)	**panameño(-a)** (pah-nah-MEH-nyoh[-nyah])
Paraguay	**Paraguay** (pah-rah-GWY)	**paraguayo(-a)** (pah-rah-GWAH-yoh[-yah])
Peru	**el Perú** (ehl peh-ROO)	**peruano(-a)** (peh-RWAH-noh[-nah])
Poland	**Polonia** (poh-LOH-nyah)	**polaco(-a)** (poh-LAH-koh[-kah])
Portugal	**Portugal** (pohr-too-GAHL)	**portugués(-guesa)** (pohr-too-GEHS[-GEH-sah])
Puerto Rico	**Puerto Rico** (PWEHR-toh RREE-koh)	**puertorriqueño(-a)** (pwehr-toh-rree-KEH-nyoh[-nyah])

175

Russia	**Rusia** (RROO-syah)	**ruso(-a)** (RROO-soh[-sah])
Spain	**España** (ehs-PAH-nyah)	**español(-a)** (ehs-pah-NYOHL[-NYOH-lah])
Sweden	**Suecia** (SWEH-syah)	**sueco(-a)** (SWEH-koh[-kah])
Switzerland	**Suiza** (SWEE-sah)	**suizo(-a)** (SUEE-soh[-sah])
Turkey	**Turquía** (toor-KEE-ah)	**turco(-a)** (TOOR-koh[-kah])
United States	**los Estados Unidos** (lohs ehs-TAH-dohs oo-NEE-dohs)	**estadounidense** (ehs-tah-doh-oo-nee-DEHN-seh)
Uruguay	**el Uruguay** (ehl oo-roo-GWY)	**uruguayo(-a)** (oo-roo-GWAH-yoh[-yah])
Venezuela	**Venezuela** (veh-neh-SWEH-lah)	**venezolano(-a)** (veh-neh-soh-LAH-noh[-nah])

LANGUAGES

Names of languages—*lenguas* (LEHN-gwahs), or *idiomas* (ee-DYOH-mahs)—are usually the same as the masculine form of the nationality. For example, the words for the German and Italian languages are *alemán* (ah-leh-MAHN) and *italiano* (ee-tah-LYAH-noh). Likewise, to say, "I speak Spanish," you say, "Yo hablo español" (yoh AH-bloh ehs-pah-NYOHL), or for "I speak English," you say, "Yo hablo inglés" (yoh AH-bloh een-GLEHS).

COLORS

red	**rojo**	RROH-hoh
yellow	**amarillo**	ah-mah-REE-yoh
green	**verde**	VEHR-deh

blue	**azul**	ah-SOOL
white	**blanco**	BLAHN-koh
brown	**café** (*or*) **marrón**	kah-FEH mah-RROHN
orange	**anaranjado**	ah-nah-rahn-HAH-doh
purple	**morado**	moh-RAH-doh
black	**negro**	NEH-groh
gold	**dorado**	doh-RAH-doh
silver	**plateado**	plah-teh-AH-doh

OCCUPATIONS

Professions	**Profesiones**	pro-feh-SYOH-nehs
architect	**arquitecto(-a)**	ahr-kee-TEHK-toh (-tah)
artist	**artista**	ahr-TEES-tah
cardiologist	**cardiólogo(-a)**	kahr-DYOH-loh-goh (-gah)
dentist	**dentista**	dehn-TEES-tah
doctor	**médico(-a)**	MEH-dee-koh(-kah)
engineer	**ingeniero(-a)**	een-heh-NYEH-roh (-rah)
eye doctor	**optometrista**	ohp-toh-meh-TREES-tah
lawyer	**abogado(-a)**	ah-boh-GHAH-doh
neurologist	**neurólogo(-a)**	nehw-ROH-log-goh (-gah)
ophthalmologist	**oftalmólogo(-a)**	ohf-tahl-MOH-loh-goh(-gah)

painter	**pintor(-a)**	peen-TOHR(-TOH-rah)
sculptor	**escultor(-a)**	ehs-kool-TOHR(-TOH-rah)
writer	**escritor(-a)**	ehs-kree-TOHR(-TOH-rah)
Occupations	**Oficios**	oh-FEE-syohs
accountant	**contador(-a)**	kohn-tah-DOHR (-DOH-rah)
baker	**panadero(-a)**	pah-nah-DEH-roh (-rah)
blacksmith	**herrero**	eh-RREH-roh
butcher	**carnicero(-a)**	kahr-nee-SEH-roh (-rah)
carpenter	**carpintero**	kahr-peen-TEH-roh
clerk	**oficinista**	oh-fee-see-NEES-tah
cook	**cocinero(-a)**	koh-see-NEH-roh (-rah)
electrician	**electricista**	eh-lehk-tree-SEES-tah
locksmith	**cerrajero**	seh-rrah-HEH-roh
maid	**serviente(-a)**	seer-VYEHN-teh(-tah)
nurse	**enfermero(-a)**	ehn-fehr-MEH-roh (-rah)
plumber	**plomero**	ploh-MEH-roh
salesperson	**vendedor(-a)**	vehn-deh-DOHR (-DOH-rah)
shoemaker	**zapatero**	sah-pah-TEH-roh
shopkeeper	**negociante**	neh-goh-SYAHN-teh
waiter	**mesero(-a) (*Mexico*)**	meh-SEH-roh(-rah)
	(*or*) mozo (*Spain*)	moh-soh

SIGNS

Abierto	ah-BYEHR-toh	Open
Arriba	ah-RREE-bah	Up
Alto	AHL-toh	Stop
Ascensor	ah-sehn-SOHR	Elevator
Bienvenidos	byen-veh-NEE-dohs	Welcome
Caballeros	kah-bah-YEH-rohs	Gentlemen
Caja	KAH-hah	Cashier
Caliente (C)	kah-LYEHN-teh	Hot
Cambio	KAHM-byoh	Exchange
Cerrado	seh-RRAH-doh	Closed
Completo	kohm-PLEH-toh	Full
Cuidado	kwee-DAH-doh	Watch Out
Damas	DAH-mahs	Ladies
Empuje	ehm-POO-heh	Push
Entrada	ehn-TRAH-dah	Entrance
Frío (F)	FREE-oh	Cold
Jale	HAH-leh	Pull
Libre	LEE-breh	Vacant
Liquidación	lee-kee-dah-SYOHN	Close-out Sale
No fumar	Noh foo-MAHR	No Smoking
No hay paso	noh ahy PAH-soh	Do Not Enter
No pisar el césped	noh pee-SAHR ehl SEHS-pehd	Keep Off the Grass
No pisar el zacate (*Mexico*)	noh pee-SAHR ehl sah-KAH-teh	Keep Off the Grass
No tocar	noh toh-KAHR	Do Not Touch
Ocupado	oh-koo-PAH-doh	Busy, Occupied
Pase	PAH-seh	Walk, Cross

179

Peligro	peh-LEE-groh	Danger
Prohibido	proh-ee-BEE-doh	Forbidden
Prohibido el paso	proh-ee-BEE-doh ehl PAH-soh	No Entrance, Keep Out
Prohibido tomar fotografías	proh-ee-BEE-doh toh-MAHR foh-toh-grah-FEE-ahs	No Pictures Allowed
Rebajas	rreh-BAH-hahs	Sale
Remate	rreh-MAH-teh	Auction
Reservado	rreh-sehr-VAH-doh	Reserved
Salida	sah-LEE-dah	Exit
Se alquila	seh ahl-KEE-lah	For Rent
Se vende	seh VEHN-deh	For Sale
Tire	TEE-reh	Pull
Veneno	veh-NEH-noh	Poison
Venta	VEHN-tah	Sale

ABBREVIATIONS

Sr.	**señor**	Mr.
Sra.	**señora**	Mrs.
Srta.	**señorita**	Miss/Ms.
Dr.	**Doctor**	Dr. (Doctor)
Prof.	**Profesor**	Prof. (Professor)
Ud.	**usted**	you
Uds.	**ustedes**	you (*plural*)
Tel.	**teléfono**	Tel. (telephone)
Apdo.	**Apartado de correos**	P.O. Box
Av.	**Avenida**	Ave. (Avenue)

c/	**Calle**	St. (Street)
Edo.	**Estado**	State
EE.UU.	**Estados Unidos**	U.S. (United States)
Cía.	**Compañía**	Co. (Company)
S.A.	**Sociedad Anónima**	Inc. (Incorporated)
Ltda.	**Limitada**	Ltd. (Limited)
FF.CC.	**Ferrocarriles**	Railroads
RENFE	**Red Nacional de Ferrocarriles Españoles**	National Railroad Network (*Spain*)

EMERGENCIES

Look!	**¡Mire!**	MEE-reh!
Listen!	**¡Eschuche!**	ehs-KOO-cheh!
Watch out!	**¡Cuidado!**	kuee-DAH-doh!
Fire!	**¡Fuego!**	FWEH-goh!
Help!	**¡Ayuda!**	ah-YOO-dah!
Help me!	**¡Socorro!**	soh-KOH-rroh!
Hurry!	**¡Dése prisa!**	DEH-seh PREE-sah!
Stop!	**¡Alto!**	AHL-toh!
I need help quick!	**¡Necesito ayuda, pronto!**	neh-seh-SEE-toh ah-YOO-dah, PROHN-toh!
Can you help me?	**¿Puede ayudarme?**	PWEH-deh ah-yoo-DAHR-meh?
Police!	**¡Policía!**	poh-lee-SEE-ah!
I need a policeman!	**¡Necesito un policía!**	neh-seh-SEE-toh oon poh-lee-SEE-ah!
It's an emergency!	**¡Es una emergencia!**	ehs OO-nah eh-mehr-HEHN-syah!

181

Leave me alone!	¡Déjeme en paz!	DEH-heh-meh ehn pahs!
That man's a thief!	¡Ese hombre es un ladrón!	EH-seh OHM-breh ehs oon-lah-DROHN!
Stop him!	¡Deténganlo!	deh-TEHN-gahn-loh!

He's stolen my
- pocketbook.
- wallet.
- passport.

- watch.

Me ha robado
- **la cartera.**
- **la billetera.**
- **el pasaporte.**

- **el reloj.**

meh ah rroh-BAH-doh
- lah kahr-teh-rah
- lah bee-yeh-TEH-rah
- ehl pah-sah-POHR-teh
- ehl rreh-LOH

I've lost my
- suitcase.
- money.
- glasses.

car keys.

He perdido
- **mi maleta.**
- **mi dinero.**
- **los anteojos.**

- **las llaves de mi automóvil.**

eh pehr-DEE-doh
- mee mah-LEH-tah
- mee dee-neh-roh
- lohs ahn-teh-OH-hohs
- lahs YAH-vehs deh mee ow-toh-MOH-beel

182

15/GRAMMAR IN BRIEF

The format of this book allows you to find and use essential phrases without formal study of the grammar. However, by learning some of the basic patterns of the language, you will also be able to construct your own sentences. No book can predict or contain every sentence a traveler may need to use or understand, so any time you invest in learning grammatical patterns will contribute to your ability to communicate.

DEFINITE AND INDEFINITE ARTICLES

Spanish articles have several different forms because Spanish nouns have gender—which means that they are viewed as either masculine or feminine—and an article must agree in gender with its noun. The article must also agree with its noun in number—singular or plural. For example, *pasaporte* (passport) is masculine; hence the article it takes might be either *un* or *el* (*un pasaporte* or *el pasaporte*). Likewise, *maleta* (suitcase) is feminine, and its article might be *una* or *la*. The plural form of the masculine or feminine articles would be used if the nouns were plural. Finally, Spanish definite articles contract with prepositions in two cases, which occur frequently. The chart below outlines the uses of the various articles.

	Indefinite Definite	Definite with	Prepositions *de* (of) *a* (to)	
Masculine, singular	**un** (a)	**el** (the)	**del** (of the) [*de* + *el* = *del*]	**al** (to the) [*a* + *el* = *al*]
Feminine, singular	**una** (a)	**la** (the)	**de la** (of the)	**a la** (to the)
Masculine, plural	**unos** (some)	**los** (the)	**de los** (of the)	**a los** (to the)
Feminine, plural	**unas** (some)	**las** (the)	**de las** (of the)	**a las** (to the)

Definite articles are used in Spanish more than they are in English. They are used with:

1. abstract nouns	**la libertad**
2. certain countries and cities	**el Japón; la Habana; el Ecuador**
3. countries and cities when qualified	**el Brasil hermoso; la Lima señorial**
4. days of weeks, seasons	**llegó el lunes; voy en la primavera**
5. verbal nouns	**el viajar es muy costoso**
6. names of languages	**el español es fácil**
7. titles (when not in direct address)	**éste es el señor Fernández**
8. parts of the body and articles of clothing (instead of the possessive adjective used in English)	**me duele la cabeza** (my head hurts); **me puse la camisa** (I put on my shirt)

Articles are omitted:

1. with simple predicate nouns [Except: when the predicate noun is modified by an adjective]	**mi tío es abogado** (my uncle is a lawyer) **[mi tío es un buen abogado** (my uncle is a good lawyer)]
2. with otro(-a)	**quiero otro libro** (I want another book)

Other aspects of articles in Spanish to take into account are:
1. Definite and indefinite articles are used to convert adjectives into nouns: *un joven* (a young man); *la vieja* (the old woman).
2. There is also a neutral (no gender), definite article, *lo*, which is used with adjectival nouns (which always appear with a masculine ending), as in *lo bello* (the beautiful).
3. The neutral, definite article, *lo* (in both singular and plural forms), is also used to convert possessive pronouns into nouns: *lo mío* (that which is mine); *lo tuyo* (that which is yours).

NOUNS

Nouns in Spanish are either masculine or feminine. As a general rule, words ending in *-o* are masculine, while words ending in *-a, -d,* or *-cion* are feminine. [Two exceptions worth nothing: *el día* (the day) and *la mano* (the hand), which are masculine and feminine, respectively.] With other endings, you simply have to learn the gender when you learn the words.

To form the plural of nouns ending in *-o* or *-a,* just add *-s.* If a word ends in a consonant, then add *-es.*

el pasaporte (the passport) **los pasaportes** (the passports)

la oficina (the office) **las oficinas** (the offices)
un boleto (a ticket) **unos boletos** (some tickets)
una maleta (a suitcase) **unas maletas** (some suitcases)

ADJECTIVES
Descriptive Adjectives

Most adjectives agree in number and gender with the noun they accompany. Unlike English adjectives, adjectives in Spanish, with few exceptions (e.g., *gran* and *buen*), usually follow the noun.

el señor viejo (the old man)
la señora vieja (the old woman)
los señores viejos (the old men)
las señoras viejas (the old women)

When an adjective ends in *-e* it does not change to agree with the noun in gender. The plural is formed by adding *-s* to the singular.

el señor inteligente (the intelligent man)
la señora inteligente (the intelligent woman)
los señores inteligentes (the intelligent men)
las señoras inteligentes (the intelligent women)

If an adjective ends in a consonant, such as: *difícil* (difficult), *común* (common), *cruel* (cruel), there is no change for gender. Plurals of both masculine and feminine are formed by adding *-es* to the singular.

un ejercicio difícil (a difficult exercise)
una tarea difícil (a difficult task)
unos ejercicios difíciles (some difficult exercises)
unas tareas difíciles (some difficult tasks)

[Exception: Adjectives ending in *-ón*, *-án*, or *-or* add *-a* form the feminine, as in *trabajador, trabajadora*.]

Demonstrative Adjectives

Singular		Plural	
este, esta	this (near me)	**estos, estas**	these (near me)
ese, esa	this (near you)	**esos, esas**	these (near you)
aquel, aquella	that (remote)	**aquellos, aquellas**	those (remote)

Possessive Adjectives

Singular	Plural	
mi	**mis**	my
tu	**tus**	your (sing., familiar)
nuestro(-a)	**nuestros(-as)**	our
vuestro(-a)	**vuestros(-as)**	your (pl., familiar/Spain only)
su	**sus**	his, her, its, their, your (sing., formal; and pl.)

186

The possessive adjective must agree in gender and number with the noun it modifies:

Mi cuarto es bonito.	(My room is pretty.)	
Mis cuartos son bonitos.	(My rooms are pretty.)	
Su hija es bonita.	(Her/his daughter is pretty.) [or]	(your [sing., formal; or pl.] daughter is pretty.)
Sus hijas son bonitas.	(Her/his daughters are pretty.)	(your [sing., formal; or pl.] daughter is pretty.)

ADVERBS

Adverbs of Manner

In English, -*ly* is added to an adjective to form an adverb. Spanish forms adverbs by adding -*mente* to the feminine form of an adjective.

Adjective		Adverb
(Masc.)	**(Fem.)**	
lento	**lenta**	**lentamente** (slowly)
rápido	**rápida**	**rápidamente** (rapidly)
fácil	**fácil***	**fácilmente** (easily)

[Exceptions: *despacio* (slow or slowly), *demasiado* (too much).]

**Note:* The feminine and masculine forms of this word are the same.

Affirmative and Interrogative Adverbs

donde (where)	**dónde** (where?)
como (how, as)	**cómo** (how?)

| **cuando** (when) | **cuándo** (when?) |
| **cuanto** (as much as) | **cuánto** (how much?) |

COMPARISONS WITH ADJECTIVES AND ADVERBS

In Spanish, you form the comparative by placing the word *más* (more) before the noun, adjective, or adverb compared, followed by the word *que*.

más caro que (more expensive than)
más antiguo que (older than)
más·despacio que (more slowly than)

Most adjectives and adverbs are regular in the formation of their comparatives, as above.

The superlative is formed by adding the corresponding definite article before the comparative.

el (libro) más caro (the most expensive book)
la (casa) más antigua (the oldest house)
los libros más caros (the most expensive books)
las casas más antiguas (the oldest houses)

A common exception, however, is *bueno* (good), whose comparative form is *mejor* (better).

The superlative is formed by adding the definite article before *mejor.*

PRONOUNS

Personal Pronouns

The pronoun takes the place of the subject in a sentence, and assumes its gender and number.

188

Subject Pronoun		Indirect Object Pronouns		Direct Object Pronouns	
yo	I	**me**	to me	**me**	me
tú	you (familiar)	**te**	to you	**te**	you
vos	you (familiar/Arg., Uru., & Central America)	**te**	to you	**te**	you
usted	you (formal)	**le**	to you	**lo** (m.) **la** (f.)	you
él	he	**le**	to him	**lo**	him
ella	she	**le**	to her	**la** **lo**	her it
nosotros	we	**nos**	to us	**nos**	us
vosotros	you (familiar/Spain only)	**os**	to you	**os**	you
ustedes	you (formal or familiar in Latin America; formal in Spain)	**les**	to you	**los** (m.) **las** (f.)	you
ellos	they (m.)	**les**	to them	**los** (m.)	them
ellas	they (f.)	**les**	to them	**las** (f.)	them

Note: With plural pronouns, the masculine form is used when referring both to a group (more than one) of males and to a group composed of both males and females.

Reflexive Pronouns

Reflexive pronouns are used when the action of the verb reflects back on the subject. Prepositional reflexive pronouns are used following prepositions.

	Simple Reflexive	Prepo-sitional	
(yo)	me	mí	myself
(tú)	te	ti	yourself
(vos)	te	vos	yourself
(él/ella)	se	sí	himself herself itself
(usted)	se	usted	yourself
(nosotros)	nos	nosotros	ourselves
(vosotros) [Spain]	os	vosotros	yourselves
(ustedes) [Lat. Amer.]	se	ustedes	themselves
(ellos/ellas)	se	sí	themselves
(ustedes)	se	sí	yourselves

Some common verbs can become reflexive by adding -se to the infinitive, producing changes such as:

lavar (to wash)
despertar (to wake up)

vestir (to dress)

lavarse (to wash [oneself])
despertarse (to wake [oneself] up)

vestirse (to dress [oneself])

Here are some common reflexive verbs:

despertarse (to wake up)
levantarse (to get up)
lavarse (to get washed)
bañarse (to bathe oneself)
peinarse (to get combed)

arreglarse (to fix oneself up)
vestirse (to get dressed)
desvestirse (to get undressed)
acostarse (to go to bed)
irse (to go away)

Relative Pronouns

Relative pronouns must always be expressed in Spanish. They are:

que	who, whom, which, that (invariable; refers to persons or things)
quien, quienes	who, whom, that (inflected for number only, and refers to persons only)
(el/la) cual (que); (los/las) cuales (que)	whom, which (used for clarity)
cuyo, cuya, cuyos, cuyas	whose (possessive, and must precede and agree in gender and number with person or thing possessed)

Interrogative Pronouns

The interrogative pronouns are relative pronouns used to ask questions. They differ from relative pronouns in that they bear an accent mark:

Singular	Plural	
¿quién?	¿quiénes?	who?, whom?
¿cuál?	¿cuáles?	which?
¿qué?		what?
¿cuánto(-a)?	¿cuántos(-as)?	how much?/how many?

Demonstrative Pronouns

Demonstrative pronouns have written accents to distinguish them from the demonstrative adjectives:

Singular		Plural	
éste, ésta	this (near me)	**éstos, éstas**	these (near me)
ése, ésa	that (near you)	**ésos, ésas**	those (near you)
aquél, aquélla	that (yonder)	**aquéllos, aquéllas**	those (yonder)

PREPOSITIONS

Some of the most common prepositions in Spanish are:

a (at, to, with time)
con (with)
contra (against)
de (from, of, about)
en (in, on)
entre (between, among)
hacia (towards)

hasta (until, up to)
para (for, in order to, to)
por (for, by, through, because)
según (according to)
sin (without)
sobre (on, about)

Some prepositions combine with other words to form compounds.

además de (besides, in addition to)
al lado de (beside, at the side of)
antes de (before [references to time])
cerca de (near)
debajo de (under, underneath)
delante de (in front of)
dentro de (inside of, within)

después de (after)
detrás de (behind)
en vez de (instead of)
encima de (on top of)
enfrente de (in front of, facing, opposite)
fuera de (outside of)
lejos de (far from)

NEGATIVE SENTENCES

To form the negative in Spanish, place the word *no* in front of the verb. For example:

Yo hablo español. (I speak Spanish.)
Yo **no** *hablo español.* (I don't speak Spanish.)

When the personal subject pronoun is omitted, then the phrase starts with *no*.

Viajo mañana. (I travel tomorrow.)
No *viajo mañana.* (I don't travel tomorrow.)

Other negative words are:

nada (nothing)   **ninguno**(-a) (none)
nadie (no one/nobody)   **tampoco** (neither)
nunca (never)

Unlike *no*, all of these words can go before or after the verb. They can also be used along with the negative *no*. Sometimes there may even be as many as three negatives in a single sentence:

No dio nada a nadie. (He did not give anything to anyone. [literally: He did *not* give *nothing* to *no one.*])

QUESTIONS

Questions are easy to form in Spanish, and can be done in several ways. The simplest form is to raise your voice at the end of a statement to indicate a question, similar to what is done in English. For example: *"Vas a México"* (You are going to Mexico) becomes: *"¿Vas a México?"* (You are going to Mexico?). Notice, however, that Spanish includes an "upside-down" question mark in front of the written sentence as well as the "right-side-up" one at the end.

A second easy way to form a question is to invert the order of the subject and verb. This again is similar to what is done in English. *"Usted tiene un boleto"* (You have a ticket) becomes: *"¿Tiene usted un boleto?"* (Do you have a ticket?).

VERBS

There are three verb conjugations in Spanish. In the infinitive, all verbs end in either *-ar, -er,* or *-ir.* Regular verbs are conjugated as follows:

-ar hablar (I) (to talk)	*-er* comer (II) (to eat)	*-ir* vivir (III) (to live)
Present Tense		
yo **hablo**	**como**	**vivo**
tú **hablas**	**comes**	**vives**
usted **habla**	**come**	**come**
él/ella **habla**	**come**	**vive**
nosotros **hablamos**	**comemos**	**vivimos**
vosotros **habláis**	**coméis**	**vivís**
ustedes **hablan**	**comen**	**viven**
ellos/ellas **hablan**	**comen**	**viven**
Past Tense (Preterite)		
yo **hablé**	**comí**	**viví**
tú **hablaste**	**comiste**	**viviste**
usted **habló**	**comió**	**vivió**
él/ella **habló**	**comió**	**vivió**
nosotros **hablamos**	**comimos**	**vivimos**
vosotros **hablasteis**	**comisteis**	**vivisteis**
ustedes **hablaron**	**comieron**	**vivieron**
ellos/ellas **hablaron**	**comieron**	**vivieron**

Other regular verbs which follow these patterns are: **comprar** (to buy), **viajar** (to travel), **beber** (to drink), **perder** (to lose), **partir** (to leave), and **pedir** (to ask for).

Irregular Verbs

Some commonly used verbs which do not follow the patterns given above, and have slightly irregular forms, are:

dar (to give)	*hacer* (to do/make)	*decir* (to tell/say)
Present Tense		
yo **doy**	**hago**	**digo**
tú **das**	**haces**	**dices**
usted **da**	**hace**	**dice**
él/ella **da**	**hace**	**dice**
nosotros **damos**	**hacemos**	**decimos**
vosotros **dais**	**hacéis**	**decís**
ustedes **dan**	**hacen**	**dicen**
ellos/ellas **dan**	**hacen**	**dicen**
Past Tense (Preterite)		
yo **di**	**hice**	**dije**
tú **diste**	**hiciste**	**dijiste**
usted **dio**	**hizo**	**dijo**
él/ella **dio**	**hizo**	**dijo**
nosotros **dimos**	**hicimos**	**dijimos**
vosotros **disteis**	**hicisteis**	**dijisteis**
ustedes **dieron**	**hicieron**	**dijeron**
ellos/ellas **dieron**	**hicieron**	**dijeron**

tener (to have)	*poder* (to be able/can)	*ver* (to see)
Present Tense		
yo **tengo**	puedo	veo
tú **tienes**	puedes	ves
usted **tiene**	puede	ve
él/ella **tiene**	puede	ve
nosotros **tenemos**	podemos	vemos
vosotros **tenéis**	podéis	véis
ustedes **tienen**	pueden	ven
ellos/ellas **tienen**	pueden	ven
Past Tense (Preterite)		
yo **tuve**	pude	vi
tú **tuviste**	pudiste	viste
usted **tuvo**	pudo	vio
él/ella **tuvo**	pudo	vio
nosotros **tuvimos**	pudimos	vimos
vosotros **tuvisteis**	pudisteis	visteis
ustedes **tuvieron**	pudieron	vieron
ellos/ellas **tuvieron**	pudieron	vieron

ir (to go)

Present Tense

yo **voy**	nosotros **vamos**
tú **vas**	vosotros **váis**
usted **va**	ustedes **van**
él/ella **va**	ellos/ellas **van**

196

Future Tense

There are two ways of forming the future in Spanish. One is the simple future, which requires only a spelling change; the other is formed with the verb "to go to" plus an infinitive. Use depends on the region of the Spanish-speaking world you are in. Although both convey the idea of the future, the meanings are slightly different:

Hablaré con el gerente. (I will speak to the manager.)
Voy a hablar con el gerente. (I am going to speak to the manager.)

The endings for the simple future of regular verbs for all three conjugations are demonstrated below.

yo **hablaré**	**comeré**	**viviré**
tú **hablarás**	**comerás**	**vivirás**
usted **hablará**	**comerá**	**vivirá**
él/ella **hablará**	**comerá**	**vivirá**
nosotros **hablaremos**	**comeremos**	**viviremos**
vosotros **hablaréis**	**comeréis**	**viviréis**
ustedes **hablarán**	**comerán**	**vivirán**
ellos/ellas **hablarán**	**comerán**	**vivirán**

To form the future with "going to," just add the preposition *a* and leave the verb in the infinitive:

Voy a comer. (I am going to eat.)
Voy a viajar. (I am going to travel.)

Note that the personal subject pronoun is sometimes omitted. This is possible since the verb ending indicates the person referred to. An exception is made sometimes when there is need to clarify or stress the persons referred to. This is common, for example, when the third person singular or plural is involved *(él, ella, ellos, ellas)*, in which case one might say:

Ella va a comer. (She is going to eat.)

197

Verbs *Ser* and *Estar*

The verb "to be" is expressed in Spanish by two different verbs: **ser** and **estar**.

Ser is conjugated as follows:		*Estar* is conjugated as follows:	
yo **soy**	I am	yo **estoy**	I am
tú **eres**	you are	tu **estás**	you are
usted **es**	you are	usted **está**	you are
él/ella **es**	he/she/it is	el/ella **está**	he/she/it is
nosotros **somos**	we are	nosotros **estamos**	we are
vosotros **sois**	you are	vosotros **estáis**	you are
ustedes **son**	you are	ustedes **están**	you are
ellos/ella **son**	they are	ellos/ellas **están**	they are

These examples show how the verbs are used:

ser

1. Used in impersonal expressions:

¿Qué hora es? (What time is it?)
Es hermoso. (It's beautiful.)

2. With prepositions, except those expressing temporary place at, or location in:

Es para mí. (It's for me.)
El es de Colombia. (He's from Colombia.)

3. With a predicate noun or pronoun:

Son nuestros. (They're ours.)

4. With predicate adjectives to express an inherent quality:

Es bueno. (It's good.)
Somos mexicanos. (We're Mexicans.)

estar

1. To express temporary location:

Estoy aquí. (I'm here.)
Está en la casa. (He's in the house.)

2. With an adjective that does not express an inherent quality:

Está contento. (He's happy.)
Estoy cansado. [temporary condition] (I'm tired.)

3. To form progressive tenses:

Estoy comiendo.* (I'm eating.)
Estoy viajando.* (I'm traveling.)
Estoy viviendo.* (I'm living.)

Note: *The gerund (present participle) is formed as follows:
-ar verbs drop the -ar ending from the infinitive and add -ando.
-er verbs drop the -er ending from the infinitive and add -iendo.
-ir verbs drop the -ir ending and add -iendo.

Special Uses of *Tener* and *Hacer*

Tener is used to express *to be* in cases such as: to be thirsty, to be hungry, to be cold, to be warm, to be . . . years old.

Tengo hambre. (I am hungry.)
¿Tienes sed? (Are you thirsty?)
Tenemos calor. (We are hot/warm.)
Tienen frío. (They are cold.)
Tiene veinte años. (He is twenty years old.)

Hacer is also used to express the idea of *to be.* It is always used in the third person singular.

Hace frío. (It is cold.)
Hace calor. (It is hot/warm.)

Finally, *hacer* is used in expressions of time, as when referring to the length of time since an event took place or to the continuation of an action through time.

Hace tres meses leí ese libro. (I read that book three months ago.)
Hace diez años que vivo en esta casa. (I have lived in this house for ten years.)

ENGLISH-SPANISH DICTIONARY

List of Abbreviations

abbr. *abbreviated as*
adj. *adjective*
conj. *conjunction*
f. *feminine noun*
m. *masculine noun*
Mex. *Mexico usage*

pl. *plural*
pron. *pronoun*
sing. *singular*
Sp. *Spain usage*
v. *verb*
w/ *with*

A

a, an un, una (f.) *(oon, OO-nah)*

able, to be poder *(poh-DEHR)*

about acerca de *(ah-SEHR-kah deh)*

above arriba, encima de *(ah-RREE-bah, ehn-SEE-mah deh)*

abscess abceso (m.) *(ahb-SEH-soh)*

accelerator acelerador (m.) *(ah-seh-leh-rah-DOHR)*

accept aceptar *(ah-sehp-TAHR)*

accident accidente (m.) *(ahk-see-DEHN-teh)*

ache, head dolor de cabeza (m.) *(doh-LOHR deh kah-BEH-sah)*

stomachache dolor de estómago *(doh-LOHR deh ehs-TOH-mah-goh)*

toothache dolor de muelas *(doh-LOHR deh MWEH-lahs)*

across a través de *(ah trah-VEHS deh)*

address dirección (f.) *(dee-rehk-SYOHN)*

adhesive tape esparadrapo (m.) *(ehs-pah-rah-DRAH-poh)*

adjust ajustar, arreglar *(ah-hoos-TAHR, ah-rreh-GLAHR)*

admittance, no se prohibe la entrada *(seh proh-EE-beh lah ehn-TRAH-dah)*

afraid, to be tener miedo *(teh-NEHR MYEH-doh)*

after después de *(dehs-PWEHS deh)*

afternoon tarde (f.) *(TAHR-deh)*

again otra vez, de nuevo *(OH-trah vehs, deh NWEH-voh)*

against contra *(KOHN-trah)*

ago hace (with time expressions) *(AH-seh)*

agree estar de acuerdo *(ehs-TAHR deh ah-KWEHR-doh)*

ahead adelante *(ah-deh-LAHN-teh)*

aid ayuda (f.) *(ah-YOO-dah)*; **first aid** primeros auxilios (m.pl.) *(pree MEH rohs owk-SEE-lyohs)*

air aire (m.) *(AHY-reh)*; **airmail** correo aéreo (m.) *(koh-RREH-oh ah-EH-reh-oh)*

airline línea aérea (f.) *(LEE-neh-ah ah-EH-reh-ah)*

airplane avión (m.)*(ah-VYOHN)*

airport aeropuerto (m.) *(ah-eh-roh-PWEHR-toh)*

alarm clock despertador (m.) *(dehs-pehr-tah-DOHR)*

all todo *(TOH-doh)*

allow permitir *(pehr-mee-TEER)*

almond almendra (f.) *(ahl-MEHN-drah)*

almost casi *(KAH-see)*

alone solo *(SOH-loh)*

already ya *(yah)*

also también *(tahm-BYEHN)*

always siempre *(SYEHM-preh)*

a.m. de (por) la mañana *(deh [pohr] lah mah-NYAH-nah)*

am, I soy, estoy *(sohy, ehs-TOHY)*

American norteamericano (-a) *(nohr-teh-ah-meh-ree-KAH-noh)(-nah)*

among entre *(EHN-treh)*

and y *(ee)*

ankle tobillo (m.) *(toh-BEE-yoh)*

annoy molestar *(moh-lehs-TAHR)*

another otro *(OH-troh)*

answer (response) respuesta (f.) *(rrehs-PWEHS-tah)*

any algún *(ahl-GOON)*

anybody (anyone) alguien *(AHL-gyehn)*

anything algo *(AHL-goh)*; **anything else?** ¿algo más? *(AHL-goh mahs?)*

apartment piso (m./Sp.), apartamento (m.) *(PEE-soh, ah-pahr-tah-MEHN-toh)*

aperitif aperitivo (m.) *(ah-peh-ree-TEE-voh)*

appetizers entremeses (m.pl.), bocadillos (m.pl.) *(ehn-treh-MEH-sehs, boh-kah-DEE-yohs)*

apple manzana (f.) *(mahn-SAH-nah)*

apricot albaricoque (m.) *(ahl-bah-ree-KOH-keh)*

April abril (m.) *(ah-BREEL)*

Arab árabe *(AH-rah-beh)*

are, they son; están *(sohn; ehs-TAHN)*

Argentine argentino(-a) *(ahr-hehn-TEE-noh)(-nah)*

arm brazo (m.) *(BRAH-soh)*

armchair sillón (m.) *(see-YOHN)*

around alrededor de *(ahl-reh-deh-DOHR deh)*

arrival llegada (f.) *(yeh-GAH-dah)*

article artículo (m.) *(ahr-TEE-koo-loh)*

as como *(KOH-moh)*

ashtray cenicero (m.) *(seh-nee-SEH-roh)*

ask (a question) preguntar *(preh-goon-TAHR);*
  ask for pedir *(peh-DEER)*
asparagus espárragos (m.pl.) *(ehs-PAH-rrah-gohs)*
aspirin aspirina (f.) *(ahs-pee-REE-nah)*
at en; a *(ehn; ah);*
  at once en seguida *(ehn seh-GEE-dah)*
attention atención (f.); cuidado (m.) *(ah-tehn-SYOHN; kuee-DAH-doh)*
August agosto (m.) *(ah-GOHS-toh)*
aunt tía (f.) *(TEE-ah)*
Austrian austríaco(-a) *(ows-TREE-ah-koh)(-kah)*
automobile automóvil (m.), carro (m.), coche (m.) *(ow-toh-MOH-veel, KAH-rroh, KOH-cheh)*
autumn otoño (m.) *(oh-TOH-nyoh)*
avoid evitar *(eh-vee-TAHR)*
awful terrible *(teh-RREE-bleh)*

B

baby bebé (m./f.), nene(-a) (m.,f.) *(beh-BEH, NEH-neh [-nah])*
back (body part) espalda (f.) *(ehs-PAHL-dah);*
  (behind) detrás de *(deh-TRAHS deh);*
  (direction, movement) atrás *(ah-TRAHS)*
bacon tocino (m.) *(toh-SEE-noh)*
bad malo *(MAH-loh)*

badly mal *(mahl)*
bag bolsa (f.) *(BOHL-sah);*
  handbag cartera (f.) *(kahr-TEH-rah);*
  (valise) maleta (f.) *(mah-LEH-tah)*
baggage equipaje (m.) *(eh-kee-PAH-heh)*
baked al horno *(ahl OHR-noh)*
balcony (theater) galería (f.) *(gah-leh-REE-ah);*
  (house) balcón (m.) *(bahl-KOHN)*
ball pelota (f.) *(peh-LOH-tah)*
banana plátano (m.) *(PLAH-tah-noh)*
bandage venda (f.) *(VEHN-dah)*
bank banco (m.) *(BAHN-koh)*
barber peluquero (m.) *(peh-loo-KEH-roh)*
barbershop peluquería (f.) *(peh-loo-keh-REE-ah)*
bargain ganga (f.) *(GAHN-gah)*
basket cesta (f.), canasta (f.) *(SEHS-tah, kah-NAHS-tah)*
bath baño *(BAH-nyoh)*
bathe bañarse *(bah-NYAR-seh)*
bathing suit traje de baño (m.) *(TRAH-heh deh BAH-nyoh)*
bathroom cuarto de baño (m.) *(KWAHR-toh deh BAH-nyoh)*
battery (automobile) acumulador (m.), batería (f.) *(ah-koo-moo-lah-DOHR, bah-teh-REE-ah)*

be ser; estar *(sehr; ehs-TAHR)*;
to be back estar de
vuelta *(ehs-TAHR deh VWEHL-tah)*

beach playa (f.) *(PLAH--yah)*

beautiful bello, hermoso
(BEH-yoh, ehr-MOH-soh)

beauty salon salón de
belleza (m.) *(sah-LOHN deh beh-YEH-sah)*

because porque *(POHR-keh)*

bed cama (f.) *(KAH-mah)*

bedroom alcoba (f.), dor-
mitorio (m.) *(ahl-KOH-bah, dohr-mee-TOH-ryoh)*

beef carne de res (f.)
(KAHR-neh deh rehs);
roast beef rosbif *(rrohs-BEEF)*

beer cerveza (f.) *(sehr-VEH-sah)*

beet remolacha (f.),
betabel (f./Mex.) *(rreh-moh-LAH-chah, beh-tah-BEHL)*

before antes de *(AHN-tehs deh)*

begin comenzar *(koh-mehn-SAHR)*

behind detrás de *(deh-TRAHS deh)*

Belgian belga *(BEHL-gah)*

believe creer *(kreh-EHR)*

bell (door) timbre (m.)
(TEEM-breh)

bellhop botones (m.) *(boh-TOH-nehs)*

belong pertenecer *(pehr-teh-neh-SEHR)*

belt cinturón (m.) *(seen-too-ROHN)*

best el/la mejor *(ehl/lah meh-HOHR)*

bet apuesta (f.) *(ah-PWEHS-tah)*;
I'll bet apuesto a que *(ah-PWEHS-toh ah keh)*

better mejor *(meh-HOHR)*

between entre *(EHN-treh)*

bicarbonate of soda bi-
carbonato de soda (m.)
(bee-kahr-boh-NAH-toh deh SOH-dah)

big grande *(GRAHN-deh)*

bill (restaurant check)
cuenta (f.) *(KWEHN-tah)*

billion mil millones *(meel mee-YOH-nehs)*

bird pájaro (m.) *(PAH-hah-roh)*

bite mordida (f.) *(mohr-DEE-dah)*;
to bite morder *(mohr-DEHR)*

bitter amargo *(ah-MAHR-goh)*

black negro *(NEH-groh)*

blade, razor hoja de
afeitar (f.) *(OH-hah deh ah-fay-TAHR)*

blank form formulario
(m.) *(fohr-moo-LAH-ryoh)*

block (city) cuadra (f.)
(KWAH-drah);
square (city) block
manzana (f.) *(mahn-SAH-nah)*

blood sangre (f.) *(SAHN-greh)*

blouse blusa (f.) *(BLOO-sah)*

blue azul *(ah-SOOL)*

boat bote (m.) *(BOH-teh)*

203

body cuerpo (m.) *(KWEHR-poh)*

boiled hervido *(ehr-VEE-doh)*

bolt perno (m.) *(PEHR-noh)*

bone hueso (m.) *(WEH-soh)*

book libro (m.) *(LEE-broh)*;
  guidebook guía (f.) *(GEE-ah)*

bookstore librería (f.) *(lee-breh-REE-ah)*

booth, phone cabina telefónica (f.) *(kah-BEE-nah teh-leh-FOH-nee-kah)*

born, to be nacer *(nah-SEHR)*

borrow pedir prestado *(peh-DEER prehs-TAH-doh)*

bother molestar *(moh-lehs-TAHR)*;
  don't bother no se moleste *(noh seh moh-LEHS-teh)*

bottle botella (f.) *(boh-TEH-yah)*

box caja (f.) *(KAH-hah)*

box office (theater) taquilla (f.) *(tah-KEE-yah)*

boy muchacho (m.), chico (m.) *(moo-CHAH-choh, CHEE-koh)*

bra; brassiere sostén (m.) *(sohs-TEHN)*

bracelet pulsera (f.) *(pool-SEH-rah)*

brakes (automobile) frenos (m.pl.) *(FREH-nohs)*

Brazilian brasileño(-a) *(brah-see-LEH-nyoh)(-nyah)*

bread pan (m.) *(pahn)*

break romper *(rrohm-PEHR)*

breakdown (car) avería (f.) *(ah-veh-REE-ah)*

breakfast desayuno (m.) *(deh-sah-YOO-noh)*

breathe respirar *(rrehs-pee-RAHR)*

bridge puente (m.) *(PWEHN-teh)*

bring traer *(trah-EHR)*

broiled a la parrilla *(ah lah pah-RREE-yah)*

broken roto, quebrado *(RROH-toh, keh-BRAH-doh)*

brother hermano *(ehr-MAH-noh)*

brown pardo, castaño *(PAHR-doh, kahs-TAH-nyoh)*

bruise (injury) contusión (f.) *(kohn-too-SYOHN)*

brush cepillo (m.) *(seh-PEE-yoh)*;
  shaving brush brocha de afeitar (f.) *(BROH-chah deh ah-fay-TAHR)*;
  to brush cepillar *(seh-pee-YAHR)*

building edificio (m.) *(eh-dee-FEE-syoh)*

bulb (electric) bombilla (f.), foco (m.) *(bohm-BEE-yah, FOH-koh)*

bullfight corrida de toros (f.) *(koh-RREE-dah deh TOH-rohs)*

bumper (automobile) parachoques (m.) *(pah-rah-CHOH-kehs)*

burn (injury) quemadura (f.) *(keh-mah-DOO-rah)*;
  to burn quemar *(keh-MAHR)*

bus autobús (m.) *(ow-toh-BOOS)*

busy ocupado *(oh-koo-PAH-doh)*

but pero *(PEH-roh)*

butter mantequilla (f.) *(mahn-teh-KEE-yah)*

button botón (m.) *(boh-TOHN)*

buy comprar *(kohm-PRAHR)*

by de; por *(deh; pohr)*

C

cab taxi (m.) *(TAHK-see)*

cabaret cabaret (m.) *(kah-bah-REHT)*

cabbage col (f.), repollo (m./Mex.) *(kohl, rreh-POH-yoh)*

cable (telegram) cable-grama (m.) *(kah-bleh-GRAH-mah)*

cake torta (f.), pastel (m./Mex.) *(TOHR-tah, pahs-TEHL)*

call llamar *(yah-MAHR)*; **telephone call** llamada telefónica (f.) *(yah-MAH-dah teh-leh-FOH-nee-kah)*

camera cámara (f.) *(KAH-mah-rah)*

can (container) lata (f.) *(LAH-tah)*; **can opener** abrelatas (m.) *(ah-breh-LAH-tahs)*; **(to be able)** poder *(poh-DEHR)*

Canadian canadiense *(kah-nah-DYEHN-seh)*

cancel cancelar *(kahn-seh-LAHR)*

candle vela (f.) *(VEH-lah)*

candy dulces (m.pl.), bombones (m.pl.) *(DOOL-sehs, bohm-BOH-nehs)*

cap gorra (f.) *(GOH-rrah)*

captain capitán (m.) *(kah-pee-TAHN)*

car (automobile) au-tomóvil (m.), coche (m.) *(ow-toh-MOH-veel, KOH-cheh)*; **railroad car** vagón **(m.)** *(vah-GOHN)*; **streetcar** tranvía (m.) *(trahn-VEE-ah)*

carburetor carburador (m.) *(kahr-boo-rah-DOHR)*

card (playing) carta (f.), naipe (m.) *(KAHR-tah, NAH-ee-peh)*

care (caution) cuidado (m.) *(kwee-DAH-doh)*

careful, to be tener cuidado *(teh-NEHR kwee-DAH-doh)*

carefully con cuidado *(kohn kwee-DAH-doh)*

carrot zanahoria (f.) *(sah-nah-OH-ryah)*

carry llevar *(yeh-VAHR)*

carry-on luggage equipaje de mano *(eh-kee-PAH-heh deh MAH-noh)*

cash (money) dinero en efectivo (m.) *(dee-NEH-roh ehn eh-fehk-TEE-voh)*

cash cobrar *(koh-BRAHR)*

cashier cajero(-a) *(kah-HEH-roh)(-rah)*

castle castillo (m.) *(kahs-TEE-yoh)*

cat gato (m.) *(GAH-toh)*

catch coger, agarrar (Mex.) *(koh-HEHR, ah-gah-RRAHR)*

cathedral catedral (f.) *(kah-teh-DRAHL)*

Catholic católico(-a) *(kah-TOH-lee-koh)(-kah)*

cauliflower coliflor (f.) *(koh-lee-FLOHR)*

caution cuidado (m.), precaución (f.) *(kwee-DAH-doh, preh-kow-SYOHN)*

ceiling techo (m.) *(TEH-choh)*

celery apio (m.) *(AH-pyoh)*

center centro (m.) *(SEHN-troh)*

certainly ciertamente *(syehr-tah-MEHN-teh)*

certificate certificado (m.) *(sehr-tee-fee-KAH-doh)*

chain cadena (f.) *(kah-DEH-nah)*

chair silla (f.) *(SEE-yah)*

change (money) cambio (m.) *(KAHM-byoh)*

charge, cover cobro de entrada (m.) *(KOH-broh deh ehn-TRAH-dah)*;

   minimum charge consumo mínimo (m.) *(kohn-SOO-moh MEE-nee-moh)*;

   to charge cobrar *(koh-BRAHR)*

cheap barato *(bah-RAH-toh)*

check, baggage talón (m.) *(tah-LOHN)*;

   traveler's check cheque de viajero (m.) *(CHEH-keh deh vyah-HEH-roh)*;

   to check (luggage) facturar, revisar *(fahk-too-RAHR, rre-vee-SAHR)*

checkroom sala de equipaje (f.) *(SAH-lah deh eh-kee-PAH-heh)*

cheek mejilla (f.) *(meh-HEE-yah)*

cheese queso (m.) *(KEH-soh)*

cherry cereza (f.) *(seh-REH-sah)*

chest (body part) pecho (m.) *(PEH-choh)*

chestnut castaña (f.) *(kahs-TAH-nyah)*

chicken pollo (m.) *(POH-yoh)*

child niño(-a) *(NEE-nyoh (-nyah)*

Chilean chileno(-a) *(chee-LEH-noh)(-nah)*

chill escalofrío (m.) *(ehs-kah-loh-FREE-oh)*

chin barba (f.) *(BAHR-bah)*

Chinese chino(-a) *(CHEE-noh)(-nah)*

chiropodist pedicuro *(peh-dee-KOO-roh)*

chocolate chocolate (m.) *(choh-koh-LAH-teh)*

choose escoger *(ehs-koh-HEHR)*

chop (cutlet) chuleta (f.) *(choo-LEH-tah)*

Christmas Navidad (f.) *(nah-vee-DAHD)*

church iglesia (f.) *(ee-GLEH-syah)*

cigar cigarro (m.), puro (m.) *(see-GAH-rroh, POO-roh)*

cigarette cigarrillo (m.) *(see-gah-RREE-yoh)*

cigar store tabaquería (f.) *(tah-bah-keh-REE-ah)*

city cuidad (f.) *(syoo-DAHD)*

class clase (f.) *(KLAH-seh)*

clean limpio *(LEEM-pyoh)*;

to clean limpiar *(leem-PYAHR)*

cleaner, dry tintorería (f.) *(teen-toh-reh-REE-ah)*

clear (transparent) claro *(KLAH-roh)*

climb trepar *(treh-PAHR)*

clock reloj (m.) *(rreh LOH)*

close (near) cerca *(SEHR-kah)*;
    to close cerrar *(seh-RRAHR)*;
    closed cerrado *(seh-RRAH-doh)*

cloth tela (f.) *(TEH-lah)*

clothes ropa (f.) *(RROH-pah)*

cloud nube (f.) *(NOO-beh)*;
    cloudy nublado *(noo-BLAH-doh)*

club, night cabaret (m.) *(kah-bah-REHT)*

clutch (automobile) embrague (m.) *(ehm-BRAH-geh)*

coach (railroad) coche (m.), vagón (m.) *(KOH-cheh, vah-GOHN)*

coat saco (m.), americana (f.) *(SAH-koh, ah-meh-ree-KAH-nah)*

coat hanger colgador (m.) *(kohl-gah-DOHR)*

cocktail cóctel (m.) *(KOHK-tehl)*

coffee café (m.) *(kah-FEH)*

coin (money) moneda (f.) *(moh-NEH-dah)*

cold (temperature) frío *(FREE-oh)*;
    (illness) resfrío (m.) *(rrehs-FRY-oh)*

cold cuts fiambres (m.), carnes frías (f.) *(FYAHM-brehs, KAHR-nehs FREE-ahs)*

collar cuello (m.) *(KWEH-yoh)*

collect cobrar *(koh-BRAHR)*

cologne agua de colonia (f.) *(AH-gwah deh koh-LOH-nyah)*

color color (m.) *(koh-LOHR)*

color film película de color (f.) *(peh-LEE-koo lah deh koh-LOHR)*

comb peine (m.) *(PAY-neh)*

come venir *(veh-NEER)*;
    to come in entrar *(ehn-TRAHR)*

comedy comedia (f.) *(koh-MEH-dyah)*

comfortable cómodo *(KOH-moh-doh)*

company compañía (f.) *(kohm-pah-NYEE-ah)*

compartment compartimiento (m.) *(kohm-pahr-tee-MYEHN-toh)*

complaint queja (f.) *(KEH-hah)*

concert concierto (m.) *(kohn-SYEHR-toh)*

conductor (train) conductor (m.), revisor (m.) *(kohn-dook-TOHR, rreh-vee-SOHR)*

congratulations felicitaciones (f.pl.) *(feh-lee-see-tah-SYOH-nehs)*

consul cónsul (m.) *(KOHN-sool)*

consulate consulado (m.) *(kohn-soo-LAH-doh)*

continue continuar, seguir *(kohn-tee-NWAHR, seh-GEER)*

convent convento (m.) *(kohn-VEHN-toh)*

cooked cocido *(koh-SEE-doh)*

cool fresco *(FREHS-koh)*

corkscrew sacacorchos (m.) *(sah-kah-KOHR-chohs)*

corn maíz (m.) *(mah-EES)*

corner esquina (f.) *(ehs-KEE-nah)*

cost (amount) precio (m.) *(PREH-syoh)*;
   to cost costar *(kohs-TAHR)*

cotton algodón (m.) *(ahl-goh-DOHN)*

cough tos (f.) *(tohs)*;
   to cough toser *(toh-SEHR)*

count contar *(kohn-TAHR)*

country (nation) país (m.) *(pah-EES)*

countryside campo (m.) *(KAHM-poh)*

course (in meals) plato (m.) *(PLAH-toh)*

crazy loco *(LOH-koh)*

cream crema (f.) *(KREH-mah)*

crystal cristal (m.) *(krees-TAHL)*

Cuban cubano(-a) *(koo-BAH-noh)(-nah)*

cucumber pepino (m.) *(peh-PEE-noh)*

cup taza (f.) *(TAH-sah)*

curtain cortina (f.) *(kohr-TEE-nah)*;
   (stage) telón (m.) *(teh-LOHN)*

curve curva (f.) *(KOOR-vah)*

customs aduana (f.) *(ah-DWAH-nah)*

cut cortar *(kohr-TAHR)*;
   cut it out! ¡basta! *(BAHS-tah!)*

cutlet chuleta (f.) *(choo-LEH-tah)*

Czech checo(-a) *(CHEH-koh)(-kah)*

D

daily (by the day) por día, al día *(pohr DEE-ah, ahl DEE-ah)*

damp húmedo *(OO-meh-doh)*

dance baile (m.) *(BAHY-leh)*;
   to dance bailar *(bah-ee-LAHR)*

danger peligro (m.) *(peh-LEE-groh)*

dangerous peligroso *(peh-lee-GROH-soh)*

Danish danés(-esa) *(dah-NEHS)(-NEH-sah)*

dark oscuro *(ohs-KOO-roh)*

darn it! ¡caramba! *(kah-RAHM-bah!)*

date (calendar) fecha (f.) *(FEH-chah)*

daughter hija (f.) *(EE-hah)*

day día (m.) *(DEE-ah)*

dead muerto(-a) *(MWEHR-toh)(-tah)*

death muerte (f.) *(MWEHR-teh)*

December diciembre (m.) *(dee-SYEHM-breh)*

declaration declaración (f.) *(deh-klah-rah-SYOHN)*

declare declarar *(deh-klah-RHAR)*

deep profundo *(proh-FOON-doh)*

deliver entregar *(ehn-treh-GAHR)*

delivery entrega (f.) *(ehn-TREH-gah)*;
   special delivery entrega inmediata (f.) *(ehn-TREH-gah een-men-DYAH-tah)*

dental dental *(dehn-TAHL)*

dentist dentista (m./f.) *(dehn-TEES-tah)*

denture dentadura (f.) *(dehn-tah-DOO-rah)*

deodorant desodorante (m.) *(deh-soh-doh-RAHN-teh)*

department store almacén (m.) *(ahl-mah-SEHN)*

desk, information mostrador de información (m.) *(mohs-trah-DOHR deh een-fohr-mah-SYOHN)*

dessert postre (m.) *(POHS-treh)*

detour desvío (m.) *(dehs-VEE-oh)*

develop (film) revelar *(rreh-veh-LAHR)*

devil diablo (m.), demonio (m.) *(DYAH-bloh, deh-MOH-nyoh)*

diapers pañales (m.pl.) *(pah-NYAH-lehs)*

dictionary diccionario (m.) *(deek-syoh-NAH-ryoh)*

different diferente *(dee-feh-REHN-teh)*

difficult difícil *(dee-FEE-seel)*

difficulty dificultad (f.) *(dee-fee-kool-TAHD)*

dining car coche-comedor (m.) *(KOH-cheh koh-meh-DOHR)*

dining room comedor (m.) *(koh-meh-DOHR)*

dinner comida (f.) *(koh-MEE-dah)*

direct directo *(dee-REHK-toh)*;
   to direct indicar, dirigir *(een-dee-KAHR, dee-ree-HEER)*

direction dirección (f.) *(dee-rehk-SYOHN)*

dirty sucio *(SOO-syoh)*

discount descuento (m.) *(dehs-KWEHN-toh)*

dish plato (m.) *(PLAH-toh)*

district barrio (m.) *(BAH-rryoh)*

disturb molestar *(moh-lehs-TAHR)*

dizzy, to feel estar mareado *(ehs-TAHR mah-reh-AH-doh)*

do hacer *(ah-SEHR)*

dock muelle (m.) *(MWEH-yeh)*

doctor médico(-a), doctor(-a) *(MEH-dee-koh[-kah], dohk-TOHR[-TOH-rah])*

document documento (m.) *(doh-koo-MEHN-toh)*

dog perro (m.) *(PEH-rroh)*

dollar dólar (m.) *(DOH-lahr)*

domestic nacional, doméstico *(nah-syoh-NAHL, doh-MEHS-tee-koh)*

door puerta (f.) *(PWEHR-tah)*

doorman portero (m.)
(pohr-TEH-roh)

double room habitación
para dos (f.) *(ah-bee-tah-
SYOHN PAH-rah dohs)*

down abajo *(ah-BAH-hoh)*

dozen docena (f.) *(doh-
SEH-nah)*

draw dibujar *(dee-boo-
HAHR)*

drawer cajón (m.) *(kah-
HOHN)*

dress (garment) vestido
(m.) *(vehs-TEE-doh);*
to dress vestirse *(vehs-TEER-
seh)*

dressing gown bata (f.)
(BAH-tah)

drink (beverage) bebida
(f.) *(beh-BEE-dah);*
to drink beber *(beh-BEHR)*

drinkable potable *(poh-
TAH-bleh)*

drive (ride) paseo en
coche (m.) *(pah-SEH-oh ehn
KOH-cheh);*
to drive conducir *(kohn-
doo-SEER)*

driver chofer (m.) *(cho-
FEHR)*

drugstore farmacia (f.)
(fahr-MAH-syah)

drunk borracho *(boh-RRAH-
choh)*

dry seco *(SEH-koh);*
dry cleaning limpieza en
seco (f.) *(leem-PYEH-sah ehn SEH-
koh)*

duck pato (m.) *(PAH-toh)*

Dutch holandés(-esa) *(oh-
lahn-DEHS)(-DEH-sah)*

dysentery disentería (f.)
(dee-sehn-teh-REE-ah)

E

each cada *(KAH-dah);*
each one cada uno *(KAH-
dah OO-noh)*

ear (outer) oreja (f.) *(oh-
REH-hah);*
(inner) ear oído (m.) *(oh-
EE-doh);*
earache dolor de oído
(m.) *(doh-LOHR deh oh-EE-doh)*

early temprano *(tehm-PRAH-
noh)*

easy fácil *(FAH-seel);*
take it easy! ¡no se preocupe! *(noh seh preh-oh-KOO-
peh!)*

Easter Pascua *(PAHS-kwah)*

eat comer *(koh-MEHR)*

egg huevo (m.) *(WEH-voh)*

eight ocho *(OH-choh)*

eighteen dieciocho *(dyeh-
SYOH-choh)*

eighth octavo *(ohk-TAH-voh)*

eighty ochenta *(oh-CHEHN-
tah)*

elbow codo (m.) *(KOH-doh)*

electric eléctrico *(eh-LEHK-
tree-koh)*

elevator elevador (m.),
ascensor (m.) *(eh-leh-vah-
DOHR, ah-sehn-SOHR)*

eleven once *(OHN-seh)*

else, nothing nada más
(NAH-dah mahs);
what else? ¿qué más?
(keh mahs?)

empty vacío *(vah-SEE-oh)*
end (conclusion) fin (m.)
(feen);
  to end terminar *(tehr-mee-NAHR)*
endorse endosar *(ehn-doh-SAHR)*
engine motor (m.), máquina
(f.) *(moh TOHR, MAH-kee-nah)*
English inglés(-esa) *(een-GLEHS)(-GLEH-sah)*
enlargement ampliación
(f.) *(ahm-plyah-SYOHN)*
enough bastante *(bahs-TAHN-teh)*
evening tarde (f.) *(TAHR-deh)*
every cada *(KAH-dah)*
everybody todo el mundo
(m.), todos (m.pl.) *(TOH-doh
ehl MOON-doh, TOH-dóhs)*
everything todo *(TOH-doh)*
examine examinar *(ehk-sah-mee-NAHR)*
exchange cambiar *(kahm-BYAHR)*;
  exchange office casa
de cambio (f.) *(KAH-sah deh
KAHM-byoh)*
excursion excursión (f.)
(ehs-koor-SYOHN)
excuse perdonar *(pehr-doh-NAHR)*
exhaust (automobile)
escape (m.) *(ehs-KAH-peh)*
exit salida (f.) *(sah-LEE-dah)*
expect esperar *(ehs-peh-RAHR)*
expensive caro *(KAH-roh)*
express train expreso
(m.) *(ehks-PREH-soh)*
extra extra *(EHKS-trah)*

extract (v.) sacar *(sah-KAHR)*
eye ojo (m.) *(OH-hoh)*
eyebrow ceja (f.) *(SEH-hah)*
eyeglasses gafas (f.pl.),
anteojos (m.pl.) *(GAH-fahs,
anh-teh-OH-hohs)*
eyelash pestaña (f.) *(pehs-TAH-nyah)*
eyelid párpado (m.)
(PAHR-pah-doh)

F

face (body part) cara (f.)
(KAH-rah);
  face powder polvo para
la cara (m.) *(POHL-voh PAH-rah
lah KAH-rah)*
facial (massage) masaje
facial (m.) *(mah-SAH-heh fah-SYAHL)*
fall (autumn) otoño (m.)
(oh-TOH-nyoh);
  (injury) caída (f.) *(kah-EE-dah)*;
  to fall caer *(kah-EHR)*
false falso *(FAHL-soh)*
family familia (f.) *(fah-MEE-lyah)*;
  family name (surname)
apellido (m.) *(ah-peh-YEE-doh)*
fan (car or electric) ventilador (m.) *(vehn-tee-lah-DOHR)*;
  (hand) abanico (m.) *(ah-bah-NEE-koh)*
far lejos *(LEH-hohs)*
fare (fee) tarifa (f.) *(tah-REE-fah)*

fast de prisa, pronto *(deh PREE-sah, PROHN-toh)*

faster más de prisa, más rápido *(mahs deh PREE-sah, mahs RRAH-pee-doh)*

father padre (m.), papá (m.) *(PAH-dreh, pah-PAH)*

faucet grifo (m.) *(GREE-foh)*

fear miedo (m.) *(MYEH-doh);*
to fear tener miedo *(teh-NEHR MYEH-doh)*

February febrero (m.) *(feh-BREH-roh)*

feel (sick, tired, happy, etc.) sentirse *(sehn-TEER-seh);*
to feel like (doing something) tener ganas de *(teh-NEHR GAH-nahs deh)*

felt (cloth) fieltro (m.) *(FYEHL-troh)*

fender guardafango (m.), guardabarro (m.) *(gwahr-dah-FAHN-goh, gwahr-dah-BAH-rroh)*

festival fiesta (f.) *(FYEHS-tah)*

fever fiebre (f.) *(FYEH-breh)*

few pocos *(POH-kohs);*
a few unos cuantos *(OO-nohs KWAHN-tohs)*

fifteen quince *(KEEN-seh)*

fifth quinto *(KEEN-toh)*

fig higo (m.) *(EE-goh)*

fill llenar *(yeh-NAHR);*
(a tooth) empastar *(ehm-pahs-TAHR);*
filling (tooth) empaste (m.), arreglo (m.) *(ehm-PAHS-teh, ah-RREH-gloh)*

film (movie) película (f.) *(peh-LEE-koo-lah)*

find encontrar, hallar *(ehn-kohn-TRAHR, ah-YAHR)*

fine (good quality) fino, bueno *(FEE-noh, BWEH-noh)*

fine (penalty) multa (f.) *(MOOL-tah)*

finger dedo (m.) *(DEH-doh)*

finish acabar, terminar *(ah-kah-BAHR, tehr-mee-NAHR)*

fire fuego (m.) *(FWEH-goh);*
(destructive) incendio (m.) *(een-SEHN-dyoh)*

first primero *(pree-MEH-roh);*
first aid primeros auxilios (m.pl.) *(pree-MEH-rohs owk-SEE-lyohs)*

fish (in water) pez (m.) *(pehs);*
(when caught) pescado (m.) *(pehs-KAH-doh)*

fit (shoes) calzar *(kahl-SAHR);*
(clothes) quedar *(KEH-dahr)*

fix componer, reparar, arreglar *(kohm-poh-NEHR, rreh-pah-RAHR, ah-rreh-GLAHR);*
fixed price precio fijo (m.) *(PREH-syoh FEE-hoh)*

flashlight linterna (f.) *(leen-TEHR-nah)*

flat (level) llano *(YAH-noh);*
flat tire neumático desinflado (m.), llanta reventada (f./Mex.) *(neoo-MAH-tee-koh deh-seen-FLAH-doh, YAHN-tah rreh-vehn-TAH-dah)*

flight (plane) vuelo (m.) *(VWEH-loh)*

floor piso (m.), suelo (m.) *(PEE-soh, SWEH-loh)*

flower flor (f.) *(flohr)*
fog niebla (f.) *(NYEH-blah)*
follow seguir *(seh-GEER)*
foot pie (m.) *(pyeh)*
for (purpose, destination)
para *(PAH-rah)*;
  (exchange) por *(pohr)*
forbidden prohibido *(pro-ee-BEE-doh)*
forehead frente (f.)
(FREHN-teh)
  foreign extranjero(-a)
  (m.,f.) *(ehks-trahn-HEH-roh)*;
  foreigner extranjero(-a)
  (m.,f.) *(ehks-trahn-HEH-roh)(-rah)*
forget olvidar *(ohl-vee-DAHR)*
fork tenedor (m.) *(teh-neh-DOHR)*
form (document) formu-
lario (m.) *(fohr-moo-LAH-ryoh)*
forty cuarenta *(kwah-REHN-tah)*
forward (direction) adelante *(ah-deh-LAHN-teh)*;
  **to forward (to a farther
  destination)** reexpedir
  (rreh-ehks-peh-DEER)
fountain fuente (f.)
(FWEHN-teh)
  fountain pen pluma de
  fuente *(ploo-mah deh FWEHN-teh)*
four cuatro *(KWAH-troh)*
fourteen catorce *(kah-TOHR-seh)*
fourth cuarto *(KWAHR-toh)*
fracture (injury) fractura
(f.) *(frahk-TOO-rah)*
free (independent) libre
(LEE-breh);

(free of charge) gratis
(GRAH-tees)
French francés(-esa)
(frahn SEHS)(-SEH-sah)
Friday viernes (m.) *(VYEHR-nehs)*
fried frito *(FREE-toh)*
friend amigo(-a) *(ah-MEE-goh)(-gah)*
from de; desde *(deh; DEHS-deh)*
front (position) delantero
(deh-lahn-TEH-roh);
  **in front (facing the
  street)** que de a la calle
  (keh dah ah lah KAH-yeh)
fruit fruta (f.) *(FROO-tah)*
fuel pump bomba de
combustible (f.) *(BOHM-bah
deh kohm-boos-TEE-bleh)*
full lleno *(YEH-noh)*
furnished amueblado,
amoblado *(ah-mweh-BLAH-doh, ah-moh-BLAH-doh)*

G

game juego (m.) *(HWEH-goh)*;
  (sports contest) partido
  (m.) *(pahr-TEE-doh)*
garage garaje (m.) *(gah-RAH-heh)*
garden jardín (m.) *(hahr-DEEN)*
garlic ajo (m.) *(AH-hoh)*
garter liga (f.) *(LEE-gah)*
gas (fuel) gasolina (f.)
(gah-soh-LEE-nah);
  gas station gasolinera
  (gah-soh-lee-NEH-rah)

gate (railroad station) barrera (f.) *(bah-RREH-rah)*

gauze gasa (f.) *(GAH-sah)*

gear (car) engranaje (m.) *(ehn-grah-NAH-heh)*

gentleman caballero, señor *(kah-bah-YEH-roh, seh-NYOHR)*

German alemán(-ana) *(ah-leh-MAHN)(-MAH-nah)*

get (obtain) conseguir *(kohn-seh-GEER)*;
  to get back (recover) recobrar *(rreh-koh-BRAHR)*;
  to get dressed vestirse *(vehs-TEER-se)*;
  to get off bajarse *(bah-HAHR-seh)*;
  to get out irse, salir *(EER-seh, sah-LEER)*;
  to get up levantarse *(leh-vahn-TAHR-seh)*

gift regalo (m.) *(rreh-GAH-loh)*

gin ginebra (f.) *(hee-NEH-brah)*

girl muchacha (f.), chica (f.) *(moo-CHAH-chah, CHEE-kah)*

give dar *(dahr)*
  to give back devolver *(deh-vohl-VEHR)*

glad contento *(kohn-TEHN-toh)*

gladly con mucho gusto *(kohn MOO-choh GOOS-toh)*

glass (drinking) vaso *(VAH-soh)*;
  (material) vidrio *(VEE-dryoh)*

glasses (eye) gafas, anteojos *(GAH-fahs, ahn-teh-OH-hohs)*

glove guante *(GWAHN-teh)*

go ir *(eer)*;
  to go away irse, marcharse *(EER-seh, mahr-CHAHR-seh)*;
  to go shopping ir de compras *(eer deh KOHM-prahs)*;
  to go down bajar *(bah-HAHR)*;
  to go home ir a casa *(eer ah KAH-sah)*;
  to go in entrar *(ehn-TRAHR)*;
  to go out salir *(sah-LEER)*;
  to go to bed acostarse *(ah-kohs-TAHR-seh)*;
  to go up subir *(soo-BEER)*

gold oro *(OH-roh)*

good bueno *(BWEH-noh)*

good-bye! ¡hasta la vista! ¡adiós! *(AHS-tah lah VEES-tah!, ah-DYOHS!)*

goose ganso (m.) *(GAHN-soh)*

grade (on road) cuesta (f.) *(KWEHS-tah)*;
  grade crossing paso a nivel (m.) *(PAH-soh ah nee-VEHL)*

gram gramo (m.) *(GRAH-moh)*

grapefruit toronja (f.), pomelo (m.) *(toh-ROHN-hah, poh-MEH-loh)*

grapes uvas (f.pl.) *(OO-vahs)*

grass hierba (f.), zacate (m.) (m./Mex.) *(YEHR-bah, sah-KAH-teh)*

grateful agradecido *(ah-grah-deh-SEE-doh)*

gravy (or sauce) salsa (f.) *(SAHL-sah)*

gray gris *(grees)*

grease (lubricate) engrasar *(ehn-grah-SAHR)*

Greek griego(-a) *(GRYEH-goh)(-gah)*

green verde *(VEHR-deh)*

greeting saludo (m.) *(suh-LOO-doh)*

guide guía (m./f.) *(GEE-ah)*;
guidebook guía (f.) *(GEE-ah)*

gum, chewing chicle (m.) *(CHEE-kleh)*

guy tipo (m.) *(TEE-poh)*

H

hair pelo (m.), cabello (m.) *(PEH-loh, kah-BEH-yoh)*;
hair lotion loción para el cabello (f.) *(loh-SYOHN PAH-rah ehl kah-BEH-yoh)*;
hair rinse enjuague (m.) *(ehn-HWAH-geh)*

hairbrush cepillo (m.) *(seh-PEE-yoh)*

haircut corte de pelo (m.) *(KOHR-teh deh PEH-loh)*

hairnet redecilla (f.) *(rreh-deh-SEE-yah)*

hairpin gancho (m.), horquilla (f.) *(GAHN-choh, ohr-KEE-yah)*

half medio (adj.), mitad (f.) *(MEH-dyoh, mee-TAHD)*

halt! ¡alto! *(AHL-toh!)*

ham jamón (m.) *(hah-MOHN)*

hammer martillo (m.) *(mahr-TEE-yoh)*

hand mano (f.) *(MAH-noh)*

handbag cartera (f.), bolsa (f.) *(kahr-TEH-rah, BOHL-sah)*

handkerchief pañuelo (m.) *(pah-NYWEH-loh)*

handmade hecho a mano *(EH-choh ah MAH-noh)*

hanger (clothes) colgador (m.), gancho (m.) *(kohl-gah-DOHR, GAHN-choh)*

happen pasar, suceder, ocurrir, resultar *(pah-SAHR, soo-seh-DEHR, oh-koo-RREER, rreh-sool-TAHR)*

happy feliz *(feh-LEES)*

Happy New Year! ¡Feliz Año Nuevo! *(feh-LEES AH-nyoh NWEH-voh!)*

harbor puerto (m.) *(PWEHR-toh)*

hard (difficult) difícil *(dee-FEE-seel)*;
(tough) duro *(DOO-roh)*

hat sombrero (m.) *(sohm-BREH-roh)*

hat shop sombrerería (f.) *(sohm-breh-reh-REE-ah)*

have tener *(teh-NEHR)*;
to have to deber, tener que *(deh-BEHR, teh-NEHR keh)*

hazelnut avellana (f.) *(ah-veh-YAH-nah)*

he él *(ehl)*

head cabeza (f.) *(kah-BEH-sah)*;
headache dolor de cabeza (f.) *(doh-LOHR deh kah-BEH-sah)*

215

headlight luz delantera (f.) *(loos deh-lahn-TEH-rah)*
headwaiter jefe de comedor (m.) *(HEH-feh deh koh-meh-DOHR)*
health salud (f.) *(sah-LOOD)*;
health certificate certificado de salud (m.) *(sehr-tee-fee-KAH-doh deh sah-LOOD)*
hear oír *(oh-EER)*;
to hear from tener noticias de *(teh-NEHR noh-TEE-syahs deh)*
heart corazón (m.) *(koh-rah-SOHN)*
heat calor (m.) *(kah-LOHR)*
heaven cielo (m.) *(SYEH-loh)*
heavy pesado *(peh-SAH-doh)*
Hebrew hebreo(-a) *(eh-BREH-oh)(-ah)*
heel (of foot) talón (m.) *(tah-LOHN)*;
(of shoe) tacón (m.) *(tah-KOHN)*
hell infierno (m.) *(een-FYEHR-noh)*
hello! ¡hola! *(OH-lah!)*
help ayudar *(ah-yoo-DAHR)*
here aquí *(ah-KEE)*
high alto *(AHL-toh)*
highway carretera (f.) *(kah-rreh-TEH-rah)*
hip cadera (f.) *(kah-DEH-rah)*
hire contratar *(kohn-trah-TAHR)*
his su *(soo)*;
(w/pl.) sus *(soos)*;
(pron.) suyo *(SOO-yoh)*;
(w/pl.) suyos *(SOO-yohs)*
home casa (f.), hogar (m.) *(KAH-sah, oh-GAHR)*;
to go home ir a casa *(eer ah KAH-sah)*;
to be at home estar en casa *(ehs-TAHR ehn KAH-sah)*
hood (car) capó (m.) *(kah-POH)*
hook gancho (m.) *(GAHN-choh)*
hope esperar *(ehs-peh-RAHR)*
horn (car) bocina (f.) *(boh-SEE-nah)*
hors d'oeuvres extremeses (m.pl.), tapas (f.pl./Sp.), botanas (f.pl./Mex.) *(ehn-treh-MEH-sehs, TAH-pahs, boh-TAH-nahs)*
horse caballo (m.) *(kah-BAH-yoh)*
hospital hospital (m.) *(ohs-pee-TAHL)*
hostel, youth albergue de jóvenes *(ahl-BEHR-geh deh HOH-veh-nehs)*
hostess (plane) azafata (f.) *(ah-sah-FAH-tah)*;
(home) anfitriona *(ahn-fee-TRYOH-nah)*
hot caliente *(kah-LYEHN-teh)*;
(piquant) picante *(pee-KAHN-teh)*
hotel hotel (m.) *(oh-TEHL)*
hour hora (f.) *(OH-rah)*
house casa (f.) *(KAH-sah)*
how? ¿cómo? *(KOH-moh?)*;
how far? ¿a qué distancia? *(ah keh dees-TAHN-syah?)*;
how long? ¿cuánto tiempo?, ¿desde cuándo? *(KWAHN-toh TYEHM-poh?, DEHS-deh KWAHN-doh?)*;

ENGLISH-SPANISH

how many? ¿cuántos? *(KWAHN-tohs?);*
how much? ¿cuánto? *(KWAHN-toh?)*

hundred cien *(SYEHN);*
a hundred and . . .
ciento . . . *(SYEHN-toh . . .)*

Hungarian húngaro(-a) *(OON-gah-roh)(-rah)*

hungry, to be tener hambre *(teh-NEHR AHM-breh)*

hurry (v.) darse prisa *(DAHR-seh PREE-sah);*
to be in a hurry tener prisa *(teh-NEHR PREE-sah)*

hurt (v.) lastimar *(lahs-tee-MAHR)*

husband esposo (m.) *(ehs-POH-soh)*

I

I yo *(yoh)*

ice hielo (m.) *(YEH-loh);*
ice cream helado (m.) *(eh-LAH-doh);*
ice water agua helada (f.) *(AH-gwah eh-LAH-dah)*

identification identificación (f.) *(ee-dehn-tee-fee-kah-SYOHN)*

if si *(see)*

ignition (car) encendido (m.) *(ehn-sehn-DEE-doh)*

ill enfermo *(ehn-FEHR-moh)*

illness enfermedad (f.) *(ehn-fehr-meh-DAHD)*

imported importado *(eem-pohr-TAH-doh)*

in en *(ehn)*

included incluido *(een-KLUEE doh)*

indigestion indigestión (f.) *(een-dee-hehs-TYOHN)*

indisposed indispuesto *(een-dees-PWEHS-toh)*

information información (f.) *(een-fohr-mah-SYOHN);*
information desk mostrador de información (m.) *(mohs-trah-DOHR deh een-FOHR-mah-SYOHN)*

injection inyección (f.) *(een-yehk-SYOHN)*

ink tinta (f.) *(TEEN-tah)*

inner tube tubo interior (m.) *(TOO-boh een-teh-RYOHR)*

inquire preguntar, averiguar *(preh-goon-TAHR, ah-veh-ree-GWAHR)*

insect insecto (m.) *(een-SEHK-toh)*

insecticide insecticida (m.) *(een-sehk-tee-SEE-dah)*

inside dentro de *(DEHN-troh deh)*

instead of en vez de *(ehn vehs deh)*

insurance seguro (m.) *(seh-GOO-roh)*

insure asegurar *(ah-seh-goo-RAHR)*

interest interés (m.) *(een-teh-REHS)*

interpreter intérprete (m./f.) *(een-TEHR-preh-teh)*

intersection intersección (f.) *(een-teer-sehk-SYOHN)*

into en; dentro de *(ehn; DEHN-troh deh)*

217

introduce presentar *(preh-sehn-TAHR)*

iodine yodo (m.) *(YOH-doh)*

iron (metal) hierro (m.) *(YEH-rroh)*;
  (flatiron) plancha (f.) *(PLAHN-chah)*;
  to iron planchar *(plahn-CHAHR)*

is es; está *(ehs; ehs-TAH)*

Italian italiano(-a) *(ee-tah-LYAH-noh)(-nah)*

J

jack (auto) gato (m.) *(GAH-toh)*;
  to jack up (car) alzar (levantar) con el gato *(ahl-SAHR (leh-vahn-TAHR) kohn ehl GAH-toh)*

jam (fruit) mermelada (f.) *(mehr-meh-LAH-dah)*

January enero (m.) *(eh-NEH-roh)*

Japanese japonés(-esa) *(ha-poh-NEHS)(-NEH-sah)*

jaw quijada (f.) *(kee-HAH-dah)*

jeweler joyero (m.) *(hoh-YEH-roh)*

jewelry joyas (f.pl.) *(HOH-yahs)*;
  jewelry store joyería (f.) *(hoh-yeh-REE-ah)*

Jewish judío(-a) *(joo-DEE-oh)(-ah)*

journey viaje (m.) *(VYAH-heh)*

juice jugo (m.), zumo (m./Sp.) *(HOO-goh, SOO-moh)*

July julio (m.) *(HOO-lyoh)*

June junio (m.) *(HOO-nyoh)*

K

keep guardar *(gwahr-DAHR)*;
  (to hold on to) quedarse con *(keh-DAHR-seh kohn)*;
  to keep right seguir a la derecha *(seh-GEER ah lah deh-REH-chah)*

key llave (f.) *(YAH-veh)*

kilogram kilogramo (m.) *(kee-loh-GRAH-moh)*

kilometer kilómetro (m.) *(kee-LOH-meh-troh)*

kind (nice) bueno, amable *(BWEH-noh, ah-mah-BLEH)*;
  (type) clase (f.), género (m.) *(KLAH-seh, HEH-neh-roh)*

kiss beso (m.) *(BEH-soh)*;
  to kiss besar *(beh-SAHR)*

kitchen cocina (f.) *(koh-SEE-nah)*

knee rodilla (f.) *(rroh-DEE-yah)*

knife cuchillo (m.) *(koo-CHEE-yoh)*

knock (v.) llamar *(yah-MAHR)*

know (a fact, how) saber *(sah-BEHR)*;
  (a person or thing) conocer *(koh-noh-SEHR)*

L

label etiqueta (f.) *(eh-tee-KEH-tah)*

lace encaje (m.) *(ehn-KAH-heh)*

laces (shoe) cordones (m.pl.) *(kohr-DOH-nehs)*

ladies' room baño de señoras (m.) *(BAH nyoh deh seh-NYOH-rahs)*

lady dama (f.), señora (f.) *(DAH-mah, seh-NYOH-rah)*

lamb cordero (m.) *(kohr-DEH-roh)*

lamp lámpara (f.) *(LAHM-pah-rah)*

land (ground) tierra (f.) *(TYEH-rrah)*;
   to land (by ship) desembarcar *(dehs-ehm-bahr-KAHR)*;
   to land (by plane) aterrizar *(ah-teh-rree-SAHR)*

language idioma (m.), lengua (f.) *(ee-DYOH-mah, LEHN-gwah)*

large grande *(GRAN-deh)*

last último *(OOL-tee-moh)*;
(preceding) pasado *(pah-SAH-doh)*;
   to last durar *(doo-RAHR)*

late tarde *(TAHR-deh)*

latest, at the a más tardar *(ah mahs tahr-DAHR)*

laugh (v.) reír, reírse *(reh-EER, reh-EER-seh)*

laundry lavandería (f.) *(lah-vahn-deh-REE-ah)*

laundry woman lavandera (f.) *(lah-vahn-DEH-rah)*

lavatory lavabo (m.) *(lah-VAH-boh)*

laxative laxante (m.) *(lahk-SAHN-teh)*

leak escape (m.) *(ehs-KAH-peh)*;

to leak escapar *(ehs-KAH-pahr)*

lean on apoyarse en *(ah poh-YAHR-seh ehn)*

learn aprender *(ah-prehn-DEHR)*

least, at al (por lo/a lo) menos *(ahl [pohr loh/ah loh] MEH-nos)*

leather cuero (m.) *(KWEH-roh)*

leave (behind) (v.) dejar *(deh-HAHR)*;
   (to depart) salir *(sah-LEER)*

left (direction) izquierda (f.) *(ees-KYEHR-dah)*

leg pierna (f.) *(PYEHR-nah)*

lemon limón (m.) *(lee-MOHN)*

lemonade limonada (f.) *(lee-moh-NAH-dah)*

lend prestar *(prehs-TAHR)*

length largo (m.) *(LAHR-goh)*

lens lente (m.) *(LEHN-teh)*

less menos *(MEH-nohs)*

let dejar, permitir *(deh-HAHR, pehr-mee-TEER)*

letter carta (f.) *(KAHR-tah)*;
   (of the alphabet) letra *(LEH-trah)*

letterbox buzón (m.) *(boo-SOHN)*

lettuce lechuga (f.) *(leh-CHOO-gah)*

library biblioteca (f.) *(bee-blyoh-TEH-kah)*

lie (down) acostarse *(ah-kohs-TAHR-seh)*

life vida (f.) *(VEE-dah)*;

lifeboat bote salvavidas (m.) *(BOH-teh sahl-vah-VEE-dahs);*
lifeguard salvavidas (m./f.) *(sahl-vah-VEE-dahs);*
life preserver salvavidas (m.) *(sahl-vah-VEE-dahs)*
lift levantar *(leh-vahn-TAHR)*
light (color) claro *(KLAH-roh);*
(brightness) luz (f.) *(loos);*
to light encender *(ehn-sehn-DEHR)*
lighter (cigarette) encendedor (m.) *(ehn-sehn-deh-DOHR)*
lighting relámpago (m.) *(rreh-LAHM-pah-goh)*
like (as) como *(KOH-moh);*
to like gustar *(goos-TAHR)*
limit, speed velocidad máxima (f.) *(veh-loh-see-DAHD MAHK-see-mah)*
line línea (f.) *(LEE-neh-ah)*
linen lino (m.); ropa blanca (f.) *(LEE-noh; RROH-pah BLAHN-kah)*
lip labio (m.) *(LAH-byoh)*
lipstick lápiz de labios (m.) *(LAH-pees deh LAH-byohs)*
liqueur licor (m.) *(lee-KOHR)*
liquor bebida alcohólica (f.) *(beh-BEE-dah ahl-KOH-lee-kah)*
list (wine, food) lista (f.) *(LEES-tah)*
listen (listen to) escuchar *(ehs-koo-CHAHR)*
liter litro (m.) *(LEE-troh)*
little pequeño *(peh-KEH-nyoh)*
live (v.) vivir *(vee-VEER)*
liver hígado (m.) *(EE-gah-doh)*

living room sala (f.) *(SAH-lah)*
lobby vestíbulo (m.) *(vehs-TEE-boo-loh)*
lobster langosta (f.) *(lahn-GOHS-tah)*
local (train) el tren local (m.) *(ehl trehn loh-KAHL)*
local phone call llamada local (f.) *(yah-MAH-dah loh-KAHL)*
lock cerradura (f.) *(seh-rrah-DOO-rah)*
long largo *(LAHR-goh);*
how long? ¿cuánto tiempo? *(KWAHN-toh TYEHM-poh?)*
long-distance call llamada de larga distancia (f.) *(yah-MAH-dah deh LAHR-gah dees-TAHN-syah)*
look (look at) mirar *(mee-RAHR);*
to look for buscar *(boos-KAHR);*
to look out tener cuidado *(teh-NEHR kwee-DAH-doh)*
lose perder *(pehr-DEHR)*
lost-and-found objetos perdidos (m.pl.) *(ohb-HEH-tohs pehr-DEE-dohs)*
lotion loción (f.) *(loh-SYOHN)*
lots of (much) mucho *(MOO-choh);*
(many) muchos *(MOO-chohs)*
lounge salón (m.) *(sah-LOHN)*
low bajo *(BAH-hoh)*
lower berth litera baja (f.) *(lee-TEH-rah BAH-hah)*

luck suerte (f.) *(SWEHR-teh)*

lunch almuerzo (m.), co-mida (f.) *(ahl MWEHR-soh, koh-MEE-dah)*;
  to lunch almorzar, comer *(ahl-mohr-SAHR, koh-MEHR)*

lung pulmón (m.) *(pool-MOHN)*

M

maid sirvienta (f.) *(seer-VYEHN-tah)*;
  chamber maid camar-era (f.) *(kah-mah-REH-rah)*

mail correo (m.) *(koh-RREH-oh)*

mailbox buzón (m.) *(boo-SOHN)*

magazine revista (f.) *(rreh-VEES-tah)*

make hacer *(ah-SEHR)*

man hombre (m.) *(OHM-breh)*

manager director(-a), gerente (m./f.), adminis-trador(-a) *(dee-rehk-TOHR) (-TOH-rah), (heh-REHN-teh), (-ahd-mee-nees-trah-DOHR) (-DOH-rah)*

manicure manicura (f.) *(mah-nee-KOO-rah)*

many muchos *(MOO-chohs)*

map (road) mapa (de carreteras) (m.) *(MAH-pah [deh kah-rreh-TEH-rahs])*

March marzo (m.) *(MAHR-soh)*

market mercado (m.) *(mehr-KAH-doh)*

mashed (food) puré de (m.) *(poo-REH deh)*

mass misa (f.) *(MEE-sah)*;
  high mass misa cantada (f.) *(MEE-sah kahn-TAH-dah)*

massage masaje (m.) *(mah-SAH-heh)*

match fósforo (m.), cerillo (m.) *(FOHS foh-roh, seh-REE-yoh)*

matter, it doesn't no im-porta *(noh eem-POHR-tah)*;
  what's the matter? ¿qué pasa? *(keh PAH-sah?)*

mattress colchón (m.) *(kohl-CHOHN)*

May mayo (m.) *(MAH-yoh)*

maybe quizás, tal vez *(kee-SAHS, tahl-VEHS)*

meal comida (f.) *(koh-MEE-dah)*

mean (v.) significar, querer decir *(seeg-nee-fee-KAHR, keh-REHR deh-SEER)*

measurement medida (f.) *(meh-DEE-dah)*

meat carne (f.) *(KAHR-neh)*

mechanic mecánico (m.) *(meh-KAH-nee-koh)*

medical médico *(MEH-dee-koh)*

medicine medicina (f.) *(meh-dee-SEE-nah)*

meet encontrarse *(ehn-kohn-TRAHR-seh)*;
  (for the first time) conocer *(koh-noh-SEHR)*

melon melón (m.) *(meh-LOHN)*

mend remendar *(rreh-mehn-DAHR)*

men's room baño de señores (m.) *(BAH-nyoh deh seh-NYOH-rehs)*

menu menú (m.) *(meh-NOO)*

merry alegre *(ah-LEH-greh)*

Merry Christmas! ¡Feliz Navidad! *(feh-LEES nah-vee-DAHD!)*

message mensaje (m.) *(mehn-SAH-heh)*

meter (length) metro (m.) *(MEH-troh);*
   taxi meter taxímetro (m.) *(tahk-SEE-meh-troh)*

Mexican mexicano(-a) *(meh-hee-KAH-noh)(-nah)*

middle (center) medio (m.); centro (m.) *(MEH-dyoh; SEHN-troh)*

midnight medianoche (f.) *(meh-dyah-NOH-cheh)*

mild ligero, suave *(lee-HEH-roh, SWAH-veh)*

milk leche (f.) *(LEH-cheh)*

million millón *(mee-YOHN)*

mind mente (f.) *(MEHN-teh);*
   never mind no importa *(noh eem-POHR-tah)*

mine mío *(MEE-oh);*
   (w./pl) míos *(MEE-ohs)*

mineral water agua mineral (f.) *(AH-gwah mee-neh-RAHL)*

minister ministro (m.) *(mee-NEES-troh)*

mirror espejo (m.) *(ehs-PEH-hoh)*

Miss señorita *(seh-nyoh-REE-tah)*

miss (a train, bus, etc.) perder *(pehr-DEHR)*

missing, to be faltar *(fahl-TAHR)*

mistake error (m.) *(eh-RROHR)*

monastery monasterio (m.) *(moh-nahs-TEH-ryoh)*

Monday lunes (m.) *(LOO-nehs)*

money dinero (m.) *(dee-NEH-roh);*
   money order giro (m.) *(HEE-roh)*

month mes (m.) *(mehs)*

monument monumento (m.) *(moh-noo-MEHN-toh)*

moon luna (f.) *(LOO-nah)*

more más *(mahs)*

morning mañana (f.) *(mah-NYAH-nah)*

mosquito mosquito (m.) *(mohs-KEE-toh)*

mother madre (f.) *(MAH-dreh)*

motion picture cine (m.), película (f.) *(SEE-neh, peh-LEE-koo-lah)*

motor motor (m.) *(moh-TOHR)*

mouth boca (f.) *(BOH-kah);*
   mouthwash enjuague (m.) *(ehn-HWAH-geh)*

move mover *(moh-VEHR);*
   (to change residence) mudarse *(moo-DAHR-seh)*

movie película (f.) *(peh-LEE-koo-lah)*

Mr. (Mister) señor *(seh-NYOHR)*

Mrs. señora *(seh-NYOH-rah)*

much mucho *(MOO-choh)*

museum museo (m.) *(moo-SEH-oh)*

mushroom seta (f./Sp.),
hongo (m./M x.) *(SEH-tah,
OHN-goh)*
must deber, tener que
(deh-BEHR, teh-NEHR keh)
my mi *(mee)*;
(w/pl.) mis *(mees)*

N

nail (finger, toe) uña (f.)
(OO-nyah)
name nombre (m.) *(NOHM-
breh)*;
surname apellido (m.)
(ah-peh-YEE-doh)
napkin servilleta (f.) *(sehr-
vee-YEH-tah)*
narrow estrecho, angosto
(ehs-TREH-choh, ahn-GOHS-toh)
nationality nacionalidad
(f.) *(nah-syoh-nah-lee-DAHD)*
nausea nauseas (f.pl.)
(NOW-seh-ahs)
near cerca *(SEHR-kah)*
nearly casi *(KAH-see)*
necessary necesario *(neh-
seh-SAH-ryoh)*
neck cuello (m.) *(KWEH-
yoh)*
necklace collar (m.) *(koh-
YAHR)*
necktie corbata (f.) *(kohr-
BAH-tah)*
need (v.) necesitar *(neh-
seh-see-TAHR)*
needle aguja (f.) *(ah-GOO-
hah)*
nerve nervio (m.) *(NEHR-
vyoh)*

net (hair) redecilla (f.)
(rreh-deh-SEE-yah)
never nunca *(NOON-kah)*
new nuevo *(NWEH-voh)*
new year año nuevo (m.)
(AH-nyoh NWEH-voh)
newspaper periódico
(m.) *(peh-RYOH-dee-koh)*
newsstand quiosco (m.)
(KYOHS-koh)
next próximo, siguiente
*(PROHK-see-moh, see-GYEHN-
teh)*
night noche (f.) *(NOH-cheh)*
night rate tarifa nocturna
(f.) *(tah-REE-fah nohk-TOOR-
nah)*
nightclub cabaret (m.)
(kah-bah-REHT)
nightgown camisón (m.)
(kah-mee-SOHN)
nightlife vida nocturna
(f.) *(VEE-dah nohk-TOOR-nah)*
nine nueve *(NWEH-veh)*
nineteen diecinueve *(dyeh-
see-NWEH-veh)*
ninety noventa *(no-VEHN-
tah)*
ninth noveno *(noh-VEH-noh)*
no no *(noh)*;
no one nadie, ninguno
(NAH-dyeh, neen-GOO-noh)
noise ruido (m.) *(RRUEE-
doh)*
noisy ruidoso *(rruee-DOH-
soh)*
none ninguno *(neen-GOO-
noh)*
noon mediodía (m.) *(meh-
dyoh-DEE-ah)*
north norte (m.) *(NOHR-teh)*

Norwegian noruego(-a) *(noh-RWEH-goh)(-gah)*

nose nariz (f.) *(nah-REES)*

not no *(noh)*

nothing nada *(NAH-dah)*;
nothing else nada más *(NAH-dah mahs)*

notice (announcement) aviso (m.) *(ah-VEE-soh)*

novel (book) novela (f.) *(noh-VEH-lah)*

November noviembre (m.) *(noh-VYEM-breh)*

now ahora *(ah-OH-rah)*

number número (m.) *(NOO-meh-roh)*

nurse enfermera (f.) *(ehn-fehr-MEH-rah)*

nut (food) nuez (f.) *(nwehs)*;
(for a bolt or screw) tuerca (f.) *(TWEHR-kah)*

O

occupied ocupado *(oh-koo-PAH-doh)*

October octubre (m.) *(ohk-TOO-breh)*

oculist oculista (m./f.) *(oh-koo-LEES-tah)*

of de *(deh)*

of course naturalmente, desde luego, por supuesto *(nah-too-rahl-MEHN-teh, DEHS-deh LWEH-goh, pohr soo-PWEHS-toh)*

office oficina (f.) *(oh-fee-SEE-nah)*;
box office taquilla (f.) *(tah-KEE-yah)*;

post office correo (m.) *(koh-RREH-oh)*

often a menudo *(ah meh-NOO-doh)*

oil aceite (m.) *(ah-SAY-teh)*

okay, it's está bien *(ehs-TAH byehn)*

old viejo, anciano *(VYEH-hoh, ahn-SYAH-noh)*;
how old are you? ¿qué edad tiene? *(keh eh-DAHD TYEH-neh?)*

olive aceituna (f.) *(ah-say-TOO-nah)*

omelet tortilla de huevos (f.) *(tohr-TEE-yah deh WEH-vohs)*

on en, sobre *(ehn, SOH-breh)*

once (one time) una vez *(OO-nah vehs)*;
at once en seguida *(ehn seh-GEE-dah)*

one un (uno, una) *(oon [OO-noh, OO-nah])*;
one-way (traffic) dirección única *(dee-rehk-SYOHN OO-nee-kah)*

onion cebolla (f.) *(seh-BOH-yah)*

only solamente, sólo *(soh-lah-MEHN-teh, SOH-loh)*

open abierto *(ah-BYEHR-toh)*;
to open abrir *(ah-BREER)*

opera ópera (f.) *(OH-peh-rah)*

operator (phone) operadora (f.) *(oh-peh-rah-DOH-rah)*

optician óptico(-a) *(OHP-tee-koh)(-kah)*

orange naranja (f.) *(nah-RAHN-hah)*

orangeade naranjada (f.) *(nah-rahn-HAH-dah)*

orchestra (band) orquesta (f.) *(ohr-KEHS-tah)*

order encargo (m.) *(ehn-KAHR-goh)*;
to order encargar *(ehn-kahr-GAHR)*

other otro *(OH-troh)*;
(w/pl.) otros *(OH-trohs)*

ouch! ¡ay! *(ahy!)*

our, ours nuestro *(NWEHS-troh)*;
(w/pl.) nuestros *(NWEHS-trohs)*

out afuera *(ah-FWEH-rah)*

outlet (electrical) toma corriente (m.), enchufe (m.) *(toh-mah-koh-RRYEHN-teh, ehn-CHOO-feh)*

outside afuera *(ah-FWEH-rah)*

over (above) encima *(ehn-SEE-mah)*;
(finished) terminado *(tehr-mee-NAH-doh)*;
it's over ya terminó *(yah tehr-mee-NOH)*

overcoat abrigo (m.), sobretodo (m.) *(ah-BREE-goh, soh-breh-TOH-doh)*

overdone requemado *(rreh-keh-MAH-doh)*

overheat (motor) recalentar *(rreh-kah-lehn-TAHR)*

overnight por la noche *(pohr lah NOH-cheh)*

owe deber *(deh-BEHR)*

own (v.) poseer *(poh-seh-EHR)*

oyster ostra (f.) *(OHS-trah)*

P

pack (luggage) (v.) hacer las maletas *(ah-SEHR lahs mah-LEH-tahs)*

package paquete (m.), bulto (m.) *(pah-KEH-teh, BOOL-toh)*

packet paquete (m.) *(pah-KEH-teh)*

page (of book) página (f.) *(PAH-hee-nah)*;
to page llamar *(yah-MAHR)*

pain dolor (m.) *(doh-LOHR)*

paint, wet pintura fresca (f.) *(peen-TOO-rah FREHS-kah)*

pair par (m.) *(pahr)*

pajamas pijama (f.) *(pee-HAH-mah)*

palace palacio (m.) *(pah-LAH-syoh)*

panties bragas (f.pl./Sp.), pantaletas (f.pl./Mex.) *(BRAH-gahs, pahn-tah-LEH-tahs)*

pants pantalones (m.pl.) *(pahn-tah-LOH-nehs)*

paper papel (m.) *(pah-PEHL)*;
toilet paper papel higiénico *(pah-PEHL ee-HYEH-nee-koh)*;
wrapping paper papel de regalo *(pah-PEHL deh rreh-GAH-loh)*

parcel paquete (m.) *(pah-KEH-teh)*

225

parcel post paquete postal (m.) *(pah-KEH-teh pohs-TAHL)*

pardon (v.) perdonar *(pehr-doh-NAHR)*

park (v.) estacionar *(ehs-tah-syoh-NAHR)*

parking, no prohibido estacionar *(proh-ee-BEE-doh ehs-tah-syoh-NAHR)*

part (section) parte (f.) *(PAHR-teh)*;
   to part hair hacer la raya *(ah-SEHR lah RRAH-yah)*;
   to separate separar, dividir *(seh-pah-RAHR, dee-vee-DEER)*

parts (spare) piezas de repuesto (f.pl.) *(PYEH-sahs deh rreh-PWEHS-toh)*

pass (permit) permiso (m.) *(pehr-MEE-soh)*;
   to pass pasar *(pah-SAHR)*

passenger pasajero(-a) (m.,f.) *(pah-sah-HEH-roh)(-rah)*

passport pasaporte (m.) *(pah-sah-POHR-teh)*

past pasado (m.) *(pah-SAH-doh)*

pastry pasteles (m.pl.) *(pahs-TEH-lehs)*

pay (v.) pagar *(pah-GAHR)*

pea guisante (m.), chícharo (m.) *(gee-SAHN-teh, CHEE-chah-roh)*

peach melocotón (m.), durazno (m.) *(meh-loh-koh-TOHN, doo-RAHS-noh)*

pear pera (f.) *(PEH-rah)*

pedestrian peatón (m.) *(peh-ah-TOHN)*

pen pluma (f.) *(PLOO-mah)*

pencil lápiz (m.) *(LAH-pees)*

people gente (f.) *(HEHN-teh)*

pepper, black pimienta negra (f.) *(pee-MYEHN-tah NEH-grah)*

peppers pimientos (m.pl.), chiles (m.pl./Mex.) *(pee-MYEHN-tohs, CHEE-lehs)*

performance función (m.) *(foon-SYOHN)*

perfume perfume (m.) *(pehr-FOO-meh)*

perhaps quizás, tal vez *(kee-SAHS, tahl VEHS)*

permanent (wave) permanente (f.) *(pehr-mah-NEHN-teh)*

permit (pass) permiso (m.) *(pehr-MEE-soh)*;
   to permit permitir *(pehr-mee-TEER)*

Persian persa (m./f.) *(PEHR-sah)*

personal personal *(pehr-soh-NAHL)*

phone teléfono (m.) *(teh-LEH-foh-noh)*;
   to phone telefonear *(teh-leh-foh-neh-AHR)*

photograph fotografía (f.) *(foh-toh-grah-FEE-ah)*;
   to take a photo tomar una foto *(toh-MAHR OO-nah FOH-toh)*

pickle encurtido (m.) *(ehn-koor-TEE-doh)*

picnic gira (f.), picnic (m.) *(HEE-rah, PEEK-neek)*

picture (art) cuadro (m.),

pintura (f.) *(KWAH-droh, peen-TOO-rah)*;

motion picture película (f.) *(peh-LEE-koo-lah)*

pie pastel (m.) *(pahs-TEHL)*

piece pedazo (m.) *(peh-DAH-soh)*

pier muelle (f.) *(MWEH-yeh)*

pill píldora (f.) *(PEEL-doh-rah)*

pillow almohada (f.) *(ahl-moh-AH-dah)*

pillowcase funda (f.) *(FOON-dah)*

pilot piloto (m.) *(pee-LOH-toh)*

pin alfiler (m.) *(ahl-fee-LEHR)*;

safety pin imperdible (m.) *(eem-pehr-DEE-bleh)*

pineapple piña (f.), ananá (m.) *(PEE-nyah, ah-nah-NAH)*

pink rosado *(rroh-SAH-doh)*

pipe (smoking) pipa (f.) *(PEE-pah)*

pitcher jarro (m.), cántaro (m.) *(HAH-rroh, KAHN-tah-roh)*

pity!, what a ¡qué lástima! *(keh-LAHS-tee-mah!)*

place (site) sitio (m.) *(SEE-tyoh)*;

to place colocar *(koh-loh-KAHR)*

plane (air) avión (m.) *(ah-VYOHN)*

plate plato (m.) *(PLAH-toh)*

platform andén (m.), plataforma (f.) *(ahn-DEHN, plah-tah-FOHR-mah)*

play drama (m.) *(DRAH-mah)*;

to play (a game) jugar *(hoo-GAHR)*;

to play (an instrument) tocar *(toh-KAHR)*

playing cards naipes (m.pl.) *(NAH-ee-pehs)*

pleasant agradable *(ah-grah-DAH-bleh)*;

(person) simpático *(seem-PAH-tee-koh)*

please por favor, haga el favor de *(pohr fah-VOHR, AH-gah ehl fah-VOHR deh)*

pleasure gusto (m.), placer (m.) *(GOOS-toh, plah-SEHR)*

pliers alicates (m.pl.) *(ah-lee-KAH-tehs)*

plug (spark) bujía (f.) *(boo-HEE-ah)*

plum ciruela (f.) *(see-RWEH-lah)*

p.m. de la tarde, de la noche *(deh lah TAHR-deh, deh lah NOH-cheh)*

pocket bolsillo (m.) *(bohl-SEE-yoh)*

pocketbook bolsa (f.) *(BOHL-sah)*

point (place) punto (m.) *(POON-toh)*

poison veneno (m.) *(veh-NEH-noh)*

police policía (f.) *(poh-lee-SEE-ah)*

policeman policía (m.), agente de policía (m.) *(poh-lee-SEE-ah, ah-HEHN-teh deh poh-lee-SEE-ah)*

Polish polaco(-a) *(poh-LAH-koh)(-kah)*

227

polish (nail) esmalte (m.) *(ehs-MAHL-teh);*
polish remover acetona (f.) *(ah-seh-TOH-nah)*
polite cortés *(kohr-TEHS)*
politeness cortesía (f.) *(kohr-teh-SEE-ah)*
poor pobre *(POH-breh)*
pork carne de cerdo (f.) *(KAHR-neh deh SEHR-doh)*
port (harbor) puerto (m.) *(PWEHR-toh)*
porter mozo (m.) *(MOH-soh)*
portion porción (f.), ración (f.) *(pohr-SYOHN, rrah-SYOHN)*
Portuguese portugués (-esa) *(pohr-too-GEHS)(-GEH-sah)*
possible posible *(poh-SEE-bleh)*
postcard tarjeta postal (f.) *(tar-HEH-tah pohs-TAHL)*
postage porte (m.), franqueo (m.) *(POHR-teh, frahn-KEH-oh)*
potato papa (f.), patata (f./Sp.) *(PAH-pah, pah-TAH-tah)*
pour (rain) llover a cántaros *(yoh-VEHR ah KAHN-tah-rohs)*
powder polvo (m.) *(POHL-voh);*
face powder polvo para la cara (m.) *(POHL-voh PAH-rah lah KAH-rah)*
prefer preferir *(pre-feh-REER)*
prepare preparar *(preh-pah-RAHR)*
prescription receta (f.) *(rreh-SEH-tah)*

press (iron) planchar *(plahn-CHAHR)*
pretty bonito, lindo *(boh-NEE-toh, LEEN-doh)*
price precio (m.) *(PREH-syoh)*
priest cura (m.), sacerdote (m.) *(KOO-rah, sah-sehr-DOH-teh)*
print (photo) copia (f.) *(KOH-pyah)*
program programa (m.) *(proh-GRAH-mah)*
promise (v.) prometer *(proh-meh-TEHR)*
Protestant protestante (m./f.) *(proh-tehs-TAHN-teh)*
prune ciruela pasa (f.) *(see-RWEH-lah PAH-sah)*
pudding budín (m.) *(boo-DEEN)*
pump (fuel) bomba de combustible (f.) *(BOHM-bah deh kohm-boos-TEE-bleh)*
puncture (tire) pinchazo (m.) *(peen-CHAH-soh)*
purchase (item) compra (f.) *(KOHM-prah)*
purple morado *(moh-RAH-doh)*
purse bolsa (f.) *(BOHL-sah)*
purser contador de barco *(kohn-tah-DOHR deh BAHR-koh)*
push (v.) empujar *(ehm-poo-HAHR)*
put poner *(poh-NEHR);*
put in meter en *(meh-TEHR ehn);*
put (clothes) on ponerse *(poh-NEHR-seh)*

Q

quarter (fraction) cuarto (m.) *(KWAHR-toh)*

quick; quickly pronto *(PROHN-toh)*

quiet quieto, tranquilo *(KYEH-toh, trahn-KEE-loh)*

quinine quinina (f.) *(kee-NEE-nah)*

quite bastante *(bahs-TAHN-teh)*

R

rabbi rabino (m.) *(rrah-BEE-noh)*

rabbit conejo (m.) *(koh-NEH-hoh)*

rack (train or bus) rejilla (f.) *(rreh-HEE-yah)*

radiator radiador (m.) *(rrah-dyah-DOHR)*

radio radio (m.) *(RRAH-dyoh)*

radish rábano (m.) *(RRAH-bah-noh)*

railroad ferrocarril (m.) *(feh-rroh-kah-RREEL)*

rain lluvia (f.) *(YOO-vyah)*

raincoat impermeable (m.) *(eem-pehr-meh-AH-bleh)*

rare (meat) poco asada *(POH-koh ah-SAH-dah)*

rate of exchange tipo de cambio *(TEE-poh deh KAHM-byoh)*

rather (prefer) preferir *(preh-feh-REER)*

razor navaja de afeitar (f.) *(nah-VAH-hah deh ah-fay-TAHR)*

razor blade hojilla de afeitar (f.) *(oh-HEE-yah deh ah-fay-TAHR)*

read leer *(leh-EHR)*

ready, to be estar listo *(ehs-TAHR LEES-toh)*

real verdadero *(vehr-dah-DEH-roh)*

really de veras, de verdad *(deh VEH-rahs, deh vehr-DAHD)*

reasonable razonable *(rrah-soh-NAH-bleh)*

receipt recibo (m.) *(rreh-SEE-boh)*

receiver (on package) destinatario (m.) *(dehs-tee-nah-TAH-ryoh)*

recommend recomendar *(rreh-koh-mehn-DAHR)*

record (phonograph) disco (m.) *(DEES-koh)*

recover (get back) recobrar *(rreh-koh-BRAHR);* **(health)** reponerse *(rreh-poh-NEHR-seh)*

red rojo *(RROH-hoh)*

refund (payment) reembolso (m.) *(rreh-ehm-BOHL-soh);* **to refund** reembolsar *(rreh-ehm-bohl-SAHR)*

refuse (v.) rehusar, rechazar *(rreh-oo-SAHR, rreh-chah-SAHR)*

regards recuerdos (m.pl.), saludos (m.pl.) *(rreh-KWEHR-dohs, sah-LOO-dohs)*

registered (mail) certificado *(sehr-tee-fee-KAH-doh)*

registry window ventanilla de los certificados (f.) *(vehn-tah-NEE-yah deh lohs sehr-tee-fee-KAH-dohs)*

regular (ordinary) ordinario *(ohr-dee-NAH-ryoh)*

remedy remedio (m.) *(rreh-MEH-dyoh)*

remember recordar, acordarse de *(rreh-kohr-DAHR, ah-kohr-DAHR-seh deh)*

rent alquiler (m.) *(ahl-kee-LEHR)*;
    to rent alquilar *(ahl-kee-LAHR)*

repair reparación (f.) *(rreh-pah-rah-SYOHN)*

repeat repetir *(rreh-peh-TEER)*

reply (v.) responder *(rrehs-pohn-DEHR)*

reservation reservación (f.), reserva (f./Sp.) *(rreh-sehr-vah-SYOHN, rreh-SEHR-vah)*

reserve reservar *(rreh-sehr-VAHR)*

reserved seat asiento reservado (m.) *(ah-SYEHN-toh rreh-sehr-VAH-doh)*

rest (v.) descansar *(dehs-kahn-SAHR)*

restroom lavabo (m.), retrete (m.) *(lah-VAH-boh, rreh-TREH-teh)*

restaurant restaurante (m.) *(rrehs-tow-RAHN-teh)*

return (give back) devolver *(deh-vohl-VEHR)*;
    (go back) volver *(vohl-VEHR)*

rib costilla (f.) *(kohs-TEE-yah)*

ribbon cinta (f.) *(SEEN-tah)*

rice arroz (m.) *(ah-RROHS)*

rich rico *(RREE-koh)*

ride paseo (m.) *(pah-SEH-oh)*;
    to ride (on a car, train, etc.) pasear en, ir en *(pah-seh-AHR ehn, EER ehn)*

right (direction) derecha (f.) *(deh-REH-chah)*;
    to be right tener razón *(teh-NEHR rrah-SOHN)*;
    all right está bien *(ehs-TAH byehn)*;

right now ahora mismo *(ah-OH-rah MEES-moh)*

ring (on finger) anillo, sortija *(ah-NEE-yoh, sohr-TEE-hah)*

rinse enjuague (m.) *(ehn-HWAH-geh)*

river río (m.) *(RREE-oh)*

road camino (m.) *(kah-MEE-noh)*;
    (highway) carretera (f.) *(kah-rreh-TEH-rah)*;
    road map mapa de carreteras (m.) *(MAH-pah de kah-rreh-TEH-rahs)*

roast asado (m.) *(ah-SAH-doh)*;
    roast beef rosbif (m.) *(rohs-BEEF)*

rob robar *(rroh-BAHR)*

robe bata (f.) *(BAH-tah)*

roll (bread) panecillo (m.), bolillo (m./Mex.) *(pah-neh-SEE-yoh, boh-LEE-yoh)*;
    (film) rollo (m.) *(RROH-yoh)*

room cuarto (m.), alcoba (f.), habitación (f.) *(KWAHR-toh, ahl-KOH-bah, ah-bee-tah-SYOHN)*

root raíz (f.) *(rrah-EES)*

rope cuerda (f.) *(KWER-dah)*

rouge colorete (m.) *(koh-loh-REH-teh)*

round redondo *(rreh-DOHN-doh)*;

round trip viaje de ida y vuelta (m.) *(VYAH-heh deh EE-dah ee VWEHL-tah)*

row (theatre) fila (f.) *(FEE-lah)*

rubber caucho (m.) *(KOW-choh)*;

rubber eraser goma de borrar (f.) *(GOH-mah deh boh-RRAHR)*;

rubber band elástico (m.) *(eh-LAHS-tee-koh)*

rug alfombra (f.) *(ahl-FOHM-brah)*

Rumanian rumano(-a) *(rroo-MAH-noh)(-nah)*

rum ron (m.) *(rrohn)*

run correr *(koh-RREHR)*

running water agua corriente (f.) *(AH-gwah koh-RRYEHN-teh)*

runway (plane) pista (f.) *(PEES-tah)*

Russian ruso(-a) *(RROO-soh)(-sah)*

S

salad ensalada (f.) *(ehn-sah-LAH-dah)*

sale venta (f.), oferta (f./Mex.) *(VEHN-tah, oh-FEHR-tah)*

salon (beauty) salón de belleza (m.) *(sah-LOHN deh beh-YEH-sah)*

saloon cantina (f.) *(kahn-TEE-nah)*

salt sal (f.) *(sahl)*

same mismo *(MEES-moh)*

sand arena (f.) *(ah-REH-nah)*

sandwich bocadillo (m.) *(boh-kah-DEE-yoh)*;

(in a roll) torta (f./Mex.) *(TOHR-tah)*

sardine sardina (f.) *(sahr-DEE-nah)*

Saturday sábado (m.) *(SAH-bah-doh)*

sauce salsa (f.) *(SAHL-sah)*

saucer platillo (m.) *(plah-TEE-yoh)*

sausage salchicha (f.), chorizo (m.) *(sahl-CHEE-chah, choh-REE-soh)*

say decir *(deh-SEER)*

scarf bufanda (f.) *(boo-FAHN-dah)*

school escuela (f.) *(ehs-KWEH-lah)*

scissors tijeras (f.pl.) *(tee-HEH-rahs)*

screwdriver destornillador (m.) *(dehs-tohr-nee-yah-DOHR)*

sea mar (m.) *(mahr)*

seafood mariscos (m.pl.) *(mah-REES-kohs)*

seasickness mareo (m.) *(mah-REH-oh)*

season estación (f.) *(ehs-tah-SYOHN)*

seasoned sazonado *(sah-soh-NAH-doh)*

seat asiento (m.) *(ah-SYEHN-toh)*

seat (v.) sentarse *(sehn-TAHR-seh)*

second segundo *(seh-GOON-doh)*

secretary secretario(-a) *(seh-kreh-TAH-ryoh) (-ryah)*

see ver *(vehr)*

seem parecer *(pah-reh-SEHR)*

select escoger *(ehs-koh-HEHR)*

sell vender *(vehn-DEHR)*

send mandar, enviar *(mahn-DAHR, ehn-VYAHR)*

sender (on mail) remitente (m.) *(rreh-mee-TEHN-teh)*

September septiembre (m.) *(sehp-TYEHM-breh)*

serve servir *(sehr-VEER)*

service servicio (m.) *(sehr-VEE-syoh)*;
at your service a sus órdenes *(ah soos OHR-deh-nehs)*

set (hair) (v.) arreglarse *(ah-rreh-GLAHR-seh)*

seven siete *(SYEH-teh)*

seventeen diecisiete *(dye-see-SYEH-teh)*

seventh séptimo *(SEPH-tee-moh)*

seventy setenta *(seh-TEHN-tah)*

several varios *(VAH-ryohs)*

shade, in the en la sombra *(ehn lah SOHM-brah)*

shampoo champú (m.) *(chahm-POO)*

shave (v.) afeitar *(ah-fay-TAHR)*

shawl chal (m.) *(chahl)*

she ella *(EH-yah)*

sheet sábana (f.) *(SAH-bah-nah)*

shine (v.) (shoes) lustrar *(loos-TRAHR)*;
(stars) brillar *(bree-YAHR)*

ship buque (m.) *(BOO-keh)*;
to ship enviar *(ehn-VYAHR)*

shirt camisa (f.) *(kah-MEE-sah)*

shoe zapato (m.) *(sah-PAH-toh)*

shoelaces cordones de zapato (m.pl.) *(kohr-DOH-nehs deh sah-PAH-tohs)*

shop tienda (f.) *(TYEHN-dah)*

shopping, to go ir de compras *(eer deh KOHM-prahs)*

short corto *(KOHR-toh)*

shorts (underwear) calzoncillos (m.pl.) *(kahl-sohn-SEE-yohs)*

shoulder hombro (m.) *(OHM-broh)*;
(on road) borde (m.) *(BOHR-deh)*

show (art) exposición (f.) *(ehks-poh-see-SYOHN)*;
(performance) función (f.) *(foon-SYOHN)*;
to show mostrar *(mohs-TRAHR)*

shower ducha (f.), regadera (f./Mex.) *(DOO-cha, rreh-gah-DEH-rah)*

shrimp gamba (f./Sp.), camarón (m.) *(GAHM-bah, kah-mah-ROHN)*

shrine santuario (m.) *(sahn-TWAH-ryah)*

232

shut (v.) cerrar *(seh-RRAHR)*

sick enfermo *(ehn-FEHR-moh)*

sickness enfermedad (f.) *(ehn-fehr-meh-DAHD)*

side lado (m.) *(LAH-doh)*

sidewalk acera (f.) *(ah-SEH-rah)*

sight-see hacer turismo, visitar *(ah-SEHR too-REES-moh, vee-see-TAHR)*

sign (display) letrero (m.) *(leh-TREH-roh)*;
to sign firmar *(feer-MAHR)*

silk seda (f.) *(SEH-dah)*

silver plata (f.) *(PLAH-tah)*

since desde *(DEHS-deh)*

sing cantar *(kahn-TAHR)*

single room habitación para uno (f.) *(ah-bee-tah-SYOHN PAH-rah OO-noh)*

sink (basin) lavabo (m.) *(luh-VAH-boh)*

sir señor (m.) *(seh-NYOHR)*

sister hermana (f.) *(ehr-MAH-nah)*

sit (down) (v.) sentarse *(sehn-TAHR-seh)*

sixteen dieciséis *(dyeh-see-SAYS)*

sixth sexto *(SEHKS-toh)*

sixty sesenta *(seh-SEHN-tah)*

size tamaño (m.) *(tah-MAH-nyoh)*

skin piel (f.) *(pyehl)*

skirt falda (f.) *(FAHL-dah)*

sky cielo (m.) *(SYEH-loh)*

sleep (v.) dormir *(dohr-MEER)*

sleeping car coche-cama (m.) *(KOH-cheh KAH-mah)*

sleepy, to be tener sueño *(teh-NEHR SWEH-nyoh)*

slip (garment) combinación (f.) *(kohm-bee-nah-SYOHN)*

slippers zapatillas (f.pl.) *(sah-pah-TEE-yahs)*

slow lento *(LEHN-toh)*;
the watch is slow el reloj está atrasado *(ehl rreh-LOH ehs-TAH ah-trah-SAH-doh)*

slowly despacio, lentamente *(dehs-PAH-syoh, lehn-tah-MEHN-teh)*

small pequeño *(peh-KEH-nyoh)*

smoke (v.) fumar *(foo-MAHR)*

smoking car coche fumador (m.) *(KOH-cheh foo-mah-DOHR)*

snow nieve (f.) *(NYEH-veh)*;
to snow nevar *(neh-VAHR)*

so así *(ah-SEE)*

soap jabón (m.) *(hah-BOHN)*

soccer fútbol (m.) *(FOOT-bohl)*

socks calcetines (m.pl.) *(kahl-seh-TEE-nehs)*

sofa sofá (m.) *(soh-FAH)*

soft blando, suave *(BLAHN-doh, SWAH-veh)*

soft drink refresco (m.) *(rreh-FREHS-koh)*

sole (shoe) suela (f.) *(SWEH-lah)*

some algún *(ahl-GOON)*;
(w/pl.) algunos *(ahl-GOO-nohs)*

someone alguien *(AHL-gyehn)*

something algo *(AHL-goh)*

sometimes a veces, algu-nas veces *(ah VEH-sehs, ahl-GOO-nahs VEH-sehs)*

son hijo (m.) *(EE-hoh)*

song canción (f.) *(kahn-SYOHN)*

soon pronto *(PROHN-toh)*

sore throat dolor de gar-ganta (m.) *(doh-LOHR deh gahr-GAHN-tah)*

sorry, to be sentirlo *(sehn-TEER-loh)*;

  I am sorry lo siento *(loh SYEHN-toh)*

soup sopa (f.) *(SOH-pah)*

sour agrio *(AH-gryoh)*

south sur (m.), sud (m.) *(soor, sood)*

souvenir recuerdo (m.) *(rreh-KWEHR-doh)*

Spanish español(-a) *(ehs-pah-NYOHL)(-NYOH-lah)*

spare tire neumático de repuesto (m.) *(neoo-MAH-tee-koh deh rreh-PWEHS-toh)*

spark plug bujía (f.) *(boo-HEE-ah)*

sparkling wine vino es-pumante (m.) *(VEE-noh ehs-poo-MAHN-teh)*

speak hablar *(ah-BLAHR)*

special especial *(ehs-peh-SYAHL)*

speed limit velocidad máxima (f.) *(veh-loh-see-DAHD MAHK-see-mah)*

spend (money) gastar *(gahs-TAHR)*;

  spend time pasar tiempo *(pah-SAHR TYEHM-poh)*

spinach espinaca (f.) *(ehs-pee-NAH-kah)*

spoon cuchara (f.) *(koo-CHAH-rah)*

sprain torcedura (f.) *(tohr-seh-DOO-rah)*

spring (mechanical) re-sorte (m.) *(rreh-SOHR-teh)*;

  (season) primavera (f.) *(pree-mah-VEH-rah)*

square (adj.) cuadrado *(kwah-DRAH-doh)*;

  main square plaza prin-cipal (f.), zócalo (m./Mex.) *(PLAH-sah preen-see-PAHL, SOH-kah-loh)*

stairs escalera (f.) *(ehs-kah-LEH-rah)*

stamp (postage) sello (m.), estampilla (f./Mex.) *(SEH-yoh, ehs-tahm-PEE-yah)*

stand (v.) estar de pie *(ehs-TAHR deh pyeh)*;

  stand up ponerse de pie *(poh-NEHR-seh deh pyeh)*;

  stand in line hacer cola *(ah-SEHR KOH-lah)*

star estrella (f.) *(ehs-TREH-yah)*

starch (laundry) almidón (m.) *(ahl-mee-DOHN)*

start (v.) empezar, comen-zar, principiar *(ehm-peh-SAHR, koh-mehn-SAHR, preen-see-PYAHR)*

stateroom camarote (m.) *(kah-mah-ROH-teh)*

station (gasoline) gaso-linera (f.) *(gah-soh-lee-NEH-rah)*;

(railroad) estación de tren (f.) *(ehs-tah-SYOHN deh trehn)*;

(bus) terminal de autobúses (f.) *(tehr-mee-NAHL deh ow-toh-BOO-sehs)*

stay (a visit) estancia (f.) *(ehs-TAHN-syah)*;

to stay quedarse *(keh-DAHR-seh)*

steak bistec (m.) *(bees-TEHK)*

steal (v.) robar *(rroh-BAHR)*

steel acero (m.) *(ah-SEH-roh)*

steering wheel volante (m.) *(voh-LAHN-teh)*

stew guiso (m.) *(gee-SOH)*

stewardess (airplane) azafata (f.) *(ah-sah-FAH-tah)*

stockings medias (f.pl.) *(MEH-dyahs)*

stomach estómago (m.) *(ehs-TOH-mah-goh)*;

stomachache dolor de estómago (m.) *(doh-LOHR deh ehs-TOH-mah-goh)*

stop (bus) parada (f.) *(pah-RAH-dah)*

stoplight semáforo (m.) *(seh-MAH-foh-roh)*

store tienda (f.) *(TYEHN-dah)*

straight derecho *(deh-REH-choh)*

strap correa (f.) *(koh-RREH-ah)*

straw paja (f.) *(PAH-hah)*

strawberry fresa (f.) *(FREH-sah)*

street calle (f.) *(KAH-yeh)*

streetcar tranvía (m.) *(trahn-VEE-ah)*

string cuerda (f.) *(KWEHR-dah)*

string (green) beans judías verdes (f.), ejotes (m./Mex.) *(hoo-DEE-ahs VEHR-dehs, ch-HOH tehs)*

strong fuerte *(FWEHR-teh)*

style estilo (m.) *(ehs-TEE-loh)*;

(fashion) moda (f.) *(MOH-dah)*

sudden repentino *(rreh-pehn-TEE-noh)*

suddenly de repente *(deh rreh-PEHN-teh)*

sugar azúcar (m.) *(ah-SOO-kahr)*

suit traje (m.) *(TRAH-heh)*

suitcase maleta (f.), valija (f.) *(mah-LEH-tah, vah-LEE-hah)*

summer verano (m.) *(veh-RAH-noh)*

sun sol (m.) *(sohl)*

sunglasses gafas (para sol) (f.pl.) *(GAH-fahs (PAH-rah sohl))*

Sunday domingo (m.) *(doh-MEEN-goh)*

sunny asoleado *(ah-soh-leh-AH-doh)*

supper cena (f.) *(SEH-nah)*

surgeon cirujano (m.) *(see-roo-HAN-noh)*

sweater suéter (m.) *(SWEH-tehr)*

Swedish sueco(-a) *(SWEH-koh)(-kah)*

sweet dulce *(DOOL-seh)*

swell (v.) hinchar *(een-CHAHR)*

swim nadar *(nah-DAHR)*

swimming pool piscina (f.), alberca (f./Mex.) *(pees-SEE-nah, ahl-BEHR-kah)*

Swiss suizo(-a) *(SUEE-soh)(-sah)*

switch (electric) interruptor (m.) *(een-teh-rroop-TOHR)*

swollen hinchado, inflamado *(een-CHAH-doh, een-flah-MAH-doh)*

synagogue sinagoga (f.) *(see-nah-GOH-gah)*

syrup (cough) jarabe para la tos (m.) *(hah-RAH-beh PAH-rah lah tohs)*

T

table mesa (f.) *(MEH-sah)*

tablecloth mantel (m.) *(mahn-TEHL)*

tablespoon cuchara (f.) *(koo-CHAH-rah)*

tablespoonful cucharada (f.) *(koo-chah-RAH-dah)*

tablet pastilla (f.) *(pahs-TEE-yah)*

taillight (car) luz trasera (f.) *(loos trah-SEH-rah)*

tailor sastre (m.) *(SAHS-treh)*

take (carry) llevar *(yeh-VAHR)*;
  (a person) conducir *(kohn-doo-SEER)*;
  (a thing) tomar *(toh-MAHR)*;
  takes time toma tiempo *(TOH-mah TYEHM-poh)*

take off (a garment) quitarse *(kee-TAHR-seh)*

taken (occupied) ocupado *(oh-koo-PAH-doh)*

talcum powder talco (m.) *(TAHL-koh)*

tall alto *(AHL-toh)*

tan (color) color canela (m.) *(koh-LOHR kah-NEH-lah)*

tangerine mandarina (f.) *(mahn-dah-REE-nah)*

tank tanque (m.) *(TAHN-keh)*

tap grifo (m.) *(GREE-foh)*

tape (adhesive) esparadrapo (m.) *(ehs-pah-rah-DRAH-poh)*

tasty sabroso, rico *(sah-BROH-soh, RREE-koh)*

tax impuesto (m.) *(eem-PWEHS-toh)*

tea té (m.) *(teh)*

teaspoon cucharita (f.), cucharilla (f.) *(koo-chah-REE-tah, koo-chah-REE-yah)*

teaspoonful cucharadita (f.) *(koo-chah-rah-DEE-tah)*

telegram telegrama (m.) *(teh-leh-GRAH-mah)*

telegraph (v.) telegrafiar *(tel-leh-GRAH-mah)*

telegraph (v.) telegrafíar *(teh-leh-grah-FYAHR)*

telephone teléfono (m.) *(teh-LEH-foh-noh)*;
  to telephone telefonear *(teh-leh-foh-neh-AHR)*

tell decir *(deh-SEER)*

teller (bank) cajero(-a) *(kah-HEH-roh)(-rah)*

temporarily temporalmente *(tehm-poh-rahl-MEHN-teh)*

ten diez *(dyehs)*

tenth décimo *(deh-see-moh)*

terminal terminal (f.) *(tehr-mee NAHL)*

thank agradecer, dar las gracias *(ah-grah-deh-SEHR, dahr lahs GRAH-syahs)*

thank you! ¡gracias! *(GRAH-syahs!)*

that (adj.) ese (esa), aquel (aquella) *(EH-seh [EH-sah], ah-KEHL [ah-KEH-yah]);* **(pron.)** eso *(EH-soh);* **(conj.)** que *(keh)*

the el (la), los (las) *(ehl [lah], lohs [lahs])*

theater teatro (m.) *(teh-AH-troh)*

their su *(soo);* **(w/pl.)** sus *(soos)*

there ahí, allí *(ah-EE, ah-YEE);* **there is; there are** hay *(AHY)*

thermometer termómetro (m.) *(tehr-MOH-meh-troh)*

these estos (estas) *(EHS-tohs [EHS-tahs])*

they ellos (ellas) *(EH-yohs [EH-yahs])*

thick espeso, denso, grueso *(ehs-PEH-soh, DEHN-soh, GRWEH-soh)*

thief ladrón (m.) *(lah-DROHN)*

thigh muslo (m.) *(MOOS-loh)*

thing cosa (f.) *(KOH-sah)*

think pensar *(pehn-SAHR)*

third tercero *(tehr-SEH-roh)*

thirsty, to be tener sed *(teh-NEHR sehd)*

thirteen trece *(TREH-seh)*

thirty treinta *(TRAYN-tah)*

this este (esta, esto) *(EHS-teh [EHS-tah, EHS-toh])*

those esos (esas), aquellos (aquellas) *(EH-sohs [EH-sahs], ah-KEH-yohs [ah-KEH-yahs])*

thousand mil *(meel)*

thread hilo (m.) *(EE-loh)*

three tres *(trehs)*

throat garganta (f.) *(gahr-GAHN-tah)*

through por, a través de *(pohr, a trah-VEHS deh)*

thumb pulgar (m.) *(pool-GAHR)*

thunder trueno (m.) *(TRWEH-noh);* **to thunder** tronar *(troh-NAHR)*

Thursday jueves (m.) *(HWEH-vehs)*

ticket billete (m.) *(bee-YEH-teh);* **ticket window** ventanilla (f.) *(vehn-tah-NEE-yah)*

tie (neck-) corbata (f.) *(kohr-BAH-tah)*

tighten apretar *(ah-preh-TAHR)*

till hasta (que) *(ahs-tah [keh])*

time tiempo (m.) *(TYEHM-poh);* **on time** a tiempo *(ah TYEHM-poh);* **at what time?** ¿a qué hora? *(ah keh OH-rah?)*

timetable horario (m.) *(oh-RAH-ryoh)*

tint (hair) (v.) teñir *(teh-NYEER)*

237

tip (gratuity) propina (f.)
(proh-PEE-nah)

tire (car) llanta (f.),
neumático (m.) *(YAHN-tah,
neoo-MAH-tee-koh)*

tired, to be cansado
(estar) *(kahn-SAH-doh [ehs-
TAHR])*

tissue paper papel de seda
(m.) *(pah-PEHL deh SEH-dah)*

to a; por; para *(ah; pohr;
PAH-rah)*

toast (bread) tostada (f.)
(tohs-TAH-dah);
(drink) brindis (m.)
(BREEN-dees)

tobacco tobaco (m.) *(tah-
BAH-koh)*

today hoy *(ohy)*

toe dedo (del pie) *(DEH-doh
[dehl pyeh])*

together juntos *(HOON-
tohs)*

toilet retrete (m.) *(rreh-
TREH-teh);*
toilet paper papel
higiénico (m.) *(pah-PEHL ee-
HYEH-nee-koh)*

tomato tomate (m.) *(toh-
MAH-teh)*

tomorrow mañana (f.)
(mah-;NYAH-nah)

tongue lengua (f.) *(LEHN-
gwah)*

tonic (hair) tónico para el
cabello (m.) *(TOH-nee-koh
PAH-rah ehl kah-BEH-yoh)*

tonight esta noche *(EHS-tah
NOH-cheh)*

too (also) también *(tahm-
BYEHN);*

too bad ¡qué lástima! *(keh
LAHS-tee-mah!);*

too much demasiado
(deh-mah-SYAH-doh)

tooth diente (m.) *(DHYEN-
teh);*
toothache dolor de muelas (m.) *(doh-LOHR deh MWEH-
lahs)*

toothbrush cepillo de
dientes (m.) *(seh-PEE-yoh deh
DYEHN-tehs)*

top cima (f.) *(SEE-mah)*

touch (v.) tocar *(toh-KAHR)*

tough duro *(DOO-roh)*

tourist turista (m./f.) *(too-
REES-tah)*

tow (car) remolcar *(rreh-
MOHL-kahr)*

toward hacia *(AH-syah)*

towel toalla (f.) *(toh-AH-
yah)*

town pueblo (m.) *(PWEH-
bloh)*

track (railroad) rieles
(f.pl.) *(RRYEH-lehs)*

traffic light semáforo (m.)
(seh-MAH-foh-roh)

train tren (m.) *(trehn)*

transfer (ticket) transbordo *(trahns-BOHR-doh);*
to transfer transbordar
(trahns-bohr-DAHR)

translate traducir *(trah-
doo-SEER)*

travel viajar *(vyah-HAHR);*
travel insurance seguro
de viaje (m.) *(seh-GOO-roh deh
VYAH-heh)*

traveler viajero(-a) *(vyah-
HEH-roh)(-rah);*

traveler's check cheque de viajero (m.) *(CHEH-keh deh vyah-HEH-roh)*
tree árbol (m.) *(AHR-bohl)*
trip (voyage) viaje (m.) *(VYAH-heh)*
trolley car tranvía (m.) *(trahn-VEE-ah)*
trouble, to be in tener dificultades *(teh-NEHR dee-fee-kool-TAH-dehs)*
trousers pantalones (m.pl.) *(pahn-tah-LOH-nehs)*
truck camión (m.) *(kah-MYOHN)*
true verdadero *(vehr-dah-DEH-roh)*
trunk (car) cajuela (f./Mex.), maletera (f.) *(kah-HWEH-lah, mah-leh-TEH-rah)*
try tratar *(trah-TAR);*
   try on probarse *(proh-BAHR-seh);*
   try to tratar de *(trah-TAHR-deh)*
tube (inner) cámara de aire (f.) *(KAH-mah-rah deh AH-ee-reh)*
Tuesday martes (m.) *(MAHR-tehs)*
Turkish turco(-a) *(TOOR-koh) (-kah)*
turn vuelta (f.) *(VWEHL-tah);*
   to turn doblar *(doh-BLAHR)*
tuxedo smoking (m.), traje de etiqueta (m.) *(ehs-MOH-keeng, TRAH-heh deh eh-tee-KEH-tah)*
twelve doce *(DOH-seh)*

twenty veinte *(VAYN-teh)*
twice dos veces *(dohs VEH-sehs)*
twin beds camas gemelas (f.pl.) *(KAH-mahs heh-MEH-lahs)*
two dos *(dohs)*

U

ugly feo *(FEH-oh)*
umbrella paraguas (m.) *(pah-RAH-gwahs)*
uncle tío (m.) *(TEE-oh)*
uncomfortable incómodo *(een-KOH-moh-doh)*
under debajo de *(deh-BAH-hoh deh)*
undershirt camiseta (f.) *(kah-mee-SEH-tah)*
understand comprender, entender *(kohm-prehn-DEHR, ehn-tehn-DEHR)*
underwear ropa interior (f.) *(RROH-pah een-teh-RYOHR)*
United States (of America) Estados Unidos (de América) (m.pl.) *(ehs-TAH-dohs oo-NEE-dohs [deh ah-MEH-ree-kah])*
university universidad (f.) *(oo-nee-vehr-see-DAHD)*
until hasta *(AHS-tah)*
up arriba *(ah-RREE-bah)*
upon sobre, encima de *(SOH-breh, ehn-SEE-mah deh)*
upper alto *(AHL-toh)*
upstairs arriba *(ah-RREE-bah)*

use (purpose) uso, empleo *(OO-soh, ehm-PLEH-oh)*; **to use** usar *(oo-SAHR)*

V

valise valija (f.), maleta (f.) *(vah-LEE-hah, mah-LEH-tah)*

veal ternera (f.) *(tehr-NEH-rah)*

vegetables legumbres (m.) *(leh-GOOM-brehs)*; **(greens)** verduras (f.pl.) *(vehr-DOO-rahs)*

velvet terciopelo (m.) *(tehr-syoh-PEH-loh)*

very muy *(mwee)*

vest chaleco (m.) *(chah-LEH-koh)*

veterinarian veterinario (m.) *(veh-teh-ree-NAH-ryoh)*

view vista (f.) *(VEES-tah)*

vinegar vinagre (m.) *(vee-NAH-greh)*

visit visita (f.) *(vee-SEE-tah)*; **to visit** visitar *(vee-see-TAHR)*

visitor visitante (m./f.) *(vee-see-TAHN-teh)*

W

waist cintura (f.) *(seen-TOO-rah)*

wait (for) esperar *(ehs-peh-RAHR)*

waiter mozo (m.), camarero (m.), mesero (m./Mexico) *(MOH-soh, kah-mah-REH-roh, meh-SEH-roh)*;

headwaiter jefe de comedor *(HEH-feh deh koh-meh-DOHR)*

waiting room sala de espera (f.) *(SAH-lah deh ehs-PEH-rah)*

waitress camarera (f.) *(kah-mah-REH-rah)*

wake up despertarse *(dehs-pehr-TAHR-seh)*

walk, take a dar un paseo *(dahr oon pah-SEH-oh)*

wall (interior) pared (f.) *(pah-REHD)*; **(exterior)** muro (m.) *(MOO-roh)*

wallet billetera (f.), cartera (f.) *(bee-yeh-TEH-rah, kahr-TEH-rah)*

want (v.) querer *(keh-REHR)*

warm caliente *(kah-LYEHN-teh)*

was era; estaba *(EH-rah; ehs-TAH-bah)*

wash (v.) lavar *(lah-VAHR)*; **(oneself)** lavarse *(lah-VAHR-seh)*

washroom lavabo (m.) *(lah-VAH-boh)*

watch (timepiece) reloj (m.) *(rreh-LOH)*; **to watch** mirar *(mee-RAHR)*; **watch out!** ¡cuidado! *(kwee-DAH-doh!)*

water agua (f.) *(AH-gwah)*

watermelon sandía (m.) *(sahn-DEE-ah)*

way (path) vía (f.) *(VEE-ah)*;

　(manner) manera (f.), modo (m.) *(mah-NEH-rah, MOH-doh)*;

　by way of por vía de *(pohr VEE-ah deh)*;

　one-way dirección única *(dee-rehk-SYOHN OO-nee-kah)*;

　which way? ¿por dónde? *(pohr DOHN-deh?)*

we nosotros(-as) *(noh-SOH-trohs)(-trahs)*

weak débil *(DEH-beel)*

wear llevar *(yeh VAI IR)*

weather tiempo (m.) *(TYEHM-poh)*

Wednesday miércoles (m.) *(MYEHR-koh-lehs)*

week semana (f.) *(seh-MAH-nah)*

weight peso (m.) *(PEH-soh)*

welcome, you're de nada *(deh NAH-dah)*

well bien *(byehn)*;

　well-done (meat) bien cocido *(byehn koh-SEE-doh)*

west oeste (m.) *(oh-EHS-teh)*

wet mojado *(moh-HAH-doh)*;

　wet paint pintura fresca *(peen-TOO-rah FREHS-kah)*

what? ¿qué? *(keh?)*

wheel rueda (f.) *(RRWEH-dah)*;

　steering wheel volante (m.) *(voh-LAHN-teh)*

when? ¿cuándo? *(KWAHN-doh?)*

where? ¿dónde? *(DOHN-deh?)*

which? ¿cuál? *(kwahl?)*

whiskey whiskey (m.) *(WEES-kee)*

white blanco *(BLAHN-koh)*

who? ¿quién? *(kyehn?)*;

　(pl.) ¿quiénes? *(KYEH-nehs?)*;

　why? ¿por qué? *(pohr KEH?)*

wide ancho *(AHN-choh)*

width anchura *(ahn-CHOO-rah)*

wife señora (f.), esposa (f.) *(seh-NYOH-rah, ehs-POH-sah)*

wind viento (m.) *(VYEHN-toh)*

window ventana (f.) *(vehn-TAH-nah)*;

　display window escaparate (m.) *(ehs-kah-pah-RAH-teh)*;

　(of a train station, post office, bank, etc.) ventanilla (f.) *(vehn-tah-NEE-yah)*

windshield parabrisas (m.pl.) *(pah-rah-BREE-sahs)*

windy ventoso *(vehn-TOH-soh)*;

　it's windy hace viento *(AH-seh VYEHN-toh)*

wine vino (m.) *(VEE-noh)*;

　wine list lista de vinos (f.) *(LEES-tah deh VEE-nohs)*

winter invierno (m.) *(een-VYEHR-noh)*

wish (v.) querer, desear *(keh-REHR, deh-seh-AHR)*;

　best wishes saludos (m.pl.) *(sah-LOO-dohs)*

with con *(kohn)*

241

without sin *(seen)*
woman mujer (f.) *(moo-HEHR)*
wood madera (f.) *(mah-DEH-rah)*
wool lana (f.) *(LAH-nah)*
word palabra (f.) *(pah-LAH-brah)*
work trabajo (m.) *(trah-BAH-hoh)*;
  (piece of work) obra (f.) *(OH-brah)*;
  to work trabajar *(trah-bah-HAHR)*
worry (v.) preocuparse *(preh-oh-koo-PAHR-seh)*;
  don't worry no se preocupe *(noh seh preh-oh-KOO-peh)*
worse peor *(peh-OHR)*
worst el peor *(ehl peh-OHR)*
worth, to be valer *(vah-LEHR)*
wound (injury) herida (f.) *(eh-REE-dah)*
wounded herido *(eh-REE-doh)*
wrap (up) envolver *(ehn-VOHL-vehr)*
wrapping paper papel de envolver (m.) *(pah-PEHL deh ehn-vohl-VEHR)*
wrench (tool) llave inglesa (f.) *(YAH-veh een-GLEH-sah)*
wrist muñeca (f.) *(moo-NYEH-kah)*;
  wristwatch reloj pulsera (f.) *(rreh-LOH pool-SEH-rah)*
write escribir *(ehs-kree-BEER)*

writing paper papel de carta (m.) *(pah-PEHL deh KAHR-tah)*
wrong, to be equivocarse, no tener razón *(eh-kee-voh-KAHR-seh, noh teh-NEHR RRAH-sohn)*

X

X-ray radiografía (f.) *(rrah-dyoh-grah-FEE-ah)*

Y

year año (m.) *(AH-nyoh)*
yellow amarillo *(ah-mah-REE-yoh)*
yes sí *(see)*
yesterday ayer *(ah-YEHR)*
yet todavía *(toh-dah-VEE-ah)*;
  not yet todavía no *(toh-dah-VEE-ah noh)*
you tú (familiar); usted (formal); ustedes (pl.) *(too, oos-TEHD; oos-TEH-dehs)*
young jóven *(HOH-vehn)*
your (sing./familiar) tu *(too)*;
  (w/pl.) tus *(toos)*;
  (sing./formal) su *(soo)*;
  (w/pl.) sus *(soos)*;
  your (pl.) su *(soo)*;
  (w/pl.) sus *(soos)*
yours (sing./familiar) tuyo *(TOO-yoh)*;
  (w/pl.) tuyos *(TOO-yohs)*;
  (sing./formal) suyo *(SOO-yoh)*;
  (w/pl.) suyos *(SOO-yohs)*;

yours (pl.) suyo *(SOO-yoh)*;
(w/pl.) suyos *(SOO-yohs)*
youth hostel albergue juvenil (m.) *(ahl-BEHR-geh hoo-veh-NEEL)*
Yugoslav yugoslavo(-a) *(yoo-gohs-LAH-voh)(-vah)*

Z

zipper cierre (m.) *(SYEH-rreh)*

zoo jardín zoológico (m.) *(hahr-DEEN soh-oh-LOH-hee-koh)*

SPANISH-ENGLISH DICTIONARY

A

a *(ah)* to; in; on; by

abajo *(ah-BAH-hoh)* below; down

abierto *(ah-BYEHR-toh)* open

abrigo (m.) *(ah-BREE-goh)* coat

abril (m.) *(ah-BREEL)* April

abrir *(ah-BREER)* to open

acabar *(ah-kah-BAHR)* to finish

aceite (m.) *(ah-SAY-teh)* oil

aceituna (f.) *(ah-say-TOO-nah)* olive

acero (m.) *(ah-SEH-roh)* steel

acetona (f.) *(ah-seh-TOH-nah)* nail polish remover

aclarar *(ah-klah-RAHR)* to clear up (weather); to clarify

acordarse *(ah-kohr-DAHR-seh)* to remember

acostarse *(ah-kohs-TAHR-seh)* to lie down, to go to bed

acuerdo (m.) *(ah-KWEHR-doh)* agreement

acumulador (m.) *(ah-koo-moo-lah-DOHR)* car battery

adelante *(ah-deh-LAHN-teh)* ahead, forward; come in

adiós *(ah-DYOHS)* goodbye, farewell

aduana (f.) *(ah-DWAH-nah)* customs

afuera *(ah-FWEH-rah)* out, outside

agosto (m.) *(ah-GOHS-toh)* August

agradable *(ah-grah-DAH-bleh)* pleasant

agradecido *(ah-grah-deh-SEE-doh)* grateful, thankful

agrio *(AH-gryoh)* sour

agua (m.) *(AH-gwah)* water;
   agua corriente *(. . . koh-RRYEHN-teh)* running water;
   agua potable *(. . . poh-TAH-bleh)* drinking water;
   agua mineral *(. . . mee-neh-RAHL)* mineral water

aguardar *(ah-gwahr-DAHR)* to expect, to wait for

aguja (f.) *(ah-GOO-hah)* needle

agujero (m.) *(ah-goo-HEH-roh)* hole

ahí *(ah-EE)* there

ahora *(ah-OH-rah)* now;
   ahora mismo *(ah-OH-rah MEES-moh)* right now

ajo (m.) *(AH-ho)* garlic

ajustar *(ah-hoos-TAHR)* to adjust

albaricoque (m.) *(ahl-bah-ree-KOH-keh)* apricot

alcachofa (f.) *(ahl-kah-CHOH-fah)* artichoke

alcoba (f.) *(ahl-KOH-bah)* bedroom

alegrarse *(ah-leh-GRAHR-seh)* to be glad, to rejoice

alegre *(ah-LEH-greh)* glad, merry, jolly

alemán(-ana) *(ah-leh-MAHN) (-MAH-nah)* German

alfiler (m.) *(ahl-fee-LEHR)* pin

alfombra (f.) *(ahl-FOHM-brah)* rug

algo *(AHL-goh)* something; anything

algodón (m.) *(ahl-goh-DOHN)* cotton

alguien *(AHL-gyehn)* someone, somebody; anyone, anybody

algún *(ahl-GOON)* some; any;
   algunas veces *(ahl-GOO-nahs VEH-sehs)* sometimes

alicates (m.pl.) *(ah-lee-KAH-tehs)* pliers

almacén (m.) *(ahl-mah-SEHN)* department store, store

almendra (f.) *(ahl-MEHN-drah)* almond

almidón (m.) *(ahl-mee-DOHN)* starch

almidonar *(ahl-mee-doh-NAHR)* to starch

almohada (f.) *(ahl-moh-AH-dah)* pillow

almorzar *(ahl-mohr-SAHR)* to have lunch; to have breakfast (Mex.)

almuerzo (m.) *(ahl-MWEHR-soh)* lunch; breakfast (Mex.)

alquilar *(ahl-kee-LAHR)* to rent

alquiler (m.) *(ahl-kee-LEHR)* rent

alrededor de *(ahl-reh-deh-DOHR deh)* around

alto *(AHL-toh)* tall

¡alto! *(AHL-toh!)* halt, stop

allá *(ah-YAH)* there (over there)

allí *(ah-YEE)* there (right there)

amargo *(ah-MAHR-goh)* bitter

amarillo *(ah-mah-REE-yoh)* yellow

amigo(-a) (m.,f.) *(ah-MEE-goh) (-gah)* friend

amueblado *(ah-mweh-BLAH-doh)* furnished

ancho *(AHN-choh)* wide

anchura (f.) *(ahn-CHOO-rah)* width

andén (m.) *(ahn-DEHN)* platform

angosto *(ahn-GOHS-toh)* narrow

anillo (m.) *(ah-NEE-yoh)* ring

anteojos (m.pl.) *(ahn-teh-OH-hos)* eyeglasses

antes de *(AHN-tehs-deh)* before

antipático *(ahn-tee-PAH-tee-koh)* unpleasant, not likable

año *(AN-nyoh)* year

apellido (m.) *(ah-peh-YEE-doh)* family name, surname

apio (m.) *(AH-pyoh)* celery

aprender *(ah-prehn-DEHR)* to learn

apretar *(ah-preh-TAHR)* to tighten

apuro (m.) *(ah-POO-roh)* trouble, difficulty; hurry, haste

aquel *(ah-KEHL)* that

aquí *(ah-KEE)* here

árabe *(AH-rah-beh)* Arab

árbol (m.) *(AHR-bohl)* tree

arena (f.) *(ah-REH-nah)* sand

arete (m.) *(ah-REH-teh)* earring

argentino(-a) *(ahr-hehn-TEE-noh)(-nah)* Argentine

armario (m.) *(ahr-MAH-ryoh)* closet

arreglar *(ah-rreh-GLAHR)* to fix, to repair

arroz (m.) *(ah-RROHS)* rice

asado (m.) *(ah-SAH-doh)* roast

asar *(ah-SAHR)* to roast

ascensor (m.) *(ah-sehn-SOHR)* elevator

asegurar *(ah-seh-goo-RAHR)* to insure; to ensure

así *(ah-SEE)* so, thus

asiento (m.) *(ah-SYEHN-toh)* seat;
asiento reservado *(...rreh-sehr-VAH-doh)* reserved seat

asoleado *(ah-soh-LEH-ah-doh)* sunny

aterrizar *(ah-teh-rree-SAHR)* to land (by plane)

atrás *(ah-TRAHS)* back, behind

austríaco(-a) *(ows-TREE-ah-koh)(-kah)* Austrian

avellana (f.) *(ah-veh-YAH-nah)* hazelnut

avería (f.) *(ah-veh-REE-ah)* breakdown (car)

avión (m.) *(ah-VYOHN)* airplane

aviso (m.) *(ah-VEE-soh)* notice; sign; warning

ayer *(ah-YEHR)* yesterday

ayudar *(ah-yoo-DAHR)* to help

ayutamiento (m.) *(ah-yoon-tah-MYEHN-toh)* city hall

azafata (f.) *(ah-sah-FAH-tah)* stewardess

azúcar (f.) *(ah-SOO-kahr)* sugar

azul *(ah-SOOL)* blue

B

bailar *(bahy-LAHR)* to dance

bajada (f.) *(bah-HAH-dah)* descent, path down;
de bajada *(deh . . .)* downhill

bajar *(bah-HAHR)* to go down, to come down, to step down

bajo *(BAH-hoh)* low

banderilla (f.) *(bahn-deh-REE-yah)* banderilla (long dart used to prick the bull)

bañarse *(bah-NYAHR-seh)* to bathe, to take a bath

barato *(bah-RAH-toh)* cheap

barba (f.) *(BAHR-bah)* beard, chin

barco (m.) *(BAHR-koh)* boat

barrio (m.) *(BAH-rryoh)* district, suburb

¡basta! *(BAHS-tah!)* enough!, cut it out!, stop!

bata (f.) *(BAH-tah)* robe

baúl (m.) *(bah-OOL)* trunk

beber *(beh-BEHR)* to drink

bebida (f.) *(beh-BEE-dah)* drink

belga *(BEHL-gah)* Belgian

bello *(BEH-yoh)* beautiful

besar *(beh-SAHR)* to kiss

beso (m.) *(BEH-soh)* kiss

biblioteca (f.) *(bee-blyoh-TEH-kah)* library

bien *(byehn)* well

billete (m.) *(bee-YEH-teh)* ticket

billetera (f.) *(bee-yeh-TEH-rah)* wallet

billón (m.) *(bee-YOHN)* trillion (U.S.); billion (Great Britain)

blanco *(BLAHN-koh)* white

blando *(BLAHN-doh)* soft

boca (f.) *(BOH-kah)* mouth

bocacalle (f.) *(boh-kah-KAH-yeh)* intersection

bocadillo (m.) *(boh-kah-DEE-yoh)* sandwich

bocina (f.) *(boh-SEE-nah)* car horn

bolsa (f.) *(BOHL-sah)* purse; bag

bolsillo (m.) *(bohl-SEE-yoh)* pocket

bolillo (m.) *(boh-LEE-yoh)* roll (bread) (Mex.)

bombilla(-o) (m.,f.) *(bohm-BEE-yah)(-yah)* electric bulb

bonito *(boh-NEE-toh)* pretty

borracho *(boh-RRAH-choh)* drunk

bote (m.) *(BOH-teh)* boat

botón (m.) *(boh-TOHN)* button

botones (m.) *(boh-TOH-nehs)* bellboy, bellhop

bragas (f.) *(BRAH-gahs)* panties

brasileño(-a) *(brah-see-LEH-nyoh)(-nah)* Brazilian

brazo (m.) *(BRAH-soh)* arm

brillar *(bree-YHAR)* to shine

brindis (m.) *(BREEHN-dees)* toast (as in "to drink to")

brocha de afeitar (f.) *(BROH-chah deh ah-fay-TAHR)* shaving brush

bueno *(BWEH-noh)* good

bufanda (f.) *(boo-FAHN-dah)* scarf

bujía (f.) *(boo-HEE-ah)* spark plug

buscar *(boos-KAHR)* to look for, to search

buzón (m.) *(boo-SOHN)* mailbox

C

caballero (m.) *(kah-bah-YEH-roh)* gentleman

caballo (m.) *(kah-BAH-yoh)* horse

cabello (m.) *(kah-BEH-yoh)* hair (on head)

cabeza (f.) *(kah-BEH-sah)* head

cabina (f.) *(kah-BEE-nah)* phone booth

cada *(KAH-dah)* each; **cada uno** *(. . . OO-noh)* each one

247

cadena (f.) *(kah-DEH-nah)* chain

cadera (f.) *(kah-DEH-rah)* hip

caer *(kah-EHR)* to fall

café (m.) *(kah-FEH)* coffee

caja (f.) *(KAH-hah)* box, case; cashier, cashbox

caja fuerte (f.) *(KAH-hah-FWEHR-teh)* safe

cajero(-a) *(kah-HEH-roh)(-rah)* cashier, teller

caliente *(kah-LYEHN-teh)* hot

calor (m.) *(kah-LOHR)* heat, warmth

calzoncillos (m.pl.) *(kahl-sohn-SEE-yohs)* drawers, undershorts

calle (f.) *(KAH-yeh)* street

cama (f.) *(KAH-mah)* bed

cámara fotográfica (f.) *(KAH-mah-rah foh-toh-GRAH-fee-kah)* camera

camarero(-a) *(kah-mah-REH-roh)(-rah)* waiter, waitress

camarón (m.) *(kah-mah-ROHN)* shrimp

camarote (m.) *(kah-mah-ROH-teh)* stateroom

camas gemelas (f.) *(KAH-mahs heh-MEH-lahs)* twin beds

cambiar *(kahm-BYAHR)* to change

cambio (m.) *(KAHM-byoh)* change

camino (m.) *(kah-MEE-noh)* road

camión (m.) *(kah-MYOHN)* truck

camisa (f.) *(kah-MEE-sah)* undershirt

camiseta (f.) *(kah-mee-SEH-tah)* undershirt

camisón (m.) *(kah-mee-SOHN)* nightshirt

campo (m.) *(KAHM-poh)* countryside

canadiense *(kah-nah-DYEHN-seh)* Canadian

canción (f.) *(kahn-SYOHN)* song

cansado *(kahn-SAH-doh)* tired

cantar *(kahn-TAHR)* to sing

cantina (f.) *(kahn-TEE-nah)* saloon

cara (f.) *(KAH-rah)* face

caro *(KAH-roh)* expensive

¡caramba! *(kah-RAHM-bah!)* darn it!

carne (f.) *(KAHR-neh)* meat

carta (f.) *(KAHR-tah)* letter; playing card

cartera (f.) *(kahr-TEH-rah)* pocketbook, wallet

carretera (f.) *(kah-rreh-TEH-rah)* highway

casa (f.) *(KAH-sah)* house, home

casi *(KAH-see)* almost

caso (m.) *(KAH-soh)* case (as in, "in case of")

castaña (f.) *(kahs-TAH-nyah)* chestnut

castillo (m.) *(kahs-TEE-yoh)* castle

catarro (m.) *(kah-TAH-rroh)* (common) cold

catorce *(kah-TOHR-seh)* fourteen

caucho (m.) *(KOW-choh)* rubber

cebolla (f.) *(seh-BOH-yah)* onion

ceja (f.) *(SEH-hah)* eyebrow

cena (f.) *(SEH-nah)* dinner, supper

cenicero (m.) *(seh-nee-SEH-roh)* ashtray

cepillar *(seh-pee-YAIIR)* to brush

cepillo (m.) *(seh-PEE-yoh)* brush

cerca de *(SEHR-kah deh)* near, close to

cerdo (m.) *(SEHR-doh)* pig, hog

cereza (f.) *(seh-REH-sah)* cherry

cerillo (m.) *(seh-REE-yoh)* match

certificado *(sehr-tee-fee-KAH-doh)* registered (mail)

cerveza (f.) *(sehr-VEH-sah)* beer

cerrado *(seh-RRAH-doh)* closed

cerradura (f.) *(seh-rrah-DOO-rah)* lock

cerrajero (m.) *(seh-rrah-HEH-roh)* locksmith

cerrar *(seh-RRAHR)* to close

cesta (f.) *(SEHS-tah)* basket

chal (m.) *(chahl)* shawl

chaleco (m.) *(chah-LEH-koh)* vest

checo(-a) *(CHEH-koh) (-kah)* Czech

cheque (m.) *(CHEH-keh)* check

chileno(-a) *(chee-LEH-noh) (-nah)* Chilean

chino(-a) *(CHEE-noh) (-nah)* Chinese

chorizo (m.) *(choh-REE-soh)* sausage

chuleta (f.) *(choo-LEH-tah)* chop, cutlet

cielo (m.) *(SYEH-loh)* sky; heaven

cien; ciento *(syehn; SYEHN-toh)* hundred

cima (f.) *(SEE-mah)* top

cincuenta *(seen-KWEHN-tah)* fifty

cine (m.) *(SEE-neh)* movie theater; movie

cinta (f.) *(SEEN-tah)* ribbon; (audio, video) tape

cintura (f.) *(seen-TOO-rah)* waist

cinturón (m.) *(seen-too-ROHN)* belt

ciruela (f.) *(see-RWEH-lah)* plum

　　ciruela pasa (f.) *(. . . PAH-sah)* prune

cirujano(-a) *(see-roo-HAH-noh)(-nah)* surgeon

ciudad (f.) *(syoo-DAHD)* city

claro *(KLAH-roh)* clear

cobrar *(koh-BRAHR)* to collect

cocido *(koh-SEE-doh)* cooked; stew

cocina (f.) *(koh-SEE-nah)* kitchen

cocinar *(koo-see-NAHR)* to cook

coche (m.) *(KOH-cheh)* car

249

codo (m.) *(KOH-doh)*
elbow

coger *(koh-HEHR)* to catch,
to take

colchón (m.) *(kohl-CHOHN)*
mattress

col (f.) *(kohl)* cabbage

colgador (m.) *(kohl-gah-DOHR)* coat hanger

color (m.) *(koh-LOHR)*
color

combinación (f.) *(kohm-bee-nah-SYOHN)* slip (garment)

comenzar *(koh-mehn-SAHR)*
to begin

comer *(koh-MEHR)* to eat

comida (f.) *(koh-MEE-dah)*
meal;
comida corrida *(. . . koh-RREE-dah)* a fixed menu
(Mex.)

comisaría (f.) *(koh-mee-SAH-REE-ah)* police station

como *(KOH-moh)* as, like

cómo *(KOH-moh)* how

cómodo *(KOH-moh-doh)*
comfortable

compañía (f.) *(kohm-pah-NYEE-ah)* company

compra (f.) *(KOHM-prah)*
buy

comprar *(kohm-PRAHR)* to
buy

comprender *(kohm-prehn-DEHR)* to understand

con *(kohn)* with

conducir *(kohn-doo-SEER)* to
drive

conductor (m.) *(kohn-dook-TOHR)* conductor

conferencia (f.) *(kohn-feh-REHN-syah)* conference

conocer *(koh-noh-SEHR)* to
know; to make the acquaintance of

conseguir *(kohn-seh-GEER)*
to get, to obtain

contar *(kohn-TAHR)* to
count; to tell (narrate)

contestar *(kohn-tehs-TAHR)*
to answer, to reply

contra *(KOHN-trah)*
against

contusión (f.) *(kohn-too-SYOHN)* bruise

copia (f.) *(KOH-pyah)* copy

corazón (m.) *(koh-rah-SOHN)*
heart

corbata (f.) *(kohr-BAH-tah)*
necktie

cortar *(kohr-TAHR)* to cut

corte de pelo (m.) *(KOHR-teh deh PEH-loh)* haircut

cortés *(kohr-TEHS)* polite

cortesía (f.) *(kohr-teh-SEE-ah)*
politeness, courtesy

corto *(KOHR-toh)* short
(length, distance, or time)

correo (m.) *(koh-RREH-oh)*
mail; post office;
correo aéreo *(. . . ah-EH-reh-oh)* air mail

correr *(koh-RREHR)* to run

cosa (f.) *(KOH-sah)* thing

costilla (f.) *(kohs-TEE-yah)*
rib

creer *(kreh-EHR)* to believe

crema (f.) *(KREH-mah)*
cream

cruce (m.) *(KROO-seh)*
crossroad

cuadra (f.) *(KWAH-drah)* city block

cuadrado (m.) *(kwah-DRAH-doh)* square (shape)

cuadrilla (f.) *(kwah-DREE-yah)* cuadrilla (the team of assistants to a matador)

cuadro (m.) *(KWAH-droh)* picture, printing

¿cuál? *(kwahl?)* which?, which one?

cualquier; cualquiera *(kwahl-KYEHR; kwahl-KYEH-rah)* any

¿cuándo? *(KWAHN-doh?)* when?

¿cuánto? *(KWAHN-toh?)* how much?

¿cuántos? *(KWAHN-tohs?)* how many?

cuarenta *(kwah-REHN-tah)* forty

cuarto (m.) *(KWAHR-toh)* 1. room 2. fourth

cuatro *(KWAH-troh)* four

cubano(-a) *(koo-BAH-noh)(-nah)* Cuban

cuchara (f.) *(koo-CHAH-rah)* spoon

cucharada (f.) *(koo-chah-RAH-dah)* (table) spoonful

cucharadita (f.) *(koo-chah-rah-DEE-tah)* teaspoonful

cucharilla (f.) *(koo-chah-REE-yah)* teaspoon

cuchillo (m.) *(koo-CHEE-yoh)* knife

cuello (m.) *(KWEH-yoh)* neck

cuenta (f.) *(KWEHN-tah)* bill (restaurant); count, calculation

cuerda (f.) *(KWEHR-dah)* rope, cord, string

cuero (m.) *(KWEH-roh)* leather, hide

cuerpo (m.) *(KWEHR-poh)* body

cuidado (m.) *(kwee-DAH-doh)* care; **con cuidado** *(kohn . . .)* carefully; **tener cuidado** *(teh-NEHR . . .)* to be careful; **¡cuidado!** *(kwee-DAH-doh)* be careful, watch out!

cura (m.) *(KOO-rah)* priest

D

danés(-esa) *(dah-NEHS)(-NEH-sah)* Danish

dar *(dahr)* to give; **dar las gracias** *(. . . lahs GRAH-syahs)* to thank; **dar un paseo** *(. . . oon pah-SEH-oh)* to take a walk

darse prisa *(DAHR-seh PREE-sah)* to hurry

de *(deh)* from, of

debajo de *(deh-BAH-hoh deh)* under, beneath

deber *(deh-BEHR)* to have to; to owe

deber (m.) *(deh-BEHR)* duty, obligation

débil *(DEH-beel)* weak

décimo *(DEH-see-moh)* tenth

decir *(deh-SEER)* to say, to tell

dedo (m.) *(DEH-doh)* finger

251

dejar *(deh-HAHR)* to leave behind; to let, to permit

demasiado *(deh-mah-SYAH-doh)* too much

dentadura (f.) *(dehn-tah-DOO-rah)* dentures

dentro *(DEHN-troh)* inside, within

depósito (m.) *(deh-POH-see-toh)* deposit; tank (car)

derecha (f.) *(deh-REH-chah)* right (direction)

derecho *(deh-REH-choh)* straight ahead

desayunarse *(deh-sah-yoo-NAHR-seh)* to have breakfast

desayuno (m.) *(deh-sah-YOO-noh)* breakfast

descansar *(dehs-kahn-SAHR)* to rest

descuento (m.) *(dehs-KWEHN-toh)* discount

desde *(DEHS-deh)* since; from

desear *(deh-seh-AHR)* to wish

desembarcar *(deh-sehm-bahr-KAHR)* to disembark, to land (by ship)

desodorante (m.) *(deh-soh-doh-RAHN-teh)* deodorant

despacio *(des-PAH-syoh)* slow; slowly

despejarse *(dehs-peh-HAR-seh)* to clear up (sky)

despertador (m.) *(dehs-pehr-tah-DOHR)* alarm clock

despertarse *(dehs-pehr-TAHR-seh)* to wake up

después (de) *(dehs-PWEHS [deh])* after, afterward, later

destinatario (m.) *(dehs-tee-nah-TAH-ryoh)* addressee (on mail)

destornillador (m.) *(dehs-tohr-nee-yah-DOHR)* screwdriver

desvío (f.) *(dehs-VEE-oh)* detour

detrás de *(deh-TRAHS deh)* in back of, behind

devolver *(deh-vohl-VEHR)* to return

día (m.) *(DEE-ah)* day; **por día (m.)** *(pohr . . .)* by the day; **buenos días** *(BWEH-nohs DEE-ahs)* good morning, good day

diciembre (m.) *(dee-SYEHM-breh)* December

diecinueve *(dyeh-see-NWEH-veh)* nineteen

dieciocho *(dyeh-SYOH-choh)* eighteen

dieciséis *(dyeh-see-SAYS)* sixteen

diecisiete *(dyeh-see-SYEH-teh)* seventeen

diente (m.) *(DYEHN-teh)* tooth

diez *(dyehs)* ten

difícil *(dee-FEE-seel)* difficult

dinero (m.) *(dee-NEH-roh)* money; **dinero al contado** *(. . . ahl kohn-TAH-doh)* cash

dirección (f.) *(dee-rehk-SYOHN)* address; direction; **dirección única** *(. . . OO-nee-kah)* one-way (traffic)

dirigir *(dee-ree-HEER)* to direct

disco (m.) *(DEES-koh)* (phonograph) record

disparate (m.) *(dees-pah-RAH-teh)* nonsense

dispensar *(dees-pehn-SAHR)* to excuse, to pardon

distancia (f.) *(dees-TAHN-syah)* distance

doblar *(doh-BLAHR)* to fold; to turn

doce *(DOH-seh)* twelve

docena *(doh-SEH-nah)* dozen

dolor (m.) *(doh-LOHR)* pain

domingo (m.) *(doh-MEEN-goh)* Sunday

donde *(DOHN-deh)* where

dormir *(dohr-MEER)* to sleep

dormitorio (m.) *(dohr-mee-TOH-ryoh)* bedroom

dos *(dohs)* two

ducha (f.) *(DOO-chah)* shower

dulce (m.) *(DOOL-seh)* candy

dulce *(DOOL-seh)* sweet

durar *(doo-RAHR)* to last

durazno (m.) *(doo-RAHS-noh)* peach

duro *(DOO-roh)* hard, tough

E

elástico (m.) *(eh-LAHS-tee-koh)* rubber band

el *(ehl)* the

él *(ehl)* he

ella *(EH-yah)* she

ellas *(EH-yahs)* they (f.)

ellos *(EH-yohs)* they (m.)

embrague (m.) *(ehm-BRAH-geh)* (car) clutch

empastar *(ehm-pahs-TAHR)* to fill (a tooth)

empezar *(ehm-peh-SAHR)* to begin, to start

emplear *(ehm-pleh-AHR)* to use; to hire

empleo (m.) *(ehm-PLEH-oh)* use, purpose; job

empujar *(ehm-poo-HAHR)* to push

en *(ehn)* at, in, on;
en casa *(. . . KAH-sah)* at home;
en seguida *(. . . seh-GEE dah)* at once, right away

encendedor (m.) *(ehn-sehn-deh-DOHR)* cigarette lighter

encender *(ehn-sehn-DEHR)* to light

encendido (m.) *(ehn-sehn-DEE-doh)* (car) ignition

encías (f.pl.) *(ehn-SEE-ahs)* gums (in mouth)

encima (de) *(ehn-SEE-mah [deh])* on top (of), above

encontrar *(ehn-kohn-TRAHR)* to find, to meet

encurtidos (m.pl.) *(ehn-koor-TEE-dohs)* pickles

enchufe (m.) *(ehn-CHOO-feh)* (electrical) outlet

enero (m.) *(eh-NEH-roh)* January

enfermedad (f.) *(ehn-fehr-meh-DAHD)* illness

enfermera (f.) *(ehn-fehr-MEH-rah)* nurse

enfermo *(ehn-FEHR-moh)* sick, ill

engranaje (m.) *(ehn-grah-NAH-heh)* (car) gears

engrasar *(ehn-grah-SAHR)* to grease, to lubricate

enjuague (m.) *(ehn-HWAH-geh)* rinse

ensalada (f.) *(ehn-sah-LAH-dah)* salad

enseñar *(ehn-seh-NYAHR)* to teach; to show

entender *(ehn-tehn-DEHR)* to understand

entrar *(ehn-TRAHR)* to enter, to come in

entre *(EHN-treh)* between, among

entrega (f.) *(ehn-treh-gah)* delivery

entregar *(ehn-treh-GAHR)* to deliver, to hand over

entremés (m.) *(ehn-treh-MEHS)* appetizer, hors d'oeuvre

enviar *(ehn-VYAHR)* to send

envolver *(ehn-vohl-VEHR)* to wrap

equipaje (m.) *(eh-kee-PAH-heh)* luggage

equivocarse *(eh-kee-voh-KAHR-seh)* to be mistaken

escalera (f.) *(ehs-kah-LEH-rah)* stairs

escalofrío (m.) *(ehs-kah-loh-FREE-oh)* chill

escaparate (m.) *(ehs-kah-pah-RAH-teh)* display window

escape (m.) *(ehs-KAH-peh)* exhaust (car); leak

escoger *(ehs-koh-HEHR)* to choose, to select

escribir *(ehs-kree-BEER)* to write

escuchar *(ehs-koo-CHAHR)* to listen (to)

escuela (f.) *(ehs-KWEH-lah)* school

escupir *(ehs-koo-PEER)* to spit

ese (esa, eso) *(EH-seh [EH-sah, EH-soh])* that

esmalte (m.) *(ehs-MAHL-teh)* nail polish

esos (esas) *(EH-sohs [EH-sahs])* those

espalda (f.) *(ehs-PAHL-dah)* back (body part)

español(-a) *(ehs-pah-NYOHL) (-NYOH-lah)* Spanish

esparadrapo (m.) *(ehs-pah-rah-DRAH-poh)* adhesive tape; bandage

espejo (m.) *(ehs-PEH-hoh)* mirror

esperar *(ehs-peh-RAHR)* to hope; to expect; to wait

espeso *(ehs-PEH-soh)* thick (consistency of liquid)

espinaca (f.) *(ehs-pee-NAH-kah)* spinach

esposa (f.) *(ehs-POH-sah)* wife

esposo (m.) *(ehs-POH-soh)* husband

está bien *(ehs-TAH byehn)* all right, okay

estación (f.) *(ehs-tah-SYOHN)* station; season

estacionar *(ehs-tah-syoh-NAHR)* to park

Estados Unidos de América (EE.UU.) (m.pl.) *(ehs-TAH-dohs oo-NEE-dohs deh* *ah-MEH-ree-kah)* United States of America

estanco (m.) *(ehs-TAHN-koh)* cigar store

estar *(ehs-TAHR)* to be

este (m.) *(EHS-teh)* east

este (esta, esto) *(EHS-teh [EHS-tah, EHS-toh])* this

estancia (f.) *(ehs-TAHN-syah)* stay

estofado (m.) *(ehs-toh-FAH-doh)* stew

estómago (m.) *(ehs-TOH-mah-goh)* stomach

estos (estas) *(ESH-tohs [EHS-tahs])* these

estrecho *(ehs-TREH-choh)* narrow; strait

estrella (f.) *(ehs-TREH-yah)* star

esquina (f.) *(ehs-KEE-nah)* corner

etiqueta (f.) *(eh-tee-KEH-tah)* label; etiquette;
traje de etiqueta *(TRAH-heh deh . . .)* evening gown; tuxedo

evitar *(eh-vee-TAHR)* to avoid

extranjero (m.) *(eks-trahn-HEH-roh)* foreigner

F

facturar *(fahk-too-RAHR)* to check (baggage)

faja (f.) *(FAH-hah)* girdle

falda (f.) *(FAHL-dah)* skirt

faro (f.) *(FAH-roh)* headlight

farol (m.) *(fah-ROHL)* street lamp

favor (m.) *(fah-VOHR)* favor;
por favor *(pohr . . .)* please;
haga el favor *(AH-gah ehl . . .)* please

febrero (m.) *(feh-BREH-roh)* February

fecha (f.) *(FEH-chah)* date

¡Feliz Navidad! *(feh-LEES nah-vee-DAHD!)* Merry Christmas!

felicitaciones (f.pl.) *(feh-lee-see-tah-SYOH-nehs)* congratulations

feliz *(feh-LEES)* happy;
¡feliz cumpleaños! *(. . . koom-pleh-AH-nyohs!)* happy birthday!;
¡feliz Año Nuevo! *(. . . AH-nyoh NWEH-voh!)* Happy New Year!;
¡feliz Navidad! *(. . . nah-vee-DAHD!)* Merry Christmas!

feo *(FEH-oh)* ugly

ferrocarril (m.) *(feh-rroh-kah-RREEL)* railroad

fiambre (m.) *(FYAHM-breh)* cold cut

ficha (f.) *(FEE-chah)* token (bus or phone)

fiebre (f.) *(FYEH-breh)* fever

fila (f.) *(FEE-lah)* row, queue, line

fin (m.) *(feen)* end

flor (f.) *(flohr)* flower

fósforo (m.) *(FOHS-foh-roh)* match

francés(-esa) *(frahn-SEHS) (-SEH-sah)* French

franqueo (m.) *(frahn-KEH-oh)* postage

frenos (m.pl.) *(FREH-nohs)* brakes

frente (m.) *(FREHN-teh)* front; forehead

fresa (f.) *(FREH-sah)* strawberry

fresco *(FREHS-koh)* fresh, cool

frijol (m.) *(free-HOHL)* bean (Mex.)

frío (m.) *(FREE-oh)* cold;
   hacer frío *(ah-SEHR . . .)* to be cold (weather);
   tener frío *(teh-NEHR . . .)* to be cold (person)

frito *(FREE-toh)* fried

fuego (m.) *(FWEH-goh)* fire

fuente (f.) *(FWEHN-teh)* fountain

fuera *(FWEH-rah)* outside; out

fuerte *(FWEHR-teh)* strong

fumador(-a) *(foo-mah-DOHR) (-DOH-rah)* smoker

fumar *(foo-MAHR)* to smoke

función (f.) *(foon-SYOHN)* performance, show; ceremony, function

funda (f.) *(FOON-dah)* pillowcase

G

gafas (f.pl.) *(GAH-fahs)* eyeglasses

gana (f.) *(GAH-nah)* desire;
   tener ganas de *(teh-NEHR GAH-nahs deh)* to feel like

ganado (m.) *(gah-NAH-doh)* cattle

gancho (m.) *(GAHN-choh)* hook; clothes hanger

ganga (f.) *(GAHN-gah)* bargain, sale

ganso (m.) *(GAHN-soh)* goose

garganta (f.) *(gahr-GAHN-tah)* throat

gasa (f.) *(GAH-sah)* gauze

gastar *(gahs-TAHR)* to spend; to waste

gasto (m.) *(GAHS-toh)* expense

gato (m.) *(GAH-toh)* cat

gemelos (m.pl.) *(heh-MEH-lohs)* twins; cuff links; binoculars

gente (f.) *(HEHN-teh)* people

gerente (m.) *(he-REHN-teh)* manager

ginebra (f.) *(hee-NEH-brah)* gin

gira (f.) *(HEE-rah)* tour

giro postal (m.) *(HEE-roh pohs-TAHL)* money order

gorra (f.) *(GOH-rrah)* cap

gracias (f.pl.) *(GRAH-syahs)* thanks

gracias *(GRAH-syahs)* thank you

grande *(GRAHN-deh)* large, big

granizar *(grah-nee-SAHR)* to hail (precipitation)

griego(-a) (m.) *(GRYEH-goh) (-gah)* Greek

grifo (m.) *(GREE-foh)* tap, faucet

gris *(grees)* gray

grueso *(GRWEH-soh)* thick, stout

guante (m.) *(GWAHN-teh)* glove

guardar *(gwahr-DAHR)* to keep, to look after; to put away; to guard

guardafangos (m.) *(gwahr-dah-FAHN-gohs)* fender

guía (m./f.) *(GEE-ah)* guide; guidebook

guiar *(gee-AHR)* to guide; to drive

guisante (m.) *(gee-SAHN-teh)* pea (Sp.)

guiso (m.) *(gee-SOH)* stew

gustar *(goos-TAHR)* to like

gusto (m.) *(GOOS-toh)* pleasure, taste;
con mucho gusto *(kohn MOO-choh . . .)* gladly

H

habichuela (f.) *(ah-bee-CHWEH-lah)* bean

habitación (f.) *(ah-bee-tah-SYOHN)* room

hablar *(ah-BLAHR)* to speak

hace *(AH-seh)* ago

hacer *(ah-SEHR)* to do, to make

hacerse *(ah-SEHR-seh)* to become

hacia *(AH-syah)* toward

hallar *(ah-YAHR)* to find

hasta *(AHS-tah)* until;
hasta mañana *(. . . mah-NYAH-nah)* until tomorrow;
hasta la vista *(. . . lah VEES-tah)* till we meet again

hay *(AHY)* there is, there are

hebreo(-a) *(eh-BREH-oh)(-ah)* Hebrew

hecho a mano *(EH-choh ah MAH-noh)* handmade

helado (m.) *(eh-LAH-doh)* ice cream; cold (temperature)

herida (f.) *(eh-REE-dah)* wound

herido *(eh-REE-doh)* wounded

herir *(eh-REER)* to wound

hermana (f.) *(ehr-MAH-nah)* sister

hermano (m.) *(ehr-MAH-noh)* brother

hermoso *(ehr-MOH-soh)* beautiful

hervido *(ehr-VEE-doh)* boiled

hielo (m.) *(YEH-loh)* ice

hierro (m.) *(YEH-rroh)* iron

hígado (m.) *(EE-gah-doh)* liver

higo (m.) *(EE-goh)* fig

hierba (f.) *(YEHR-bah)* grass

hilo (m.) *(EE-loh)* thread

hinchado *(een-CHAH-doh)* swollen

hinchar *(een-CHAHR)* to swell

holandés(-esa) *(oh-lahn-DEHS) (-DEH-sah)* Dutch

hombre (m.) *(OHM-breh)* man

hombro (m.) *(OHM-broh)* shoulder

hongo (m.) *(OHN-goh)* mushroom

hora (f.) *(OH-rah)* hour

horario (m.) *(oh-RAH-ryoh)* schedule, timetable

horno (m.) *(OHR-noh)* oven

horquilla (f.) *(ohr-KEE-yah)* hairpin

hoy *(ohy)* today

257

hueso (m.) *(WEH-soh)* bone
huevo (m.) *(WEH-voh)* egg
húngaro(-a) *(OON-gah-roh)*
(-rah) Hungarian

I

idioma (m.) *(ee-DYOH-mah)*
language
iglesia (f.) *(ee-GLEH-syah)*
church
impermeable (m.) *(eem-
pehr-meh-AH-bleh)* raincoat
importar *(eem-pohr-TAHR)* to
be important; to import
impuesto (m.) *(eem-PWEHS-
toh)* tax
incómodo *(een-KOH-moh-doh)*
uncomfortable
infierno (m.) *(een-FYEHR-noh)*
hell
informes (m.pl.) *(een-FOHR-
mehs)* information
inglés(-esa) *(een-GLES)(-GLEH-
sah)* English
interruptor (m.) *(een-teh-
rroop-TOHR)* electric switch
invierno (m.) *(een-VYEHR-noh)*
winter
ir *(eer)* to go
irse *(EER-seh)* to go away,
to leave
italiano(-a) *(ee-tah-LYAH-
noh)(-nah)* Italian
izquierda (f.) *(ees-KYEHR-dah)*
left

J

jabón (m.) *(hah-BOHN)* soap
jamás *(hah-MAHS)* never

jamón (m.) *(hah-MOHN)*
ham
jaqueca (f.) *(hah-KEH-kah)*
headache
japonés(-esa) *(hah-poh-
NEHS)(-NEH-sah)* Japanese
jarabe (m.) *(hah-RAH-beh)*
syrup
jardín (m.) *(hahr-DEEN)*
garden
jarra (f.) *(HAH-rrah)* pitcher
jarro (m.) *(HAH-rroh)* mug
jefe (m./f.) *(HEH-feh)* chief,
leader, boss
jóven *(HOH-vehn)* young
jóven (m./f.) *(HOH-vehn)*
youngster
joya (f.) *(HOH-yah)* jewel
joyería (f.) *(hoh-yeh-REE-ah)*
jewelry; jewelry store
joyero (m.) *(hoh-YEH-roh)*
jeweler
judías (f.pl.) *(hoo-DEE-ahs)*
green beans (Sp.)
judío(-a) *(hoo-DEE-oh)(-ah)*
Jewish
juego (m.) *(HWEH-goh)*
game
jueves (m.) *(HWEH-vehs)*
Thursday
jugar *(hoo-GAHR)* to play (a
game)
jugo (m.) *(HOO-goh)* juice
julio (m.) *(HOO-lyoh)* July
junio (m.) *(HOO-nyoh)*
June

L

la the
labio (m.) *(LAH-byoh)* lip

lado (m.) *(LAH-doh)* side

ladrón (m.) *(lah-DROHN)* thief

lámpara (f.) *(LAHM-pah-rah)* lamp

langosta (f.) *(lahn-GOHS-tah)* lobster

lápiz (m.) *(LAH-pees)* pencil

largo *(LAHR-goh)* long

lástima (f.) *(LAHS-tee-mah)* pity

lastimar *(lahs-tee-MAHR)* to hurt, to injure, to bruise

lata (f.) *(LAH-tah)* can; tin

lavabo (m.) *(lah-VAH-boh)* sink

lavandera (f.) *(lah-vahn-DEH-rah)* laundress

lavandería (f.) *(lah-vahn-deh-REE-ah)* laundry

lavar *(lah-VAHR)* to wash

lavarse *(lah-VAHR-seh)* to wash (oneself)

laxante (m.) *(lahk-SAHN-teh)* laxative

leche (f.) *(LEH-cheh)* milk

lechuga (f.) *(leh-CHOO-gah)* lettuce

leer *(leh-EHR)* to read

legumbres (f.pl.) *(leh-GOOM-brehs)* vegetables

lejos *(LEH-hohs)* far, distant

lengua (f.) *(LEHN-gwah)* tongue; language

lentamente *(lehn-tah-MEHN-teh)* slowly

lento *(LEHN-toh)* slow

letra (f.) *(LEH-trah)* letter (in alphabet); bank draft

letrero (m.) *(leh-TREH-roh)* sign, poster

levantar *(leh-VAHN-tahr)* to lift

levantarse *(leh-VAHN-tahr-seh)* to get up, to stand up

libre *(LEE-breh)* independent; free; at liberty

librería (f.) *(lee-breh-REE-ah)* bookstore

libro (m.) *(LEE-broh)* book

liga (f.) *(LEE-gah)* garter; **liga de goma** *(. . . deh GOH-mah)* rubber band

ligero *(lee-HEH-roh)* light; agile

lima de uñas (f.) *(LEE-mah deh OO-nyahs)* nail file

limpiar *(leem PYAHR)* to clean

limpieza en seco *(leem-PYEH-sah ehn SEH-koh)* dry cleaning

limpio *(LEEM-pyoh)* clean

lindo *(LEEN-doh)* pretty

línea aérea (f.) *(LEE-neh-ah ah-EH-reh-ah)* airline

lino (m.) *(LEE-noh)* linen

linterna (f.) *(leen-TEHR-nah)* flashlight

lista (f.) *(LEES-tah)* list; **lista de correo** *(. . . deh koh-RREH-oh)* general delivery; **lista de vinos** *(. . . deh VEE-nohs)* wine list

litera (f.) *(lee-TEH-rah)* berth

llamada (f.) *(yah-MAH-dah)* call (telephone)

llamar *(yah-MAHR)* to call

llamarse *(yah-MAHR-seh)* to call oneself, to be named

llanta (f.) *YAHN-tah* tire

llave (f.) *(YAH-veh)* key

llegada (f.) *(yeh-GAH-dah)* arrival

llegar *(yeh-GAHR)* to arrive

llenar *(yeh-NAHR)* to fill

lleno (m.) *(YEH-noh)* full

llevar *(yeh-VAHR)* to take

llover *(yoh-VEHR)* to rain

lluvia (f.) *(YOO-vyah)* rain

loco *(LOH-koh)* crazy

los (las) *(lohs (lahs))* the (pl.)

lograr *(loh-GRAHR)* to obtain, to get

luego *(LWEH-goh)* then, afterwards; later;
  desde luego *(DEHS-deh . . .)* of course;
  hasta luego *(AHS-tah . . .)* until later

lugar (m.) *(loo-GAHR)* place, spot

luna (f.) *(LOO-nah)* moon

lunes (m.) *(LOO-nehs)* Monday

luz (f.) *(loos)* light;
  luz delantera *(. . . deh-lahn-TEH-rah)* headlight;
  luz trasera *(. . . trah-SEH-rah)* taillight

M

madera (f.) *(mah-DEH-rah)* wood

madre (f.) *(MAH-dreh)* mother

maíz (m.) *(mah-EES)* corn

mal *(mahl)* bad

maleta (f.) *(mah-LEH-tah)* suitcase

mandar *(mahn-DAHR)* to send; to command

mandarina (f.) *(mahn-dah-REE-nah)* tangerine

manga (f.) *(MAHN-gah)* sleeve

mango (m.) *(MAHN-goh)* mango (tropical fruit)

mano (f.) *(MAH-noh)* hand

manteca (f.) *(mahn-TEH-kah)* lard

mantel (m.) *(mahn-TEHL)* tablecloth

mantequilla (f.) *(mahn-teh-KEE-yah)* butter

manzana (f.) *(mahn-SAH-nah)* apple

mañana *(mah-NYAH-nah)* morning; tomorrow;
  hasta mañana *(AHS-tah . . .)* until tomorrow;
  pasado mañana *(pah-SAH-doh . . .)* day after tomorrow

mapa (m.) *(MAH-pah)* map

mar (m.) *(mahr)* sea

mareado *(mah-reh-AH-doh)* seasick, dizzy

mareo (m.) *(mah-REH-oh)* seasickness

marido (m.) *(mah-REE-doh)* husband

mariscos (m.) *(mah-REES-kohs)* seafood

martes (m.) *(MAHR-tehs)* Tuesday

martillo (m.) *(mahr-TEE-yoh)* hammer

marzo (m.) *(MAHR-soh)* March

más *(mahs)* more

masaje (m.) *(mah-SAH-heh)* massage

matador (m.) *(mah-tah-DOHR)* matador (principal bull-fighter)

mayo (m.) *(MAH-yoh)* May

medianoche (f.) *(meh-dyah-NOH-cheh)* midnight

medias (f.pl) *(MEH-dyahs)* stockings

médico (m.) *(MEH-dee-koh)* (medical) doctor

medidas (f.pl) *(meh-DEE-dahs)* measurements; measures

medio *(MEH-dyoh)* half (adj.)

mediodía (m.) *(meh-dyoh-DEE-ah)* noon

mejilla (f.) *(meh-HEE-yah)* cheek

mejillón (m.) *(meh-hee-YOHN)* mussel

mejor *(meh-HOHR)* better

melocotón (m.) *(meh-loh-koh-TOHN)* peach

menos *(MEH-nohs)* less

menudo *(meh-NOO-doh)* small, minute;
a menudo *(ah . . .)* often

mercado (m.) *(mehr-KAH-doh)* market

mes (m.) *(mehs)* month

mesa (f.) *(MEH-sah)* table

meter *(meh-TEHR)* to put in, to insert

mexicano(-a) *(meh-hee-KAH-noh)(-nah)* Mexican

miedo (m.) *(MYEH-doh)* fear;
tener miedo *(teh-NEHR . . .)* to be afraid

miércoles (m.) *(MYEHR-koh-lehs)* Wednesday

mil *(meel)* thousand

millón *(mee-YOHN)* million

mirar *(mee-RAHR)* to look, to look at

misa (f.) *(MEE-sah)* mass

mismo *(MEES-moh)* same

mitad (f.) *(mee-TAHD)* half

moda (f.) *(MOH-dah)* fashion

mojado *(moh-HAH-doh)* wet

mojarse *(moh-HAHR-seh)* to get wet

molestar *(moh-lehs-TAHR)* to bother, to annoy

moneda (f.) *(moh-NEH-dah)* coin

monosabio (m.) *(moh-noh-SAH-byoh)* bullring attendant

morado *(moh-RAH-doh)* purple

moreno *(moh-REH-noh)* dark-complexioned; brunette

mosquitero (m.) *(mohs-kee-TEH-roh)* mosquito net

mostaza (f.) *(mohs-TAH-sah)* mustard

mostrar *(mohs-TRAHR)* to show

mozo (m.) *(MOH-soh)* waiter, porter

muchacho(-a) *(moo-CHAH-cho)(-cha)* boy, girl

mucho *(MOO-choh);* much; **mucho gusto** *(. . . GOOS-toh)* it's a pleasure (to meet you)

muchos *(MOO-chohs)* many, lots of

muelle (m.) *(MWEH-yeh)* dock pier, wharf

muerte (f.) *(MWEHR-teh)* death

muerto *(MWEHR-toh)* dead

mujer (f.) *(moo-HEHR)* woman

multa (f.) *(MOOL-tah)* fine (penalty)

muñeca (f.) *(moo-NYEH-kah)* doll; wrist

muro (m.) *(MOO-roh)* (exterior) wall

museo (m.) *(moo-SEH-oh)* museum

muslo (m.) *(MOOS-loh)* thigh

muy *(mwee)* very

N

nacer *(nah-SEHR)* to be born

nada *(NAH-dah)* nothing; **de nada** *(deh . . .)* you're welcome (it's nothing)

nadar *(nah-DAHR)* to swim

nadie *(NAH-dyeh)* nobody, no one

naranja (f.) *(nah-RAHN-hah)* orange

nariz (f.) *(nah-REES)* nose

navaja (f.) *(nah-VAH-hah)* razor; pocket knife

Navidad (f.) *(nah-vee-DAHD)* Christmas

necesitar *(neh-seh-see-TAHR)* to need

neumático (m.) *(neoo-MAH-tee-koh)* tire

nevar *(neh-VAHR)* to snow

niebla (f.) *(NYEH-blah)* fog

nieve (f.) *(NYEH-veh)* snow

ninguno(-a) *(neen-GOO-noh)(-nah)* none

niño(-a) *(NEE-nyoh) (-nyah)* boy, girl

noche (f.) *(NOH-cheh)* night; **buenas noches** *(BWEH-nahs NOH-ches)* good evening; good night

nombre (m.) *(NOHM-breh)* name

norte (m.) *(NOHR-teh)* north

norteamericano(-a) *(nohr-teh-ah-meh-ree-KAH-noh)(-nah)* (North) American

noruego(-a) *(noh-RWEH-goh)(-gah)* Norwegian

nos *(nohs)* us, ourselves

nosotros *(noh-SOH-trohs)* we; us

novela (f.) *(noh-VEH-lah)* novel

noveno *(noh-VEH-noh)* ninth

noventa *(noh-VEHN-tah)* ninety

noviembre (m.) *(noh-VYEHM-breh)* November

nube (f.) *(NOO-beh)* cloud

nublado *(noo-BLAH-doh)* cloudy

nuestro *(NWEHS-troh)* our; ours

nueve *(NWEH-veh)* nine
nuevo *(NWEH-voh)* new;
  de nuevo *(doh . . .)* again,
  anew
nuez (f.) *(nwehs)* nut (food)
número (m.) *(NOO-meh-roh)*
  number
nunca *(NOON-kah)* never

O

occidente (m.) *(ohk-see-DEHN-teh)* West, Western world
octavo *(ohk-TAH-voh)* eighth
octubre (m.) *(ohk-TOO-breh)*
  October
ocupado *(oh-koo-PAH-doh)*
  occupied, busy; occupied,
  taken
ocurrir *(oh-koo-RREER)* to
  happen
ochenta *(oh-CHEN-tah)*
  eighty
ocho *(OH-choh)* eight
oeste (m.) *(oh-EHS-teh)* west
oficina (f.) *(oh-fee-SEE-nah)*
  office;
  oficina de cambio
  (. . . deh KAHM-byoh) money
  exchange;
  oficina de informes
  (. . . deh een-FOHR-mehs) information bureau;
  oficina de objetos per-
  didos *(. . . deh ohb-HEH-tohs*
  per-DEE-dohs) lost-and-
  found
oído (m.) *(oh-EE-doh)*
  (inner) ear
oír *(oh-EER)* to hear

ojo (m.) *(OH-hoh)* eye
olvidar; olvidarse de *(ohl-vee-DAHR; ohl-vee-DAHR-seh deh)* to forget
once *(OHN-seh)* eleven
óptico (m.) *(OHP-tee-koh)*
  optician
oreja (f.) *(oh-REH-hah)*
  (outer) ear
oro (m.) *(OH-roh)* gold
ostra (f.); **ostión** (m.) *(OHS-trah; ohs-TYOHN)* oyster
otoño (m.) *(oh-TOH-nyoh)*
  autumn, fall
otra vez *(OH-trah-vehs)* again
otro *(OH-troh)* other, another

P

padre (m.) *(PAH-dreh)* father
pagar *(pah-GAHR)* to pay
página (f.) *(PAH-hee-nah)*
  page
país (m.) *(pah-EES)* country,
  nation
paja (f.) *(PAH-hah)* straw
pájaro (m.) *(PAH-hah-roh)*
  bird
palabra (f.) *(pah-LAH-brah)*
  word
pan (m.) *(pahn)* bread
panecillo (m.) *(pah-neh-SEE-yoh)* roll (bread)
pantalones (m.pl.) *(pahn-tah-LOH-nehs)* pants, trousers
pañales (m.pl.) *(pah-NYAH-lehs)* diapers
paño (m.) *(PAH-nyoh)* cloth
pañuelo (m.) *(pah-NYWEH-loh)* handkerchief

papa (f.) *(PAH-pah)* potato (Mex.)

papel (m.) *(pah-PEHL)* paper; **papel de cartas; papel de escribir** *(. . . deh KAHR-tahs; . . . deh ehs-kree-BEER)* stationery, writing paper; **papel de envolver** *(. . . deh ehn-vohl-VEHR)* wrapping paper; **papel higiénico** *(. . . ee-HYEH-nee-koh)* toilet paper

papelería (f.) *(pah-peh-leh-REE-ah)* stationer's

paquete (m.) *(pah-KEH-teh)* package, parcel, packet; **paquete postal** *(. . . pohs-TAHL)* parcel post

par (m.) *(pahr)* pair

para *(PAH-rah)* for (purpose or destination)

parabrisas (m.) *(pah-rah-BREE-sahs)* windshield

parachoques (m.) *(pah-rah-CHOH-kehs)* bumper (car)

parada (f.) *(pah-RAH-dah)* (bus) stop

paraguas (m.) *(pah-RAH-gwahs)* umbrella

parar *(pah-RAHR)* to stop

pardo *(PAHR-doh)* brown

parecer *(pah-reh-SEHR)* to seem, to appear

pared (f.) *(pah-REHD)* (interior) wall

párpado (m.) *(PAHR-pah-doh)* eyelid

partida (f.) *(pahr-TEE-dah)* game (contest)

parrilla (f.) *(pah-RREE-yah)* grill;

a la parrilla *(ah lah . . .)* broiled, grilled

pasado *(pah-SAH-doh)* last, past; **el año pasado** *(ehl AH-nyoh . . .)* last year

pasajero(-a) *(pah-sah-HEH-roh)(-rah)* passenger

pasar *(pah-SAHR)* to pass; to happen; to spend (time)

pasear; pasearse *(pah-seh-AHR; pah-seh-AHR-seh)* to take a walk

paseo (m.) *(pah-SEH-oh)* walk; **paseo en coche** *(. . . ehn KOH-cheh)* ride

pastel (m.) *(pahs-TEHL)* pie, cake

pastilla (f.) *(pahs-TEE-yah)* pill, tablet

pato (m.) *(PAH-toh)* duck

peatón (m.) *(peh-ah-TOHN)* pedestrian

pecho (m.) *(PEH-choh)* chest (body part)

pedazo (m.) *(peh-DAH-soh)* piece

pedir *(peh-DEER)* to ask for; **pedir prestado** *(. . . prehs-TAH-doh)* to borrow

peinar *(pay-NAHR)* to comb

peine (m.) *(PAY-neh)* comb

película (f.) *(peh-LEE-koo-lah)* movie; (photographic) film; **película de color** *(. . . deh koh-LOHR)* color film

peligro (m.) *(peh-LEE-groh)* danger

peligroso *(peh-lee-GROH-soh)* dangerous

pelo (m.) *(PEH-loh)* hair

pelota (m.) *(peh-LOH-tah)* ball (sports)

peluquería (f.) *(peh-loo-keh-REE-ah)* barbershop

peluquero (m.) *(peh-loo-KEH-roh)* barber

pendiente (m.) *(pehn-DYEHN-teh)* earring

pensar *(pehn-SAHR)* to think; to intend

pensión (f.) *(pehn-SYOHN)* pension, inn

peor *(peh-OHR)* worse; worst

pepino (m.) *(peh-PEE-noh)* cucumber

pequeño *(peh-KEH-nyoh)* small

pera (f.) *(PEH-rah)* pear

perder *(pehr-DEHR)* to lose; to miss (a bus or train)

¡perdón! *(pehr-DOHN)* excuse me!; pardon me!

perdonar *(pehr-don-NAHR)* to excuse; to pardon

perfumería (f.) *(pehr-foo-meh-REE-ah)* perfumery

periódico (m.) *(peh-RYOH-dee-koh)* newspaper

permiso (m.) *(pehr-MEE-soh)* pass, permit

permitir *(pehr-mee-TEER)* to permit, to allow

perno (m.) *(PEHR-noh)* bolt

pero *(PEH-roh)* but

perro (m.) *(PEH-rroh)* dog

pertenecer *(pehr-teh-neh-SEHR)* to belong (to)

pesado *(peh-SAH-doh)* heavy

pesar *(peh-SAHR)* to weigh

pescado (m.) *(pehs-KAH-doh)* fish (caught)

peso (m.) *(PEH-soh)* weight; monetary unit (Mex.)

pestaña (f.) *(pehs-TAH-nyah)* eyelash

pez (m.) *(pehs)* fish (in water)

picador (m.) *(pee-kah-DOHR)* assistant (on horseback) to matador

pie (m.) *(pyeh)* foot; **a pie** *(ah . . .)* on foot

piel (f.) *(pyehl)* skin; leather, fur

pierna (f.) *(PYEHR-nah)* leg (body part)

pieza (f.) *(PYEH-sah)* piece; play (theater)

píldora (f.) *(PEEL-doh-rah)* pill

pimienta (f.) *(pee-MYEHN-tah)* black pepper

pimientos (m.pl.) *(pee-NYEHN-tohs)* peppers

pinacoteca (f.) *(pee-nah-koh-TEH-kah)* art gallery

pinchazo (m.) *(peen-CHAH-soh)* puncture (tire)

piña (f.) *(PEE-nyah)* pineapple

piscina (f.) *(pees-SEE-nah)* swimming pool

piso (m.) *(PEE-soh)* floor; apartment

pista (f.) *(PEES-tah)* trail; (airport) runway

placer (m.) *(plah-SEHR)* pleasure

plancha (f.) *(PLAHN-chah)* (flat) iron; grill surface

planchar *(plan-CHAHR)* to iron, to press

planilla (f.) *(plah-NEE-yah)* form, document

plata (f.) *(PLAH-tah)* silver

plátano (m.) *(PLAH-tah-noh)* banana

platillo (m.) *(plah-TEE-yoh)* saucer

plato (m.) *(PLAH-toh)* plate; course (meal);
   plato del día *(. . . dehl DEE-ah)* daily special (restaurant)

playa (f.) *(PLAH-yah)* beach

plaza (f.) *(PLAH-sah)* square;
   plaza de toros *(. . . deh TOH-rohs)* bullring

pluma (f.) *(PLOO-mah)* pen; feather

poblado (m.) *(poh-BLAH-doh)* village

pobre *(POH-breh)* poor

poco *(POH-koh)* little;
   un poco *(oon. . . .)* a little

pocos *(POH-kohs)* few, a few

poder *(poh-DEHR)* to be able

polaco(-a) *(poh-LAH-koh)(-kah)* Polish

polvo (m.) *(POHL-voh)* powder, dust

pollo (m.) *(POH-yoh)* chicken

poner *(poh-NEHR)* to place, to put

ponerse *(poh-NEHR-seh)* to put on; to become

por *(pohr)* by, for

porque *(POHR-keh)* because

¿por qué? *(pohr-KEH?)* why?

porte (m.) *(pohr-TEH)* postage

portero (m.) *(pohr-TEH-roh)* porter

portugués(-esa) *(pohr-too-GEHS)(-GEH-sah)* Portuguese

poseer *(poh-seh-EHR)* to possess, to own

postre (m.) *(POHS-treh)* dessert

precio (m.) *(PREH-syoh)* price

pregunta (f.) *(preh-GOON-tah)* question

preguntar *(preh-goon-TAHR)* to ask

preocuparse *(preh-oh-koo-PAHR-seh)* to worry;
   no se preocupe *(noh seh preh-oh-KOO-peh)* don't worry

presentar *(preh-sehn-TAHR)* to present

prestar *(prehs-TAHR)* to lend

primavera (f.) *(pree-mah-VEH-rah)* spring (season)

primer(-a) *(pree-MEHR)(-MEH-rah)* first

prisa (f.) *(PREE-sah)* hurry, haste

probarse *(proh-BAHR-seh)* to try on

prohibido *(proh-ee-BEE-doh)* prohibited, forbidden

prohibir *(proh-ee-BEER)* to forbid

prometer *(proh-meh-TEHR)* to promise

pronto *(PROHN-toh)* quick, quickly, soon

propina (f.) *(proh-PEE-nah)* tip

próximo(-a) *(PROHK-see-moh)(-mah)* next

puede ser *(PWEH-deh sehr)* could be, maybe

puente (m.) *(PWEHN-teh)* bridge (span); bridge (dental)

puerta (f.) *(PWEHR-tah)* door

puerto (m.) *(PWEHR-toh)* port

pulgada (f.) *(pool-GAH-dah)* inch

pulgar (m.) *(pool-GAHR)* thumb

pulsera (f.) *(pool-SEH-rah)* bracelet;
   reloj pulsera *(reh-LOH . . .)* wristwatch

puro *(POO-roh)* pure

puro (m.) *(POO-roh)* cigar

Q

que *(keh)* that, which, who

¿qué? *(keh?)* what?

quebrado *(keh-BRAH-doh)* broken

quedarse *(keh-DAHR-seh)* to remain, to stay

queja (f.) *(KEH-hah)* complaint

quejarse *(keh-HAHR-seh)* to complain

quemadura (f.) *(keh-mah-DOO-rah)* burn

quemar *(keh-MAHR)* to burn

querer *(keh-REHR)* to desire, to want, to wish

queso (m.) *(KEH-soh)* cheese

quien *(kyehn)* who

¿quién? *(kyehn?)* who?

quijada (f.) *(kee-HAH-dah)* jaw

quince *(KEEN-seh)* fifteen

quinto *(KEEN-toh)* fifth

quitarse *(kee-TAHR-seh)* to take off

quitasol (m.) *(kee-tah-SOHL)* parasol

quizá *(kee-SAH)* maybe, perhaps

quizás *(kee-SAHS)* maybe, perhaps

R

rábano (m.) *(RRAH-bah-noh)* radish

rabino (m.) *(rrah-BEE-noh)* rabbi

radiografía (f.) *(rrah-dyoh-grah-FEE-ah)* X-ray

raíz (f.) *(rrah-EES)* root

raya (f.) *(RRAH-yah)* line; part (of hair)

razón (f.) *(rrah-SOHN)* reason

real *(rreh-AHL)* real; royal

recado (m.) *(rre-KAH-doh)* message

recalentar *(rreh-kah-lehn-TAHR)* to overheat; to reheat

receta (f.) *(rreh-SEH-tah)* prescription; recipe

recibir *(rreh-see-BEER)* to receive

recibo (m.) *(rreh-SEE-boh)* receipt

recobrar *(rreh-koh-BRAHR)* to recover, to get back

recomendar *(rreh-koh-mehn-DAHR)* to recommend

reconocer *(rreh-koh-noh-SEHR)* to recognize

recordar *(rreh-kohr-DAHR)* to remind, to remember

recuerdos (m.pl.) *(rreh-KWEHR-dohs)* regards; memories

rechazar *(rreh-chah-SAHR)* to refuse; to reject

red (f.) *(rred)* net; network

redondo *(rreh-DOHN-doh)* round

refresco (m.) *(rreh-FREHS-koh)* refreshment, soft drink

regalo (m.) *(rreh-GAH-lah)* gift

rehusar *(rreh-oo-SAHR)* to refuse

reírse *(rreh-EER-seh)* to laugh

rejilla (f.) *(rreh-HEE-yah)* (overhead) rack (in trains and buses)

relámpago (m.) *(rreh-LAHM-pah-gah)* lightning

reloj (m.) *(rreh-LOH)* clock, watch

remandar *(rreh-mehn-DAHR)* to mend

remitente *(rreh-mee-TEHN-teh)* sender

remolacha (f.) *(rreh-moh-LAH-chah)* beet

remolcar *(rreh-mahl-KAHR)* to tow

repentino *(rreh-pehn-TEE-nah)* sudden

repetir *(rreh-peh-TEER)* to repeat

reponerse *(rreh-poh-NEHR-se)* to recover (health)

resfriado *(rrehs-FRYAH-doh)* (common) cold

resorte (m.) *(rreh-SOHR-teh)* spring (mechanical)

respirar *(rrehs-pee-RAHR)* to breathe

responder *(rrehs-pahn-DEHR)* to answer, to respond

respuesta (f.) *(rrehs-PWEHS-tah)* answer

resultar *(rreh-sool-TAHR)* to result

retrete (m.) *(rreh-TREH-teh)* rest room, toilet

revelar *(rreh-veh-LAHR)* develop (film)

revisar *(rreh-vee-SAHR)* to check

revista (f.) *(rreh-VEES-tah)* magazine

rico *(RREE-kah)* rich

rieles (m.pl.) *(RRYEH-lehs)* train tracks

río (m.) *(RREE-oh)* river

robar *(rroh-BAHR)* to steal, to rob

rodilla (f.) *(rroh-DEE-yah)* knee

rojo *(RROH-hah)* red

rollo (m.) *(RROH-yoh)* roll (film)

romper *(rrohm-PEHR)* to break, to tear

ropa (f.) *(RROH-pah)* clothes;
  ropa blanca *(. . . BLAHN-kah)* linen;
  ropa interior *(. . . een-teh-RYOHR))* underwear

rosado *(rroh-SAH-doh)* pink

roto *(RROH-toh)* broken; torn

rueda (f.) *(RRWEH-dah)* wheel

ruido (m.) *(RRUEE-doh)* noise

ruidoso *(rruee-DOH-soh)* noisy

rumano(-a) *(roo-MAH-noh)*
(-nah) Rumanian
ruso(-a) *(ROO-soh)(-sah)*
Russian

S

sábana (f.) *(SAH-bah-nah)*
bedsheet
sábado (m.) *(SAH-bah-doh)*
Saturday
saber *(sah-BEHR)* to know
(a fact), to know (how)
sabroso *(sah-BROH-soh)* tasty
sacacorchos (m.) *(sah-kah-KOHR-chohs)* corkscrew
sacar *(sah-KAHR)* to take
out, to extract
sacerdote *(sah-serh-DOH-teh)*
priest
saco (m.) *(SAH-koh)* coat
sal (f.) *(sahl)* salt
sala (f.) *(SAH-lah)* living room
salado *(sah-LAH-doh)* salty
salchicha (f.) *(sahl-CHEE-chah)*
hot dog, sausage
salchichón (m.) *(sahl-chee-CHOHN)* salami, bologna
salida (f.) *(sah-LEE-dah)* exit
salir *(sah-LEER)* to leave, to
go out, to depart
salón (m.) *(sah-LOHN)* lounge;
salón de belleza *(. . . deh
beh-YEH-sah)* beauty parlor
salsa (f.) *(SAHL-sah)* sauce,
gravy
salud (f.) *(sah-LOOD)* health;
¡salud! (f.) *(sah-LOOD!)* (to
your) health! (toast)
saludo (m.) *(sah-LOO-doh)*
greeting

saludos (m.pl.) *(sah-LOO-dohs)* greetings, regards
salvavidas (m.) *(sahl-vah-VEE-dahs)* life preserver,
lifeguard
sandalia (f.) *(sahn-DAH-lyah)*
sandal
sandía (f.) *(sahn-DEE-ah)*
watermelon
sangre (f.) *(SAHN-greh)*
blood
sanidad (f.) *(sah-nee-DAHD)*
health
santuario (m.) *(sahn-TWAH-ryoh)* sanctuary, shrine
sastre (m.) *(SAHS-treh)* tailor
sazonado *(sah-soh-NAH-doh)*
seasoned (food)
se *(seh)* self, himself, her-
self, itself, themselves
seco *(SEH-koh)* dry;
limpieza en seco *(leem-PYEH-sah ehn . . .)* dry cleaning
sed (f.) *(sehd)* thirst;
tener sed *(teh-NEHR . . .)* to
be thirsty
seda (f.) *(SEH-dah)* silk
seguir *(seh-GEEHR)* to follow; to continue
segundo *(seh-GOON-doh)*
second
segundo (m.) *(seh-GOON-doh)* second (unit of time)
seguro *(seh-GOO-roh)* sure,
certain;
seguro (m.) *(seh-GOO-roh)*
insurance;
seguro de viaje *(. . . deh
VYAH-heh)* travel insurance
seis *(says)* six

269

sellar *(seh-YAHR)* to seal
sello (m.) *(SEH-yoh)* seal; postage stamp
semana (f.) *(seh-MAH-nah)* week
semáforo (m.) *(seh-MAH-foh-roh)* traffic light
sentar *(sehn-TAHR)* to seat
sentarse *(sehn-TAHR-seh)* to sit down
sentir *(sehn-TEER)* to be sorry; to feel
sentirse *(sehn-TEER-seh)* to feel (sick, tired, happy, etc.)
señor (m.) *(seh-NYOHR)* Mr., sir; gentleman
señora (f.) *(seh-NYOH-rah)* Mrs., madam; lady
señorita (f.) *(seh-nyoh-REE-tah)* Miss, Ms.; young lady
septiembre (m.) *(sehp-TYEHM-breh)* September
séptimo *(SEHP-tee-moh)* seventh
ser *(sehr)* to be
servicio (m.) *(sehr-VEE-syoh)* service
servilleta (f.) *(sehr-vee-YEH-tah)* napkin
servir *(sehr-VEER)* to serve
servirse *(sehr-VEER-seh)* to help (serve) oneself
sesenta *(seh-SEHN-tah)* sixty
setenta *(seh-TEHN-tah)* seventy
sexto *(SEHKS-toh)* sixth
si *(see)* if
sí *(see)* yes
siempre *(SYEHM-preh)* always
siete *(SYEH-teh)* seven

significar *(seeg-nee-fee-KAHR)* to signify; to mean
silla (f.) *(SEE-yah)* chair
sillón (m.) *(see-YOHN)* armchair
simpático *(seem-PAH-tee-koh)* pleasant, likable (person)
sin *(seen)* without
sinagoga (f.) *(see-nah-GOH-gah)* synagogue
sitio (m.) *(SEE-tyoh)* place, spot
smoking (m.) *(ehs-MOH-keeng)* tuxedo
sobre (m.) *(SOH-breh)* envelope
sobre *(SOH-breh)* on, upon; **sobre todo** *(. . . TOH-doh)* above all, especially
sobretodo (m.) *(soh-breh-TOH-doh)* overcoat
sol (m.) *(sohl)* sun
solamente *(soh-lah-MEHN-teh)* only, solely
solo *(SOH-loh)* alone
sólo *(SOH-loh)* only, solely
sombra (f.) *(SOHM-brah)* shadow
sombrerería (f.) *(sohm-breh-reh-REE-ah)* hat shop
sombrero (m.) *(sohm-BREH-roh)* hat
sortija (f.) *(sohr-TEE-hah)* ring
sostén (m.) *(sohs-TEHN)* bra, brassiere
su; sus (w/pl.) *(soo; soos)* his, her, its, their, your
suave *(SWAH-veh)* soft, mild
subir *(soo-BEER)* to go up, to climb

suceder *(soo-seh-DEHR)* to happen

sucio *(SOO-syoh)* dirty, soiled

sud (m.) *(sood)* south

sueco(-a) *(SWEH-koh)(-kah)* Swedish

suela (f.) *(SWEH-lah)* (shoe) sole

suelo (m.) *(SWEH-loh)* floor, ground

suelto *(SWEHL-toh)* loose

suelto (m.) *(SWEHL-toh)* small change

sueño (m.) *(SWEH-nyoh)* dream; sleep;
tener sueño *(teh-NEHR . . .)* to be sleepy

suerte (f.) *(SWEHR-teh)* luck;
¡buena suerte! *(BWEH-nah . . . !)* good luck!

suizo(-a) *(SUEE-soh)(-sah)* Swiss

supuesto *(soo-PWEHS-toh)* supposed;
por supuesto *(pohr . . .)* of course

sur (m.) *(soor)* south

suyo; suyos (w/pl.) *(SOO-yoh; SOO-yohs)* his, hers, yours, theirs, one's, its

T

taberna (f.) *(tah-BEHR-nah)* tavern

tacón (m.) *(tah-KOHN)* (shoe) heel

talón (m.) *(tah-LOHN)* baggage claim check; heel (foot)

tal vez *(tahl vehs)* perhaps, maybe

talle (m.) *(TAH-yeh)* size (clothing)

también *(tahm-BYEHN)* also, too

tapa (f.) *(TAH-pah)* lid

taquilla (f.) *(tah-KEE-yah)* ticket office

tarde *(TAHR-deh)* late

tarde (f.) *(TAHR-deh)* afternoon;
¡buenas tardes! *(BWEH-nahs TAHR-dehs!)* good afternoon!

tarifa (f.) *(tah-REE-fah)* fare, rate

tarjeta postal (f.) *(tahr-HEH-tah pohs-TAHL)* postcard

taza (f.) *(TAH-sah)* cup

té (m.) *(teh)* tea

techo (m.) *(TEH-choh)* roof

tela (f.) *(TEH-lah)* cloth

telefonista (m./f.) *(teh-leh-foh-NEES-tah)* telephone operator

temporalmente *(tehm-poh-rahl-MEHN-teh)* temporarily

temprano *(tehm-PRAH-noh)* early

tenazas (f.pl.) *(teh-NAH-sahs)* pliers

tenedor (m.) *(teh-neh-DOHR)* fork

tener *(teh-NEHR)* to have;
tener que *(. . . keh)* to have to;
tener prisa *(. . . PREE-sah)* to be in a hurry

teñir *(teh-NYEER)* to dye, to tint

271

tercero *(tehr-SEH-roh)* third
terciopelo (m.) *(tehr-syoh-PEH-loh)* velvet
ternera (f.) *(tehr-NEH-rah)* veal
tía (f.) *(TEE-ah)* aunt
tiempo (m.) *(TYEHM-poh)* time; weather
tienda (f.) *(TYEHN-dah)* store, shop
tierra (f.) *(TYEH-rrah)* dirt; soil; land; earth
tijeras (f.pl.) *(tee-HEH-rahs)* scissors
timbre (m.) *(TEEM-breh)* bell
tinta (f.) *(TEEN-tah)* ink
tintorería *(teen-toh-reh-REE-ah)* dry cleaner's
tío (m.) *(TEE-oh)* uncle
toalla (f.) *(toh-AH-yah)* towel
tobillo (m.) *(toh-BEE-yoh)* ankle
tocar *(toh-KAHR)* to touch; to play (an instrument)
tocino (m.) *(toh-SEE-noh)* bacon
todavía *(toh-dah-VEE-ah)* still, yet;
  todavía no *(. . . noh)* not yet
todo *(TOH-doh)* all, everything, every, each;
  todo el mundo *(. . . ehl MOON-doh)* everybody, everyone
todos *(TOH-dohs)* everybody, everyone, all
tomacorriente (m.) *(toh-mah-koh-RRYEHN-teh)* (electrical) outlet

tomar *(toh-MAHR)* to take; to drink
tontería (f.) *(tohn-teh-REE-ah)* nonsense
torcedura (f.) *(tohr-seh-DOO-rah)* sprain
toro (m.) *(TOH-roh)* bull
toronja (f.) *(toh-ROHN-hah)* grapefruit
toros (m.pl.) *(TOH-rohs)* bulls;
  corrida de toros (f.) *(koh-RREE-dah deh. . . .)* bullfight
torta (f.) *(TOHR-tah)* cake
tortilla (f.) *(TOHR-tee-yah)* omelet (Sp.); tortilla (a flat cornmeal cake/Mex.)
tos (f.) *(tohs)* cough
toser *(toh-SEHR)* to cough
tostada (f.) *(tohs-TAH-dah)* toast; tostada (a type of Mexican food)
trabajar *(trah-bah-HAHR)* to work
traducir *(trah-doo-SEER)* to translate
traer *(trah-EHR)* to bring
traje (m.) *(TRAH-heh)* suit;
  traje de baño *(. . . deh BAH-nyoh)* bathing suit
transbordar *(trahns-bohr-DAHR)* to transfer
transbordo (m.) *(trahns-BOHR-doh)* transfer (pass)
tranquilo *(trahn-KEE-loh)* quiet; tranquil
tranvía (m.) *(trahn-VEE-ah)* trolley, streetcar
trece *(TREH-seh)* thirteen
treinta *(TRAYN-tah)* thirty
trepar *(treh-PAHR)* to climb

tres *(trehs)* three
tronar *(troh-NAHR)* to thunder
trueno (m.) *(TRWEH-noh)* thunder
tú *(too)* you (familiar)
tuerca (f.) *(TWEHR-kah)* nut (for a bolt or screw)
turco(-a) *(TOOR-koh)(-kah)* Turkish
turismo (m.) *(too-REES-moh)* tourism

U

un (una) *(oon (OO-nah)* a/an;
  una vez *(OO-nah vehs)* once (one time)
uno(-a) *(OO-noh)(nah)* one (person), someone
uña (f.) *(OO-nyah)* nail (finger, toe)
usar *(oo-SAHR)* to use
uso (m.) *(OO-soh)* use, purpose
usted (abbr.: Ud.) *(oos-TEHD)* you (formal)
ustedes (abbre.: Uds.) *(oos-TEH-dehs)* you (pl.)
uvas (f.pl.) *(OO-vahs)* grapes

V

vacío *(vah-SEE-oh)* empty
valer *(vah-LEHR)* to be worth
válido *(VAH-lee-doh)* valid, good
variedades (f.pl.) *(vah-ryeh-DAH-dehs)* vaudeville
varios *(VAH-ryohs)* several, various

vaso (m.) *(VAH-soh)* drinking glass
¡váyase! *(VAH-yuh-seh!)* go away! scram!
veinte *(VAYN-teh)* twenty
velocidad máxima (f.) *(veh-loh-see-DAHD MAHK-see-mah)* speed limit
venda (f.) *(VEHN-dah)* bandage
vendar *(vehn-DAHR)* to bandage
vender *(vehn-DEHR)* to sell
veneno (m.) *(veh-NEH-noh)* poison
venir *(veh-NEER)* to come
venta (f.) *(VEHN-tah)* sale
ventana (f.) *(vehn-TAH-nah)* window
ventanilla (f.) *(vehn-tah-NEE-yah)* window (train, airplane); ticket window
ventilador (m.) *(vehn-tee-lah-DOHR)* (electric) fan
ver *(vehr)* to see
verano (m.) *(veh-RAH-noh)* summer
verdad (f.) *(vehr-DAHD)* truth
verdaderamente *(vehr-dah-deh-rah-MEHN-teh)* really, truly
verdadero *(vehr-dah-DEH-roh)* true
verde *(VEHR-deh)* green
verduras (f.) *(vehr-DOO-rahs)* vegetables; greens
vestido (m.) *(vehs-TEE-doh)* dress
vestirse *(vehs-TEER-seh)* to get dressed

vez (f.) *(vehs)* time (occasion);
  una vez *(OO-nah . . .)*
  once;
  en vez de *(ehn . . . deh)* instead of, in place of
viajar *(vee-ah-HAR)* to travel
viaje (m.) *(VYAH-heh)* trip, journey;
  ¡buen viaje! *(bwehn . . .)* bon voyage!
viajero(-a) *(vyah-HEH-roh)(-rah)* traveler
vida (f.) *(VEE-dah)* life
vidrio (m.) *(VEE-dryoh)* glass (material)
viejo *(VYEH-hoh)* old
viento (m.) *(VYEHN-toh)* wind;
  hace viento *(ah-seh . . .)* it's windy
viernes (m.) *(VYEHR-nehs)* Friday
vino (m.) *(VEE-noh)* wine
vista (f.) *(VEES-tah)* view
vitrina (f.) *(vee-TREE-nah)* showcase, store window
vivir *(vee-VEER)* to live
volante (m.) *(voh-LAHN-teh)* steering wheel

volver *(vohl-VEHR)* to return
vuelo (m.) *(VWEH-loh)* flight
vuelta (f.) *(VWEHL-tah)* turn

Y

y *(ee)* and
ya *(yah)* already
yo *(yoh)* I
yodo (m.) *(YOH-doh)* iodine
yugoslavo(-a) *(yoo-gohs-LAH-voh)(-vah)* Yugoslav

Z

zanahoria (f.) *(sah-nah-OH-ryah)* carrot
zapatería (f.) *(sah-pah-teh-REE-ah)* shoe store
zapatillas (f.pl.) *(sah-pah-TEE-yahs)* slippers
zapato (m.) *(sah-PAH-toh)* shoe
zarpar *(sahr-PAHR)* to sail
zarzuela (f.) *(sahr-SWEH-lah)* operetta (Sp.)
zumo (m.) *(SOO-moh)* juice (Sp.)